VIEWS

from

THE LOFT

VIEWS *from* THE LOFT

A PORTABLE WRITER'S WORKSHOP

Edited by Daniel Slager

milkweed
editions

Published 2010 by Milkweed Editions
Printed in Canada by Friesens Corporation
Cover design by Kyle Hunter
Cover photo by iStockphoto.com
Interior design by Connie Kuhnz
The text of this book is set in Adobe Caslon Pro by BookMobile Design and Publishing Services.
10 11 12 13 14 5 4 3 2 1
First Edition

Please turn to the back of this book for a list of the sustaining funders of Milkweed Editions.

Library of Congress Cataloging-in-Publication Data

Views from the loft : a portable writer's workshop edited by
    Daniel Slager. — 1st ed.
        p.   cm.
    A Who's who of writers on writing.
    ISBN-13: 978-1-57131-323-2 (pbk. : alk. paper)
    ISBN-10 (invalid) 1-57131-323-2 (pbk. : alk. paper)
    1. Authorship   I. Slager, Daniel.
    PN145.V54 2010
    808'.02—dc22
                                        2010007147

This book is printed on acid-free paper.

This book is dedicated to Marly Rusoff and to the literary community. It would not have been possible without all former and current Loft teachers, funders, board, staff, supporting members, students, and readers and writers.

VIEWS FROM THE LOFT

Introduction
Daniel Slager   1

TEACHING

Comes a Pony
Kate DiCamillo   7

Interview
Deborah Keenan   12

Interview
Michael Collier   18

Turning "Real Life" into Fiction: How to Do Justice to Grandma
Julie Schumacher   24

Why We Should Write about Things That Disappear
Nora Murphy   29

Interview
Tess Gallagher   36

Balancing Subtlety and Sledgehammers: Coming Out as a Gay Poet
William Reichard   44

Cuddling up with the Self-Censor
Kathleen Norris   50

Negotiating the Boundaries between Catharsis and Literature
Cheri Register   53

Fiction, Nonfiction, and the Woods
Rick Bass   59

Tesoros
Sandra Benítez   64

Guarding Voice
Susan Power   69

WRITING

In Favor of Uncertainty
Mark Doty   75

Working from Experience
Larry Sutin   83

Twenty-five in an Infinite Series of Numbers
Jim Moore   89

A Mentor's Words and Words on Her Words
Marilyn Chin   93

The Poem Behind the Poem
Michael Dennis Browne   98

Claiming Breath
Diane Glancy   103

Letting the Poem or Picture Book Out
Sharon Chmielarz   106

Got Them Poetry Blues?
Adrian C. Louis   112

A Few Cranky Paragraphs on Form and Content
Marilyn Hacker   118

Toward a Metaphor of Translation
Jay Miskowiec   126

Some Notes on Negative Capability
Katrina Vandenberg   132

Naming Names
David Haynes   135

A Recipe for Illusion: Memory, Imagination, Research
George Rabasa   141

Interview
Nicole Helget   145

CRITIQUE

The Sad Epiphany Poem: A Tirade For Two Voices
Brigitte Frase and Roseann Lloyd   151

A Tall White Pine: Thinking About Prophecy
Lewis Hyde   161

On Poetry
Yehuda Amichai   172

Interview
Ted Kooser   178

The Memoir as Literature
Vivian Gornick   183

Power and Powerlessness
C.J. Hribal   186

Children's Literature
Pamela Holt   189

Writing for the World
David Mura   193

Is There Life after Elegy?
Jim Moore   197

PUBLICATION

Confessions of a First Novelist
Lewis Buzbee   203

Interview
Lorna Landvik   209

What's Fiction Got to Do with It?
Karen Tei Yamashita   216

Interview
Leslie Adrienne Miller   221

The Writing of *Deadfall in Berlin*
R.D. Zimmerman   227

Interview
Michael Cunningham   230

Memoir: Don't Bite Off the Whole Elephant at Once
Laura Flynn   235

Editing the *View*
Ellen Hawley   238

Ten Questions I've Been Asked about Picture Books
John Coy   243

Why YA?
Pete Hautman   246

A View from a Slam
Bao Phi   250

On Tour
Shannon Olson   254

The Book Group Phenomenon
Faith Sullivan   259

WRITING FOR LIFE

Why I Write Fiction
Susan Straight   267

Interview
Grace Paley   272

Interview
Dorianne Laux   275

Writing about the Mysteries of Life
Mary Logue   281

Another Poet Gone to Prose: The Personal Essay as Quest
Barrie Jean Borich   284

The Making of Sense
J. Otis Powell!   287

Theories: How Life Becomes Poetry
Linda Gregg   290

Travel Writing and the Specter of Transience
Linda Watanabe McFerrin   296

Open Discovery in the Art of Creative Nonfiction
Kim R. Stafford   301

Voyeur in the House of Performance Art
Diane Wilson   305

Journal Writing: From the Inside Out
Elizabeth Jarrett Andrew   311

Up-North Literary Life
Will Weaver   318

Reading the Open Book
Nancy Gaschott   322

AFTERWORD

The Loft: Then and Now
Jim Moore   329

Contributors   333

VIEWS
from
THE LOFT

Introduction

DANIEL SLAGER

As the publisher of Milkweed Editions, I receive many submissions. Whether they arrive with the imprimatur of an agent or stuffed into a mailer by the writer who produced them, these manuscripts are a source of great pleasure and occasional exasperation. On one hand, discovering a highly original, entirely unexpected piece of writing is for me the greatest joy of editing and publishing books. On the other hand, because of their daunting number—several thousand submissions arrive in our office each year—and the time required to consider each of them carefully, it is also easy to forget the life a manuscript leads before it lands on my desk.

When I do feel overwhelmed by submissions, I often step out of my office and walk through Open Book, the singularly beautiful literary center that provides a home for Milkweed Editions, The Loft Literary Center, and the Minnesota Center for Book Arts. Beginning in the basement, I stroll the halls between old limestone walls, the faint rhythmic clack of printing presses in the Center for Book Arts softened by the warm scent of ink. From there I ascend to the first floor, where the smell of handmade paper mixes with the sounds of a poetry collective assembling the pages of their latest anthology and schoolchildren on a field trip. Walking through the Coffee Gallery, I'm surrounded by writers of diverse ages and backgrounds, crafting, critiquing, and discussing books, texts, and ideas. Up the Gail See staircase—which itself serves as an architectural metaphor joining the craft of bookmaking with literary content—aspiring screenwriters, travel writers, poets, novelists, and journalists develop and share their work with one another, or listen intently as mentors help them find their way. Emerging back onto the third floor, I reenter our office and walk past editors, publicists, and interns, cajoling and entreating authors, reviewers, and booksellers.

Back at my desk, the manuscripts are still piled high. And yet, seeing them now, with the feeling that I've just witnessed nearly the entire life cycle of a book, they don't seem so discouraging. I still sense the hard work required for their composition, of course, but I also hear the laughter-filled conversations of writers over coffee or beer, the sound of type falling into place for the broadside of someone's first poem. I see the look of wonder on a young writer's face as she gives herself over to what Kate DiCamillo describes as the "potent stew of ego and defiance and desperation and magic and faith" animating the writing process. In short, while I'm quite well aware of writers' desire for publication, after a walk through Open Book I can't help but remember that the most wondrous moment in the literary process is not a book's publication, but rather its composition.

For some, this moment is spontaneous. But for most the creative spark occurs in a communal moment of some kind, often entailing the encouragement and critique of other writers. And though the writers' workshop is a national phenomenon, for nearly four decades now The Loft Literary Center has provided this very support to more writers from more diverse backgrounds than any other program in the country. To this end, the Loft has gathered a veritable who's who of our nation's most inspiring writers, who have in turn taught classes with subjects ranging from "Food Writing for Beginners" to "Dialogue and Subtext." They administer the Mentor Series, in which established authors work with a group of students who have demonstrated extraordinary achievement and promise, and the Inroads program, where nationally acclaimed writers of color—Native Americans and Latinos, most recently—work with emerging writers from these communities. By way of these and other programs, the Loft has provided the community of writers and readers—not to mention the bards, for, as the indefatigable Bao Phi reminds us, "oral traditions of storytelling and poetry predate written literature"—with invaluable inspiration, advice, and wisdom.

Since its inception a decade ago, Open Book has been a profoundly collaborative space. And so when Jocelyn Hale, the Loft's Executive Director, approached me with an expression of interest in supplementing the experience of their students while also sharing it with the world of writers beyond the Loft's geographical reach, I leapt at the opportunity.

In 1976, the Loft began publishing a monthly newsletter for members, and in 1979 it was expanded, redesigned, and renamed *A View From the Loft*. Since then, a major component of the Loft's newsletter has been a regular column by writers from around the world. Gathering columns from the newsletter, this collection provides writers everywhere—from the most experienced workshop junky to the novice scribbler—with the tools and inspiration they need to thrive. Indeed, with sections entitled "Teaching," "Writing," "Critique," "Publication," and "Writing for Life," the contents are structured after the form of a workshop, in an attempt to bring the wonderful experience the Loft has provided for decades to an even broader audience.

Perhaps not surprisingly in light of the variety of perspectives animating our literary world, however, those who come to this collection expecting clear, unified guidance or answers for any number of age old questions facing writers will be sorely disappointed. For every contributor who suggests that you should "Write what you know," there is another who argues, as Leslie Adrienne Miller does in the context of an exchange with Heid Erdrich, that "The enemy of poetry is familiarity." And there is plenty of grist here for those with strong opinions regarding such fundamental questions as the proper role of authorial identity in literature, or the responsibility—the possibility, even—of truth and factual accuracy in memoir.

As you read through the following pieces, it is my great hope that the simple phrase, "Views from the Loft," will come to mean more. On one level, it means a building full of words, stories, and creativity. Moving through Open Book one literally moves through a book, surrounded at any moment by the genesis of countless literary and artistic experiments. Moving through this book, on the other hand, it means a perspective that encompasses and engenders the love for and importance of one of humanity's dearest and most vital tools, the creation and dissemination of good stories. I hope you enjoy the views.

Daniel Slager
August, 2010

Teaching

TOPICS ADDRESSED:

Lock Picking

Looking Long and Hard at a Fish

Absentminded Hunting

Resurrection-Based Research

First-Draft Catharsis

Doing Justice to Grandma

Conjuring Something from Nothing

Judgmental Grade School Teachers

"Major Cuts"

Ernie Kovacs and Poetry

Avoiding the Phony, Jerk, or Creep Inside

Expanding, Expanding, Expanding . . .

Comes a Pony

KATE DICAMILLO

Here is a picture of a pony. Let's start there, shall we? With the picture. Take a look. What do you see? A gravel road. Palm trees. Shadows. A barefoot girl on a pony. The roof of a house. The tailgate of a 1969 Ford.

What could this picture possibly have to do with writing?

Everything.

Listen. I will tell you a story.

I grew up in a small town in Florida. I spent a good portion of my childhood digging. I do not know, now, what I was digging for. And even then, if I had been questioned closely, I probably would have been at a loss to articulate exactly what I was hoping to find. But whatever it was, I looked for it assiduously. I had my own shovel. And every day I dug.

At the time of this story, I was eight years old and it was summer and my digging mania was at its apex. One day, under the huge magnolia tree in our backyard, I unearthed a rock. It was a white rock, worn smooth by time, and there was an indentation in the center of it that seemed to have been designed specifically for the human thumb.

I put my thumb into the hollow and took my thumb out, and I felt certain that somebody, many other people perhaps, had done the same thing before me. I was moved in a way that I could not explain to myself. All I knew was that I had found something special.

I took the rock inside and showed it to an expert: my older, rock-collecting brother.

"Look," I said to him, "I have found a very, very ancient rock."

"Ancient" seemed like exactly the right word to me: accurate, respectful, and at the same time implying a great mystery.

My brother looked up from his magazine. "Let me see," he said.

I handed him the rock.

He turned it over in his hand once, twice, and then handed it back to me. "That's not ancient," he said. "That's not even a rock."

"What is it then?" I asked.

"A bone."

"Do you think that maybe it's a special kind of bone?"

"No." He opened up his magazine. "I don't."

"Oh," I said.

But I was not convinced.

I took the bone next door and showed it to Beverly Pagoda.

"Look," I told her, "I have found an ancient, magical bone."

Beverly Pagoda was ten years old, and her mother (in what my mother referred to as "a mistake with long-term consequences") allowed her to wear makeup. Also, Beverly Pagoda owned a pair of white go-go boots with gold fringe tassels. I was forever trying to impress her; I had yet to succeed.

"A magical bone?" Beverly Pagoda said with disdain, but she opened up the screen door and stepped outside. She was wearing purple lipstick. My heart clenched in jealousy.

"Yes," I said, "magical." And then in a desperate leap born of imagination (mine was always working overtime) and belief (that something about the bone was special) and desire (to impress the sophisticated Beverly Pagoda), I said, "It makes wishes come true."

"Right," said Beverly. "I'm sure."

"Really," I said. "Here."

I held out the bone. She took it from me.

"Put your thumb in that hole. And make a wish out loud, and your wish will come true," I said.

"Oh, please," said Beverly. But she put her thumb in the hollow and with her eyes wide open, staring straight at me, she said, "I wish for a pony."

She blinked her eyes and then she made a big production out of turning her head, first to the right and then to the left. She looked around the yard and out in the street and down the hill; finally, with a sarcastic flourish, she turned and looked behind her, peering into the Pagoda carport.

"Gee," she said, "that's funny. I don't see a pony."

"Give it back," I said.

"Oh," she said, smirking, handing me the bone, "I guess it only works for you."

"Yes," I said. "It will work for me."

And I believed it.

It was summertime. I was eight years old. My heart was a small motor inside me, humming, whirring, eager to prove itself. I had faith, desperation. I believed in magic.

"Watch," I said. I held the bone in my hand. I put my thumb where it seemed to belong. I closed my eyes. "I wish for a pony," I said.

I kept my eyes closed.

I listened to the small-appliance whine of the crickets hidden in the bushes and the tall grass.

I waited.

And when I opened my eyes, I looked past Beverly Pagoda, down the hill, to where our street dead-ended into orange groves and honeysuckle vines and overgrowth.

"What's that?" I said to Beverly.

"What?" she said.

"That," I said. "There."

"Where?"

"There," I said. And I pointed at the pony that was walking out of the orange groves, toward us.

"A pony," whispered Beverly. And then she shouted it: "A pony! A pony!"

She ran down the hill screaming and whooping.

I followed behind her, more slowly, holding the bone in my hand, stunned, amazed, all powerful.

I had called a pony into being.

I had, finally, impressed Beverly Pagoda.

This is a true story.

You can ask my mother. She heard the shrieks and screams and came outside, wiping her hands on a green-and-white-checked dish towel.

"Jesus Christ," she said. "It's a pony." She went inside to get the camera. When she came back outside, she took a picture, this picture, of me sitting on the pony's back. And what is in the picture and what is not sum up most of what I know about the writing process.

First, let's talk about the things that are not visible, the unseen things standing outside of that square of light. One of those things is the man from the Penny Family Amusement Troop. He was there, standing with his hat in his hands, waiting to take the pony (whose name was Sir Alfred) back to the carnival from which he had escaped.

Also, you will note that Beverly Pagoda is not in the picture. She was standing to the right of the Penny Family Amusement Troop man. Her arms were crossed and her lower, purple lip was sticking out. She was working herself up to a considerable fit of rage: the bone, after all, had worked for me, not for her.

And the third thing you cannot see is the bone itself. It was there, however, curled in my right fist, resting in my sweating palm.

It would never work again.

And what of the things you can see? Well, there is me, atop the pony, triumphant, powerful. It did not matter to me that Beverly Pagoda was angry. It did not matter that I knew already that the bone would never work again.

What mattered was this: Somehow, through sheer audacity, through dumb luck, through willpower, through instinct, through defiance, through faith, through something unknowable, inexplicable, magical, I had conjured something from nothing.

And that is what writing is.

There is always somebody who will tell you that you cannot (the Beverly Pagodas of the world who try to work magic and fail). There is always somebody who will insist that the thing that moves you is not special (my brother, the bone). And the world (the man from the Penny Family Amusement Troop) will always (in the shape of editors and critics and the reading public and your mother and prize committees) come to claim the story. It is never, really, yours.

But when it works, none of that matters. When you find something (a word, a phrase, a name, a bone) worth wishing on, and when you believe in the magic of that thing and close your eyes and wish on it, and then suddenly where there was nothing (overgrowth, orange trees, a dead-end street, a disbeliever) there rises a story (there comes a pony) real, alive, well, there is nothing better in the world.

Part of writing is what Raymond Carver called "being at your station," showing up daily for the work, in spite of your moods or your health or your belief that the seemingly fickle muse has passed you by or is perched elsewhere, on a more deserving writer's desk. You will find reference to this, the need to do your work in spite of everything, in most manuals on writing.

Part of writing is paying attention to the world around you: listening to the gas-station attendant's story of his wife's betrayal, noting the sound that the screen door on the Fluff-o-matic Laundromat makes when it wheezes shut, knowing when the moon sets and rises and what phase it is in. And you will find reference to this need to pay attention in manuals on writing.

Part of writing is understanding the mechanics of story (narration and dialogue and transitions) and the basics of writing (punctuation, verb agreement, the elimination of dangling participles). And you will find reference to all of these things in manuals on writing.

What you will not, however, find in the manuals on writing is a discussion of the central mystery of the whole undertaking, an acknowledgment that writing is some powerful amalgam, a potent stew of ego and defiance and desperation and magic and faith.

It is a pony walking up the hill out of an orange grove.

It is a bone. The weight of it in your hand. The feel of your thumb in its groove. The knowledge that what you hold in your hand is special.

It is a wish that comes true against all odds.

And it is something that we will never fully understand.

Deborah Keenan

in dialogue with LORRAINE MEJIA-GREEN

As poets, we never know where our inspiration and support will come from. During my year in the Loft's Mentor Series, I was especially inspired by mentor Victor Hernández Cruz and by my fellow mentees. During that same time in my life, I was finishing my MFA at Hamline University, and Deborah Keenan was one of my teachers as well as my faculty adviser. Deborah has been to me an extraordinary mentor. I must begin this interview by thanking her for the path she has shown me—the unconditional belief in myself and my work that she has given to me. It was my pleasure to conduct the following interview with her.

LORRAINE MEJIA-GREEN: You are a mentor for the twenty-fifth anniversary of the Loft's Mentor Series, but years ago you yourself participated as a "mentee." What did you learn from that experience? What opportunities can be seized from the mentor-mentee relationship?

DEBORAH KEENAN: I still remember the phone call from the Loft, all those years ago, letting me know I'd been selected, along with seven other regional and local writers. As a young woman, that news gave me some confidence I'd been lacking about my journey as a writer. I learned a great deal from the other writers who were selected—we were blessed with different kinds of ambition and convivial spirits: I learned to be tougher on my own work and to begin developing the armor I would need to survive as a working writer. Two of our eight mentees were beloved by our mentors, and the rest of us needed to be at peace with that, be happy for our new friends, and not give up. Some people are gifted at being with famous people and making connections. Many are not. The Mentor Series gives you a chance to find out how you operate around writers who are farther up the food chain— this is important information to gain about oneself. Some mentees over the twenty-five-year history of the Mentor Series have developed long-lasting relationships with the visiting mentors—competitions have been won, work has been placed in good magazines, all because a personal connection was made and sustained. For many of us, the greatest opportunity was the chance to make real friendships with the other folks selected in our year. For others, it is the chance to give a great reading, to reinvent oneself as a public artist, to be seen as gifted by an artistic community. Doors open because of the Mentor Series. You just never know which doors they might be.

L.M.G: In your long career you've published six collections of poetry, edited an award-winning anthology with poet Roseann Lloyd (also a past Mentor winner), and taught thousands of people. What advice would you give emerging poets who dream of a similar life?

D.K.: I advise my students to keep writing. Too many people write a first batch of fine poems and expect those ten poems to carry them forward into a lifetime career. Keep writing. It is pretty much impossible to keep up with the extraordinary number of poetry collections published each year, not to mention studying like a demon those poets whose work has survived the vagaries of fortune and trends. Yet one must. I find poets who don't read poems or poetry collections, who don't study the extraordinary poets from past centuries, from all parts of the world, highly suspect. There's no worse moment for me in a class or with a client than to hear that a person loves to write poetry but can barely stand to read it. What does this mean, to want to be in an art form that doesn't inspire? Baffling. So, keep writing. Keep reading. Be as honest with yourself as you can be. Stop longing to be loved for your first drafts. Don't be a phony. Don't be a jerk or a creep. If entering the writing life, the competitions, the public arena in any of its forms is making you a lesser human being, stop writing immediately. Keep your eyes open for possibilities—the Mentor Series, a chance at a great internship at a press, a chance to make a real friendship with a fellow writer, a chance to write a letter to a writer you truly admire, a chance to keep a bookstore afloat by buying volumes of poetry there. Yehuda Amichai, one of my heroes, said, "Live your life, then write." There's a million things to say here, but I am stopping now!

L.M.G.: What does it take to make a career based on one's writing?

D.K.: Tenacity. Good fortune. Strangers who, as editors or judges, suddenly launch your career because they respond to your work. Different kinds of bravery. Doing good work, and never assuming that you ever get to stop proving yourself in the workplace. Continuing to write. Continuing to risk failure, rejection, indifference. Staying somewhat balanced. Walking. Having a friend. Continuing to write. Figuring out which of the many careers tied to writing is a match for your gifts, your soul, your strengths as a regular person in the world.

L.M.G: You once told me that early in your career you knew other talented, emerging poets who never went on to build writing careers. Was it the aspect of competition that stopped them? Something else?

D.K.: I think it's many different things, unique to each writer. For some, the endless placing of oneself in the marketplace, trying to be visible, to be "chosen," is so corrosive to their souls they know they have to stop. Many extraordinary young writers stop because they move on to other art forms that please them better, and poetry becomes like a first love, fondly remembered, but not practiced. Many who start as poets shift genres and claim success elsewhere. Several of my friends and colleagues have done this. Some come to a fundamental understanding about themselves—it's not the world they really want to be in; for others, the door should have opened, and it didn't, or it hasn't yet, which takes us back to tenacity.

L.M.G: What has the importance placed on being published done to the spirit of the poet?

D.K.: Lots. But extraordinary poets continue to write works of brilliance and permanence, and we don't know where they are or who they are—their stash of poems may not be found for a hundred years, if the world lasts, and we will never know the bounty we missed as readers. Being published is being published. Being a real poet is being a real poet. Sometimes they intersect.

L.M.G: I'm always amazed at the fullness of your life. Besides being an associate professor in the MFA program at Hamline University and a faculty adviser, as well as a teacher at the Loft, you have a husband, four kids, a granddaughter, you're part of a poetry collective. What have you done to maintain sacred time for your writing?

D. K.: I'm laughing as I consider this question! First, it's a blessing in my life that writing poetry is what I have always wanted to do as an American artist. My life as a poet has always been done in small moments of artistic oasis—early, early morning before a baby woke up; midday, when a child took a nap; right before dinner, when suddenly no one needed me; late at night, especially in earlier years; and always, always, while driving my old car to jobs, residencies, delivering kids to basketball practices, on my way to my mom's home in Bloomington when she was alive—driving and thinking and listening to all the radio stations. I wanted it enough. That's the simple and true answer. I wouldn't give up on myself. I didn't want other things I'd chosen, like love or kids or full-time work or friendships or my commitment to caring for my mom, to keep me from my artistic life. When I don't make poems, or my collages, I am not in good shape for the chaos and exhaustion that the world tosses at all of us every day. So I keep going, find the time.

L. M. G: What have you done to continue evolving as a poet?

D. K.: I teach amazing students. This helps enormously, as I am always in right relationship with remarkable human beings who care about what I care about. I study all the time. I read. I fold those precious voices into the poems I am struggling with—obvious evidence of this is in my new collection, *Good Heart*, which is really a book-length conversation with other writers, the living and the dead.

I judge myself more harshly as a writer each year. I keep my heroes and heroines of writing present on my writing table. I seek voices that puzzle and confound me, and drive myself to understand how they are making their poems. I try to live as if I were dying, as I say in my new book. Not a generic everyone's gonna die, but as if today were my last day on the beautiful earth. This helps me structure my poems, clean out the clutter of my life, focus on what matters to me. I try to give 100 percent to my family, friends, neighbors, and students. This giving that I try to do is returned to me in odd and remarkable ways, and this helps my poetry deepen and change.

L. M. G: Your extraordinary new book, *Good Heart*, is filled with images of death. Can you talk about the image of death from your poem "The Painting of the Amaryllis"?

D. K.: Well, my eyes have been trained on death for a long time. In this particular poem, the dead woman floating in the lake is connected to other women living underwater in my past books—this time, there's no mythic charge, and so she has to die. The living mother drags her dead self to shore, but doesn't do a good job tending this body. She straightens the nightgown, but can't bear it when the dead mother puts her arm around the little daughter. The amaryllis has died, but has sustained its beauty—we assume no such thing about the dead woman. In this poem, the living mother has a harsh and hard-won power, a clear sense of intent. She doesn't tend her dead self very well, but it seems apparent that she takes good care of the daughter. In a way, the poem passes the myths I've created in the past about women who live in water to the real woman onshore. There's loss and death here, but the daughter carries her own beauty forward. Lorraine, this was a hard question! I appreciate you asking me to reflect on this poem.

L. M. G: What kind of editing process have you developed for your work? How do you know when a poem is done?

D. K.: I am old enough now to understand that some poems are ready to be written and never altered when I finally have time to get to the computer. These poems are done, and no one can tell me differently. Because I am fifty-two, I am at peace with my own sense of the poem—it may never be accepted for publication, I don't mean that, I just mean I am done, and it is done. Some poems, one I have been working on all summer, for example, called "If You Say Luck You Can't Say God," I've revised, edited, whittled down, added to—it has been in motion and in change for four months, and yesterday, finally, it was over. I think it's done. I am much more ruthless with my work now (some of my critics will be happy to hear!) and also have much more confidence than I used to have about my voice, my talent, each poem.

L.M.G: What do you do when you think you have written a "perfect" poem, only to be surprised that the rest of the world doesn't seem to agree?

D.K.: I declare it perfect. I read it each day and feel grateful that I was allowed to write it. As I always tell my students—if you write a perfect poem, don't bring it to class. If it's perfect, you don't need us.

L.M.G: Do you think there are things in a poet's life that slaughter, either temporarily or permanently, the creative spirit? How is it regained or healed?

D.K.: Of course. Many of our greatest poets, García Lorca, Radnóti, and the numbers of greatly talented men and women poets from all world cultures—their literal slaughters have stopped them, and us, from having more of their work to treasure and learn from. And, yes. I know people every day, fantastically gifted artists, who because of struggles with depression, or cruelties inflicted on them by lovers or parents or children or strangers, are stopped in their tracks and have to do enormous amounts of personal work to survive and return again to their creative lives. For many of us, the death of an important person—my best friend who died when we were both in our twenties, my mom's death a few years ago—these deaths, for some of us, stop us. I had no interest in writing after my mom's death. I didn't write for almost three years. It is a privilege to end up in a life where one can make art and can continue making art. Those of us who have received this privilege because of the sheer assignments of fate are lucky to be able to regain our strength and talent, lucky to be able to heal and return to the blessed work of making a poem.

Michael Collier

in dialogue with GLENN FREEMAN

Michael Collier is the author of numerous collections of poetry and the editor of *The Wesleyan Tradition: Four Decades of American Poetry* and *The New American Poets: A Bread Loaf Anthology*. He has received fellowships from the Guggenheim Foundation and the National Endowment for the Arts. He has also served as director of the creative writing program at the University of Maryland and been the director of the Bread Loaf Writers' Conference since 1994. He was part of the Loft Mentor Series, which brings four nationally known writers to Minnesota to work intensively with eight local writers selected through the Mentor Series Competition.

GLENN FREEMAN: It seems, in terms of your language and your use of narrative, that you are a natural heir to a writer like Robert Frost. Would you agree?

MICHAEL COLLIER: I can't see how an American poet can avoid being some kind of Frost heir. Frost is part of our genealogy, growing out of the main trunk. He also happens to be one of my favorite poets, especially the Frost of "Neither Out Far nor In Deep" and "The Most of It," those dark lyrical poems, and then the dark narratives such as "A Servant to Servants" and "A Hill Wife," where the characters are not far from Amy Lowell's unflattering characterization of them as "leftovers of the old stock—morbid, pursued by phantoms, slowly sinking into insanity." These are poems that sound least guarded or contrived. Frost is following the language rather than taking a position or adapting the poem to his persona. I was brought into close proximity with Robert Frost through Randall Jarrell's two brilliant essays, "The Other Frost" and "To the Laodiceans." I read these in college when I still had only a high-school student's notion of Frost, and they helped me see, simply, how interesting and complex his work was. And, of course,

Jarrell's own poems are filled with Frost. Jarrell's poems spoken by women are deeply influenced by some of Frost's monologues. So that when I read Jarrell's "The Face," "Seele im Raum," and "Woman," I was also reading an aspect of Frost.

My other introduction to Frost was from William Meredith, my undergraduate teacher. Meredith had been a younger friend of Frost's and had traveled with him, in the early sixties, to the West Coast. He not only talked about Frost's poems with great love and passion, but he also gave my classmates and me a sense of what Frost was like as a man. Meredith felt, as others have, a duty to rectify the impression Lawrence Thompson created of Frost as a monster. I feel fortunate to have had Meredith's personal enthusiasm for the man; it meant I never had the problem of seeing Frost as a celebrity. Of course, you need *The Family Letters of Robert and Elinor Frost* to see how much he loved his children and family.

G.F.: I like to tell students to welcome influence and find ways to use what's important in other writers' work. How do you think you've used—or not—your influences?

M.C.: Maybe we don't really use what has influenced us as much as it uses us. I say this because of a poem, "Brave Sparrow," I wrote a couple of years ago. When I finished it, I realized that it was completely indebted to Jarrell's "The Mockingbird." Maybe all that is mine in the poem is the voice. The perception and attitude is all Jarrell. And now that I think about it, I suppose there are echoes of Roethke in the poem.

Being conscious of one's influence is an odd thing, because after a while it can become reductive. Your influences can seem more like a gallery of poets' portraits, whereas real influence happens through a network of relationships, or at any given moment in which you're working on a poem, a piece of another poet's poem might find its way into it.

But, of course, welcoming influence is one of the most important ways of establishing your own relationship to the tradition. Shortly after my wife and I were married, we went to Hawaii to visit her father, who lived in the countryside about ninety minutes from Honolulu. Outside his ramshackle house, not far from the ocean, I found an abandoned bird's nest made primarily of pine needles, but it was also threaded with many different kinds of fishing line. These pieces of different colored nylon fishing line are similar to the way poets use their influences, weaving them into the design of the poem as happenstance allows, and like the pieces of line, they are transparent, and at a distance you can't tell they exist.

G. F.: I'm impressed with the lyricism you are able to achieve using a very familiar language. The poems feel as if they're spoken in an everyday voice, yet they also manage to sing, often fluctuating between the two experiences. In the writing process, do you feel that you pay more attention to patterns of speech, trying to recreate the spoken gesture, or do you pay attention to the lyrical possibilities of the language? Do you revise more toward a naturalness of voice or toward a musicality?

M. C.: The music I am most attuned to—and I have to believe this is because of poets such as Frost and Jarrell, Roethke, Lowell and Meredith—is the one inherent in colloquial speech. I think one of the poet's jobs is to prove that the resources of colloquial speech are adequate to the demands of poetry. Another way of saying this is that we are by necessity training others—readers of poems, I presume—how to hear poetry in the bits and pieces of language everyone already uses, a language that Marianne Moore unabashedly characterized as "plain American which cats and dogs can read!" Anyway, I don't think the music inherent in language can be separated from patterns of speech. At least, I'm not able to separate them.

G. F.: I'm also impressed in your work with the precision of description. There is usually a moment in the poems which allows the image or event to open up for the reader—and that moment usually relies on something being seen clearly. The poem doesn't necessarily make a direct metaphoric connection, but allows a reader a space to step into and create meaning. I wonder how aware you are of metaphoric connections while you are writing. Do you try to consciously craft metaphor, or do you let it take its own course? Put another way, do you think the metaphors in your poems work because they're intended a certain way or because any clear description will naturally evoke other levels?

M.C.: There is a place in the middle of Bishop's "The Fish" where the "tremendous fish" she caught transforms into something else. She writes, "—It was more like the tipping / of an object toward the light. / I admired his sullen face, / the mechanism of his jaw, / and then I saw / that from his lower lip / —if you could call it a lip—" That transformation, that doubt—"if you could call it a lip"—is caused by her looking as hard and as long as possible at the fish. Never mind the flowers and wallpaper that she uses as similes earlier in the poem, most of what's preceded has described the fish. I've always aspired to that kind of transforming lucidity, which is why George Herbert was an early important influence. There's a kind of stubborn belief about it, about looking hard enough at one thing that you begin to see its manifold nature. And it seems to me there are two ways you can achieve this. You either tighten your focus on the thing, or you begin with a tight focus and move away from it.

I suppose, too, that I believe almost literally in Williams's notion of "no ideas but in things." I'm a consumer. I like things. I'm fascinated by the mechanical world. Although the virtual world doesn't yet have its hold on me, it contains all the necessary ingredients. But gears and levers and pulleys, I can't get enough of. In poems, my obsessive attraction to things ranges from Herbert's "The Collar" to Hardy's "The Workbox" and "My Father's Violin" to the very recent prose poems of Campbell McGrath. Or that Michael Ryan poem, "Switchblade."

But you asked about the origin of metaphors in things. Metaphor comes from the activity of looking, paying attention to the world in the peculiar way that poets pay attention, through language. I don't think metaphor is something inherent in things and then is somehow released from them. The work of paying attention leads us to metaphor by inviting the reader into the transformative experience of poetic language. And that's how Bishop's fish becomes an object instead of a fish and has a lip—or doesn't have a lip.

G.F.: Sometimes those metaphoric moments come as a very pointed ending of a poem, and other times they seem to be woven through the poem (and, although this is a generalization, they seem to shift toward the latter in your recent poems). Do you think this reflects a different type of process or simply a response to the needs of different types of material?

M.C.: Most of the new poems register some kind of fissure in experience. Maybe in earlier poems I still believed, against all the evidence, that I could speak about something whole and true in experience and now realize I can't. That might sound like a defeat but it actually feels like a small triumph for me as a writer. You always want your work to develop and to differentiate itself from your past work. I don't think this can be willed. When it happens, it usually coincides with changes in your life or in the way you understand your experience.

Philip Larkin wrote a preface to the reissue of his first book of poems, *The North Ship*, in which he talked about how his apprenticeship in the service of Yeats had been usurped by a conversion to Hardy. He makes it sound as if his change happened all at once and that he left Yeats behind for good. Well, it's a good story but not really true. Larkin was aware of Hardy's poetry from his earliest years, and a whiff of Yeats can be detected in Larkin. What begets his allegiance to Hardy, I think, is a reckoning with his own temperament. Larkin understands that his pessimism is not to be clarified by "Celtic Twilight." Once he understands this, he is able to write poems such as "Sad Steps," "This Be the Verse," and all those others that are undeniably what we've come to know as Larkinesque.

G.F.: There is a wonderful progression within the sections of your books and the books as a whole, so that they feel like a narrative in themselves. Do you have any comments on how you approach crafting a book? How do you know when a manuscript is complete?

M.C.: *The Folded Heart* and *The Neighbor* were finished when I wrote poems that seemed in tone and texture to be pointing away from the poems I had been writing. Both of those poems, "The Cave" and "The Water Dream," ended the volumes. I can't say that's happened with the new book. The last poems I wrote for it, "Fathom and League" and "A Last Supper," do not close the book. Those poems seem different to me in the way your previous question suggests, and yet, at the same time, I can recognize in them some of my earliest enthusiasm for surrealism; they rely on odd images and, I hope, vivid juxtapositions.

I try to approach putting together a manuscript as if I were con-
structing a single poem. I try to avoid thematic groupings. More than
anything, I want the relationship between poems to offer surprise.
Although these are my goals, I have to admit that I rely on a number
of friends to help me order the books. All of my book titles come from
suggestions made by friends or by my wife. I don't show my individual
poems to very many people, but I'm rather open, or desperate, when it
comes to soliciting ideas for the books.

G.F.: When I look at the last section of your most recent manuscript,
it feels as if you are making a new kind of poem, where the narrative is
stripped down to reveal just the skeleton of experience or thought. Do
you think those poems represent a natural ending to the progression
of that manuscript, or do they represent somewhere new you might be
heading with the work?

M.C.: You might be able to give a more accurate answer to that question than I can. Those poems are driven, I think, by the material, which
is very personal. The stripped-down aspect is probably a form of re-
sistance to the material. Those poems concentrate their drama and
tension in the mixture of the language rather than through the more
linear movement of narrative. I like the poems because they seem less
paraphrasable and yet at the same time more emotionally explicit. But
they scare me, too.

G.F.: What do you see in the future for your work?

M.C.: You might ask, "Do I see a future for my work?" While I was
finishing this last book, I was also editing two anthologies of contemporary poetry. As a result, I don't have any new poems. The future,
I guess, is always the poems you haven't written. And what might
they be like? I can't even begin to imagine. Some poets have schemes
in mind, subjects pressing them forward, obsessive habits that keep
words flowing, seemingly, day and night. I'm always blindsided by
what I write. I'll sit down without anything in mind and, if I'm lucky, I
begin to inch my way into a new poem, into the future.

Turning "Real Life" into Fiction: How to Do Justice to Grandma

JULIE SCHUMACHER

Here's a sad story: You sign up for a writing class because something is burning a hole in your heart—some dear and closely guarded experience that has been haunting you for years. You need to transfer it to the page, to unburden yourself, to translate that lovely and bitter memory into prose. So you write the story of your grandmother's demise, the tale of the cruel next-door neighbor who seduced your dad, the disillusioning account of your first love. And you turn it in. The following week you get it back from your teacher and fellow students with tactful comments: "Try to think of something more original at the end." "Could you cut the father?" "This part is corny." "It doesn't seem real."

"*Of course* the story was real," you tell yourself. "It happened to *me.*" These morons have insulted the memory of your grandma and suggested that you do away with your father. You lie awake at night composing cutting responses. Then, ten minutes before the next class begins, you approach the first unsuspecting clown. "That story wasn't unoriginal," you say. "You see, my grandmother was eighty-seven when. . . ."

Your fellow student interrupts: "So?"

This is the workshop student's worst nightmare. You have handed in a piece of your very soul, and it came back with suggestions in the margins. What should you do?

First, recognize that your experience and its fictional counterpart are not one and the same, no matter what the similarities. There is no exact prose translation for your relationship with your grandmother. In writing, she simply isn't the same woman. And this distance is good. It protects you. It protects her. Make the best use of it. Spill your guts in the first draft, then rename the old woman; give her red hair and a crooked ear and an extra fifty pounds. Acknowledge to yourself that she's someone else once she hits the page.

Second, acknowledge that "real life" and the people who inhabit it are full of uneven moments, fallow passages, unseemly habits, and clichés. Without editing and rearrangement, they're seldom fit for literature. If characters and events were enough, we would only have to list the major events of the plot and include a photograph and bio of each character. Why go to the trouble of writing the story at all?

Uneven or not, though, we can't get away from real life—usually our own—as a starting place and a source. It's not the odd thirdhand tale you overhear in the shoe store that makes you sit in a hard chair and strain your eyes at a computer screen, but your own anguish, your own doubt, affection, curiosity, and grief. So how can you do justice to Grandma? How do you translate memory into fiction? What do you change and what do you keep?

Let's say you've been hurting for years because Grandmother's house was sold out from under her and she was shipped off without ceremony to the nursing home. Rather than tackle the entire history, including a catalogue of the items sold with the clapboard house, find a crucial seed. Go back to the gesture, glance, or remark that sticks in your mind and won't go away. Remember, for example, the afternoon when the old woman came downstairs with the front of her dress buttoned wrong and announced that mice had invaded the bathroom. (She was wrong, of course.) Or the time she insisted on playing rummy but couldn't remember the difference between the jack and queen. Zero in on the moments that matter, and you'll have not a history but a story.

This next suggestion may sound strange, but when you're writing about your own experience, remember that you are not necessarily the expert. Readers get tired of a know-it-all storyteller. A story can be much more interesting if the narrator is struggling with the material—figuring it out. If you know before you start exactly who the villains are, think again. Maybe the story isn't that simple. And it will probably be more successful—less one-sided or pedantic—if you're less certain where the good and evil lie. Don't try to know all the answers before you begin.

Now, once you have a draft, ask yourself where it is strongest. Maybe the nursing home isn't well drawn. Maybe the sale of the house seems a little tedious. The real-life versions of these things haunt you, but on the page they seem flat and dull. On the other hand, buried in the middle of page four is a tiny portrait of the narrator's father— Grandmother's only son—doubled over in the vestibule as if he's about to be sick. You made that detail up, in fact. Your father was out of town during the weekend of the sale.

But here it is, a marvelous, gut-wrenching detail—a gift from heaven. Maybe you're not writing about Grandma after all, but about the narrator's unwillingness to view her father's sorrow there in the hall.

All these suggestions add up to one important point. When you rely on personal experience as a starting point for fiction, remember to be faithful to the truth and not the facts. In her essay "On Keeping a Notebook," Joan Didion talks about the difference between these two. Although she's discussing journal writing rather than fiction, the point is the same. She insists that the point of writing in a notebook is not to preserve an accurate factual record:

> In fact I have abandoned altogether that kind of pointless entry: instead I tell what some would call lies. "That's simply not true," the members of my family frequently tell me when they come up against my memory of a shared event. "The party wasn't for you, the spider was not a black widow, it wasn't that way at all." Very likely they are right, for not only have I always had trouble distinguishing between what happened and what merely might have happened, but I remain unconvinced that the distinction, for my purposes, matters. The cracked crab that I recall having for lunch the day my father came from Detroit in 1945 must certainly be embroidery, worked into the day's pattern to lend verisimilitude; I was ten years old and would not now remember the cracked crab. The day's events did not turn on cracked crab. And yet it is precisely that fictitious crab that makes me see the afternoon all over again, a home movie run all

too often, the father bearing gifts, the child weeping, an exercise in family love and guilt. Or that is what it was to me.

It is the emotional or psychological truth that matters. That brief image of the father weeping in the vestibule—you hear the stuttering intake of his breath, and focus for some unknown reason on his unbuttoned rear trouser pocket—that's the heart of your story. Make Grandma a grandpa if you need to. Make her six feet tall. Make her drink bourbon with her eggs at breakfast. It doesn't matter. Your mission is to follow that weeping fifty-one-year-old man as he staggers down the hall toward his mother's room.

Writers who begin from memory often worry that their characters or situations will be recognizable. Their mothers and fathers, in other words, will never speak to them again if their stories see daylight. The extent of this problem depends, in part, on the generosity and dispositions of your family and friends. It also depends, however, on your willingness to see the story evolve and change. This doesn't mean that your characters will speak to you in tongues or redirect the plot, or that the muse will whisper suggestions in your ear. It simply means that what you set out to do may not be what you end up with. This discrepancy doesn't imply a lack of skill, but a willingness to trust the story's strongest moments—its sense of truth—and to value fiction apart from its real-life origins.

When the story is done, chances are that your fictional parents won't quite be your parents; at least, the resemblance will be tenuous enough that they can explain to their friends, "It may sound like us, but it isn't. That was a fictional story." And they may feel uneasy, but the relatives of writers often are.

When I was an undergraduate, I wrote what I thought was a moving and romantic story about a fleeting encounter on a train in Germany: A young man gave the narrator a single red rose, and they spent the entire night on the train holding hands and talking about the meaning of love.

My teacher hated it. "Clichéd," she wrote in green Magic Marker. I was indignant. "This can't be a cliché," I said.

My teacher looked up. She actually smiled. I was probably blushing.

"Oh, it's fine as raw material," she said. "But a red rose? Think of something more original for him to give her. Maybe an empty box, or a letter from his sister."

I still had that rose pressed in a drawer, and it took me a long time to admit that a treasured romantic moment in my life was a cliché. But my teacher was right. What is wonderful in real life can be lousy in fiction. We are more generous in real life. When people tell us sad stories full of unoriginal and banal details, we don't interrupt to make stylistic suggestions. We sympathize. We cry. Not so in fiction. The word "banal" comes back to us, written in the margins.

In the end, regardless of its real-life sources, your story needs an integrity of its own; it has to feel true on the page. Your job as a writer of fiction is to start with memory, if that's what you do, but to tell the truth of the story, not the facts. At a certain point, you cut the umbilical cord and float free, leaving your autobiography—and your real-life grandma—safe at home.

Why We Should Write
about Things That Disappear

NORA MURPHY

Writing about people from the past presents the writer with a challenge or two. Even in fiction, conveying a character's experience and emotion isn't easy. What happens when the writer strives for a historical account of their character? As I struggle to write about my grandfather, I'm beginning to wonder whether it's possible to bring him back to life.

People in Saint Paul used to mistake my grandfather for Monsignor Cullinan. At least that's what my father says as we walk down Summit Avenue past Saint Luke's Church, the monsignor's old domain and the Murphy family parish. I can tell by the way my father spins the name Cullinan out into the October air—rising, not falling—that my grandfather probably took it as a compliment.

When my grandfather was hospitalized at Saint Joseph's, a nun entered the room the evening before he went in for surgery. She gasped at the sight of the revered Monsignor in bed. When she recovered enough to speak, the nun asked his forgiveness for not knowing the monsignor had taken ill and asked if there was anything she could do. My grandfather didn't let on. Instead he beckoned the nun over to his bedside, offering to hear her confession.

He didn't! He didn't really do that! I say as we stop for a light at Victoria Avenue. My father squints into the angular autumn sun and turns to answer me. *We don't really know, do we? All we know is that my father said he said that.*

Reconstructing a person who is no longer around to defend him- or herself isn't easy. I'll never know what my grandfather felt like lying in bed and pretending to be a church leader. I'll never know exactly what he said to the nun in the hospital room. But I want to.

For the past two years, I have been working on a memoir of five generations of my family and of the Irish Catholic community here in Minnesota. Understanding my grandfather is an important part of this tale. When I can't find the answers I want through research, I imagine answers. In fact, the further I get into this inquiry, the more I'm beginning to wonder if I need to know the truth in order to convey our story. This prospect raises two questions for me, both as a writer and as a Roman Catholic turned Buddhist.

First, how does a creative nonfiction writer portray his or her characters with accuracy and charisma when details are missing? For me, accuracy means sticking fast to the facts that are known about a person. To catch and maintain a reader's attention, however, writers strive to create charismatic characters. If we don't have much information about a person, we may be tempted to add details we imagined to fill in the gaps. Is this a valid enterprise for the writer of either traditional or creative nonfiction?

Second, how can a Buddhist writer write about anything except the present moment? As I understand it, Buddhism doesn't doubt the existence of the past, but it does assert that the past as single, solid entity no longer exists. Buddhists contact the past only through its manifestations in the present, like mental reruns or unresolved trauma. Writers of traditional and creative nonfiction, however, often focus on the past. Can a Buddhist writer?

Although I haven't found a sure answer to either of these questions, looking at them together has helped me find some possible avenues of reconciliation. Both questions force the writer to explore this elusive thing our language calls the past.

Imagine the past as a continuum of what we believe to be fact and what is invented. Fiction writers invent. Diehard historians stick to the facts. Creative nonfiction writers now write all along this spectrum. But in writing about my own family, I discovered that this continuum—the distance between what was and what might have been—is illusory. Writers only create images of the past. No matter how close we get to a person, our writing never precisely recreates the person we loved. Not because the writing isn't good enough, but because of the inevitable distance between life and the page, between one breath and the one that follows.

Annie Dillard writes that we can only "fashion a text." I agree, but not willingly. I can create an image of my grandfather; I can't resurrect the dead. The individual moment, my grandfather's moment, has vanished. And for me, as a Buddhist and a writer about the past, that means being willing to ask myself if it is okay to create my own version of the people I love—even of my grandfather.

Japanese Zen master Eihei Dogen offers writers a method for coming to terms with this paradox. Almost one thousand years ago, Eihei Dogen wrote the Genjokoan, a treatise on Buddhist stages of enlightenment. The Genjokoan describes this process through the use of koans, or nonlinear microcosms of Buddhist insight. You don't have to meditate crosslegged on a cushion or even be a Buddhist to glean something from the Genjokoan. It instructs Buddhists and writers alike.

Dogen opens the Genjokoan with an affirmative statement about the world around us: "When all the dharmas are the Buddha-dharma, there are delusion and enlightenment, practice, birth, death, buddhas, and sentient beings." When I read this knotty statement, I replace the word *dharma* with the word *things* and I substitute *Buddha-dharma* with *sacred reality:* "When all things are sacred reality, there are delusion and enlightenment, practice, birth, death, buddhas, and sentient beings."

In his opening line, Dogen encourages us to look at all life as sacred reality. He says there are no errors. Everything—life, even death itself—is suffused with the sacred. The trick is to develop a lens wide enough to see the sacred in the world around us. How, then, do we perceive that which surrounds our lives (or, in my case, my grandfather's life) as sacred? How do we maintain this magnanimous affirmation of life?

On this score, I think writers can teach the Buddhists. Good writers drop us deeply into the sensate world of their characters. How? Through metaphor, through precise attention to the physical world, and through created versions of the past.

In *The Walker in the City*, Alfred Kazin's memoir of growing up in New York City, Kazin lets us taste the sweetness of malted-milk candy melting on his tongue. Maxine Hong Kingston draws us into the tension between heat and cold within her aunt's laboring body in the opening chapter of *The Woman Warrior.* Smells of desperate flu cures—whiskey, camphor, garlic—deluge us in Jane Brox's lyrical essay "Influenza 1918."

What all of these writers have in common is a deep respect for the world and the people they paint, yet each must recreate a character's experience. Surely Kazin didn't remember exactly what the malted-milk candies tasted like after fifty-odd years had gone by. Kingston didn't experience her cousin's birth in a Chinese barn, nor did Brox attend patients dying in the flu epidemic. Even so, they meticulously describe tastes, feelings, smells, and sights. Are they justified in using their imaginations to create a version of the past?

In her uncompleted memoir, *A Sketch of the Past,* Virginia Woolf struggles to take the same leap. She asks herself why it is so difficult to write about the past, even about her own past:

> Witness the incident of the looking-glass. Though I have done my best to explain why I was ashamed of looking at my own face I have only been able to discover some possible reasons; there may be others; I do not suppose that I have got at the truth; yet this is a simple incident; and it happened to me personally; and I have no motive for lying about it. In spite of all this, people write what they call 'lives' of other people; that is, they collect a number of events, and leave the person to whom it happened unknown.

Woolf reminds writers that writing about the truth or the past is not a simple matter. Nor does she seem to believe that it is entirely possible. What Woolf doesn't say is that there is another option. Woolf may not be able to reconstruct her own past truthfully, but she can create a version of the past for her reader.

By willingly letting their imaginations reconstruct the past, writers like Kazin, Kingston, and Brox build versions of the past that envelop the reader in a sensate world. So I emulate these writers and try to imagine my grandfather's life through their sacred writer's lens. I let myself imagine the contained smile on my grandfather's face as the nun approaches his hospital bed for confession. I let myself imagine my grandfather's own approach to the sacred island of Iona in western Scotland near the end of his life.

"My grandfather's long, sharp nose points away from the shore we've left behind and away from the hazy outline of the island we're nearing. Instead, he hales to the west, towards an open sea and an island he can't see, Ireland. His hands, once white and now speckled in browns, grasp the side of the boat with hesitation. My grandfather appears ready to let go."

No, I'm not sure my grandfather offered to hear the nun's confession, and I don't remember exactly where my grandfather gazed into the ocean as he approached Iona. But I have a memory of the second scene—I was with my grandfather on that boat. I remember an aura of longing that surrounded his aging body. I saw his tentative hands grasp the side of the blue metal boat. And I'm willing to let myself recreate that memory as fully and with as much attention to reality as I can.

What has been harder to write about is what I didn't see and what I don't know about my grandfather. How can I paint his life and his experience when I was absent from most of it? And even if I had been there, would I remember all the details? Would I discern the details he found important? Woolf hesitated, but Kingston and Brox took the leap for their characters. Can I?

When I walk through the Minnesota State Capitol, I am struck with the solemn echoes in the marble corridors. Even my size-six feet sound imposing. What would my grandfather, a Supreme Court justice, have heard as his own feet advanced through the Capitol? I imagine his measured stride reverberating with belief in temporal justice, with trust in facts. But I can't be sure what he heard. Maybe doubt filled his mind in the empty space between each footfall.

Eihei Dogen affirms the fundamental element of impermanence in the second line of the Genjokoan. He writes, "When the myriad dharmas are without self, there is no delusion, no enlightenment, no buddhas, no sentient beings, no birth, and no death." I think Dogen means that when we acknowledge, as Woolf has done, that the past disappears with each breath, we encounter impermanence. At the most fundamental level, the girl Virginia Woolf saw in the mirror had vanished, and the boy eating chocolates had died when Kazin wrote about him.

As I rub against the sacred elements in my grandfather's life, he completely vanishes. I know he looked like Monsignor Cullinan, but I don't know what he told the nun that night in the hospital. I know he walked down the halls of the Capitol, but I don't know what he heard there. I know he survived a death warrant from tuberculosis in the 1920s, but I don't know what or whether he thought about dying as we ferried out into the Irish Sea. The man who prayed with the monsignor, who walked down the Capitol corridors, who made a pilgrimage to Iona, actually died myriad deaths along the continuum of his life. By extrapolation, then, Dogen is right: There is no grandfather.

And writers don't have to pretend otherwise. We can write about the paradox that our job as writers about the past presents us with. How? We can use our rich imagination to paint the moment-to-moment experiences in our characters' lives, and we can write about our own struggles to capture their past as our hands grip the pen, bob over the keyboard. That is, we can write about both life and death in our fashioned texts.

Dogen puts it this way: "Since originally the Buddha way goes beyond abundance and scarcity, there are birth and death, delusion and enlightenment, sentient beings and buddhas." This line helps me understand that I can rejoice in my grandfather's comings and goings, in his ebbs and flows. As his granddaughter and as a Buddhist writer, I can resuscitate his echo in the Capitol halls and I can share with you, the reader, the challenge of capturing those ephemeral sounds.

Of course, not without some sorrow or longing. In the fourth sentence of the Genjokoan, Dogen concludes that knowing life's essential impermanence doesn't change a person's, or a writer's, desire to resurrect the dead. He writes, "Yet, though it is like this, simply, flowers fall amidst our longing, and weeds spring up amidst our antipathy."

People will always dream that they can capture and define the ever-changing world we live in. As writers, we convert these dreams into the fuel we need to write about the past. Our words—like waves in constant motion—will never anchor a moment that has vanished. But that doesn't mean that what we write isn't important. Our work can describe the challenges we face squinting into the myriad possibilities the past contains. And by reanimating the sacred reality of the characters we find there, writers give birth to a new kind of present moment.

When I confess uncertainty about what my grandfather said in that hospital room long ago, I openly acknowledge that the truth isn't something a writer can always offer. When I connect my grandfather's tentative grasp on the boat with his impending death, I have imposed my own words on a shared moment long gone. But in so doing, I offer my readers a chance to travel into my grandfather's hands—not into his present, but into their own.

Tess Gallagher

in dialogue with ROSEANN LLOYD

Tess Gallagher's collections of poetry, short stories, and essays have received wide national praise and a number of awards, including the Maxine Cushing Gray Foundation Award and the Elliston Award. On July 6, 1979, she gave a reading in Saint Paul. The following day she was interviewed by Roseann Lloyd, a writer and former student of hers.

ROSEANN LLOYD: Let's begin by talking about some changes in your recent work. The poems in *Instructions to the Double* are tightly constructed with a taut syntax, even violent line breaks, and, for the most part, a short line. It seems to me that more recent poems—those at the end of *Under Stars* and those you read last night—are more open in their form and more inclusive in their subject matter. Is this the direction your work is going now?

TESS GALLAGHER: Yes, I'm working to get the poem to sing out in a very full way. And yet, at the same time I was writing these new poems, I also wrote a tight, lyrical poem, the Bird-Window-Flying poem that I read last night. I can see that I'm not giving up one kind of poem for the other, but trying to work in both forms at the same time.

R. L.: Madeline DeFrees wrote of *Instructions to the Double*, "One is repeatedly amazed at the captured life as poem after poem 'believes in its cage.'" Are you conscious of working with the poem this way?

T. G.: I don't think of that idea of cages much anymore. I feel a lot more open to the poem. I'm writing an essay now about time and the poem in which I say that the moment of the writing of the poem is the moment of all possibilities. Anything that ever happened to me in the past, anything that didn't happen that I wanted to happen, anything that I hope for yet, present motivations, the cup sitting in front of me—anything—can come into the poem. And yet I think even though you're open with what you do, you're still choosing what you allow to be possible as material. I still make definite choices.

R. L.: You've said that what you admire about Akhmatova and South American poets is that they "take in so much of the world." Do you feel that they are a present influence?

T. G.: They've continued to influence me. I know that my poems are starting to be much more concerned with others, with lives tangential to mine. At the end of "I Save Your Coat But You Lose It Later," a heart surgeon suddenly flies in at the last four lines. I'm making use of events and people that I never knew how to place in a context before, how to give some significance. Here a person from another life ends up at the end of a poem about someone losing a coat!

I don't think that it's only reading poetry in translation that has affected my work. The change has come right out of my own life, from the feeling that people don't care enough about what's going on with their neighbors, they don't look after them. It's a sadness in my life that I couldn't do enough at times for people who were very important to me or that they couldn't answer needs of mine and we drifted apart and failed one another. When I was in Ireland, I said that I thought America was becoming a place of recoveries . . . the failure of marriages and relationships, I mean. . . .

R. L.: There were individual poems about the family in *Instructions to the Double,* but the dominant theme of the book is the exploration of the self. It seems that the unifying theme in *Under Stars* is family and other close relationships, going beyond the working out of ideas about the self.

T. G.: The self, yes. I was happy that I'd begun to look at the other people in my life. I think this concern will be greater in the new work.

R. L.: The poem about your sister, "I Take Care of You: A Lantern Dashes By in the Grass," is more open technically, yet it brings along a thread from both books. It's growing.

T.G.: "I Take Care of You," you know, it's a beautiful idea. Women have been the caretakers, and I don't think that we should lose that beautiful capability of giving in that way. We should realize that we can become impoverished if we lose the spiritual and psychic capability and the sense of how we are at one another's mercy in our lives, regardless of how much on our own we can be from time to time. The self-sufficiency mode is necessary, of course, to move you out into new territory, new and necessary territory, but it can also put you right out on a limb that's bound to break.

R.L.: You said once, "Where would we be without our childhood?" It seems to me that the fact of it continues in people who knew us as children.

T.G.: I like that idea, that you could have been really important to somebody back there, that our memory continues along with them in ways that we don't even know about—a little secret legacy out there. . . .

R.L.: Many women writers admire your work because of its technical risks and the inclusiveness of concerns you just spoke of. In particular, I think, your work is a model for other writers in its ability to deal with anger. Would you comment on this?

T.G.: I've never thought of anger as the main energy of my work, but I have made use of it at times. Anger is a valid emotion in one's life. It has a certain authority that other emotions don't have at crucial moments, and there's a certain honesty to it that I like.

I can understand "feminism" as a term applied to my work, and I'm a feminist in the sense that there have been boundaries that I haven't liked having imposed on me by the society I've grown up in— economic, social, psychic boundaries.

But if you are obsessed with anger, you become very depressed and you can, in a certain way, cripple whatever creative aspects you can imagine for yourself in a situation which has so much ground to recover—where you have to gain back so many centuries of neglect of feminine talents and respect. You can become lost in the anger of it, and you can also disappear into the hatred of the forces that are believed to have caused it.

You must put the anger into a perspective or its authority is short-lived. I use the poems to do that. You know, in that poem about my uncle, "Two Stories," I actually relive his murder. I'm trying to find a way to look at it, to make that instance real to me. I had great difficulty in believing in the death of one of the people closest to me in my childhood.

R. L.: In the poem, you list the events like a chant, an exorcism.

T. G.: Yes, so that I could believe that it happened and so that I could have a context for honoring that death and that life.

R. L.: Was it a difficult poem to write?

T. G.: Oh, it was one of the most difficult. I keep thinking I should have done more for him, I should have done more for this life of his. Maybe I will. I think he still has possible life in my poems.

R. L.: It's as though you're saying that anger must have a product. It will lead you beyond your situation or beyond itself in some way.

T. G.: Yes.

R. L.: I'd like to look at your work now from a different perspective: the relationship between the poems and your interest in music. You've said that Roethke required students to memorize and speak poems out loud and that you work on new poems by saying them out loud over and over "until the music is right." Now you are learning to sing Irish ballads which you recorded from folk singers in Ireland. What effect does this way of working have on your writing?

T. G.: It makes me write a more musical line, I think. I'm really sensitive to shifts and tempo in the poems. I can tell when the poem is starting to go pianissimo, when it starts to gather impetus or when it starts to break up and fragment—all these different kinds of movement that poems make that are forms now for us more so than the traditional forms. I learned to play the piano when I was five years old, and I think I learned before I realized it how a piece of music moves and all the phases it can go through. . . . Now, by learning to sing these Irish songs, I'm reinforcing all of those movements.

R. L.: One of the strengths of your work, which goes along with your ear for music, is your knack for catching the human voice. Your mother is a great storyteller, I know. What is the connection between this aspect of your writing and your family?

T. G.: I like to hear the human voice, the way people really talk. The moment you get a voice in there as a gesture, the poem automatically perks up. I use speech as a way of enlivening the poem, as a strategy, really, at moments when there's been some description which can lull a poem, pause, soften. Then the minute the voice comes in, the poem rises again.

R. L.: When you call it a strategy, it sounds easy. It's difficult!

T. G.: Well, Yeats was doing it all the time! In that poem I love so much, "Adam's Curse," the way he renders speech and conversation is wonderful. Levertov is able to give you whole afternoons of conversation in her poems. I think it's very difficult to keep poems that are wholly conversational interesting. I tend to use conversation as a highlight, as a painter might use a color to highlight certain forms and shapes. A kind of inflection.

R. L.: Do you feel that your skill in capturing the voice is something you got from your particular family?

T. G.: After traveling, you hear the speech in your own area much more clearly. That poem I wrote entirely in my father's voice, "3 a.m. Kitchen, My Father Talking," was written after I'd been in Ireland, come home and heard the accents, my father from Oklahoma, my mother from Missouri. Their way of talking was rich for me in a new way. I think I couldn't have written that poem before traveling. And any time speech is attached to a region, as in my home, it stands out in your memory and you hear it when you go back to it.

R. L.: I wonder if your sensitivity to speech and the musical line allow you to use more repetition than someone who works with a flatter line. For example, in "Four Dancers at an Irish Wedding," a very short poem, you repeat the line "One if for sorrow" and the line that's like a refrain, "Darling, darling, darling."

T. G.: I stole that, by the way, from Vachel Lindsay. At the University of Washington we did interpretive reading, and I read one of his poems, "The Chinese Nightingale." Beautiful poem!

R. L.: Does he repeat "darling"?

T. G.: Exactly that! "Darling, darling, darling." Lindsay gave me a good love for music, too, come to think of it. He was a flamboyant poet, and he was one of the first poets to go around the country reading. I loved that repetition in his poems because the "darling" is almost like a bird sound.

R. L.: The word is so loaded, it's as though you couldn't use it once, but you can use it three times. And its excessiveness gives irony to the situation of the poem: "Sweet / gladness, I / am not yours / and you are not mine ..."

T. G.: You get away with it by making it a law unto itself in the poem. You just trust it. A lot of what people believe in poems comes through building a kind of surety in the poem, however you arrive. I always sit down very seriously to the activity of the poem, as though I believe I can make whatever I want to happen there happen.

R. L.: Other than music, what kinds of things have you been doing this year to renew your work?

T. G.: I've been reading a lot of philosophy and reading in a concentrated way about time and the way in which we experience time. That's been a preoccupation that I've carried on for a long time, and this year on the Guggenheim I've been able to pursue it in depth.

R. L.: Because of your strong drive for the narrative, you've experimented in various ways with breaking up the sequence of events so that the poem isn't locked into chronological time, most noticeably in "Songs of the Runaway Bride." "Time Lapse with Tulips" also comes to mind.

T. G.: It's been a preoccupation, on many levels, all along. It is a renewing experience for me to write essays now, and this prose will probably affect the poems in some way. I also make constant returns to familiar sources of energy. This year, for instance, I lived in a cabin by the ocean, alone for four or five months. The release of looking at water is somehow very calming, and it gets you to a good state of mind for entering into poems, and it also allows you to be in many places at once.

I've also spent time at home, just doing familiar things that I haven't done for a while, going out to places I'd been to as a child, going fishing with my father. Family activities take you back in new ways, because you're in the same place but you're different, and there's going to be an energy created from that double vision of yourself as now and then and also the people around you as now and back then. Of course, I continue to enjoy movies, reading contemporary writers, such as Jensen, Burkard, Skoyles, Carver.... I'm always reading Yeats.

R. L.: I'd like to summarize what I take to be your advice to beginning writers: "Listen for the music, don't drone, trust your jumps, and cut, cut, cut."

T. G.: Well, sometimes I say, "Expand, expand, expand." Directives are different for each person.

R. L.: Your advice for revising: "Once you've done all that, speak the words, move the lines, make it physical, run it through the typewriter a hundred times!"

T. G.: That's pretty accurate. One of the main things I try to do with students is to go into the psychology of the poem, what the poem's ambitions are, and try to get the writer to rethink them. For instance, to get the writer of a poem that kept ending in a dissolute, abject tone to go back and see what spiritual adventures the poem might have opened up, not necessarily optimism, rather, a new way of thinking about the instance of life that it had approached. If you don't have that moment of recognition by the end of the poem, it won't be exciting for the reader, let alone the writer. I know that I'm hard on endings with students, that I don't let them get out of the poems as easily as they want. I'm like that with myself—careful about endings. I know that I tend to end poems more dramatically than most contemporary poets feel is possible. Now they mostly feel they have to trail off like most American conversations.... It's unusual to find a poem ending like "On Your Own."

R. L.: Yes, I'd say there's no doubt about the closure in that poem:

> It's like this on your own: the charms
> unlucky, the employment
> solitary, the best love always
> the benefit of a strenuous doubt.

Thank you, Tess, for talking about your work today. I don't want this talk to trail off "like most American conversations"—in closing, I'd like to give you back the words you often left scribbled on your door in Missoula: *Come in, keep the fire, I'll be right back.* We welcome your return.

Balancing Subtlety
and Sledgehammers:
Coming Out as a Gay Poet

WILLIAM REICHARD

Most writers spend a great deal of time observing other people: listening to their language, watching their actions. I've always spent more time listening than speaking, especially when I'm with my family. I grew up in a large family (ten children) in a small town (population seventy), and there was always plenty to observe.

A few years ago, I sat in my mother's kitchen, surrounded by my many sisters, listening to my family talk. In the next room, my fifteen nieces and nephews ran back and forth, playing a claustrophobic game of tag. One nephew was "it." He chased his cousin, tapped him on the shoulder. The new "it" turned on his captor and screamed, "You faggot!"

Everybody—my mother, my sisters, my brothers, my brothers-in-law—laughed. Then the game went on. It was Christmas 1990. I had only to hear the word "faggot" to know I was home.

What's the worst word in the world? What word do many children, and too many adults, use when they want to verbally injure someone? My mother always thought it was "fucker." Any other profanity was acceptable, and she used most of it, but not "fucker." Yet, as I grew up in my small town, I came to see that there were worse words, and that many of those words applied to me: *faggot, queer, cocksucker, homo, fairy.* No one was around to tell me that the meanings of words are relative, that what is profanity to one person is a source of pride to another; I had to find that out on my own. And so I return to Christmas 1990 and "Faggot!"

At that time, I was engaged in my own private poetic revolution. I had not written much poetry before the fall of 1990. I was in the MA writing program at the University of Minnesota, concentrating on short fiction. But by the previous spring I had finished my course work and thesis project in fiction and was ready to move on to something new. A friend suggested poetry; she knew John Engman, a local poet, and was sure I'd benefit from his instruction. So I enrolled in his advanced workshop, not sure what to expect. To enter, I was required to submit a small sample of poems. I pulled out what little poetry I had written and chose the "best" pieces, all full of heavy-handed, convoluted images, all dense, encoded, and, from my current perspective, pretty stupid. You see, I wanted to write about my experience as a gay man, but I didn't know how. I was still afraid of being called a faggot or a queer, still afraid of being mocked if I committed my gay self to print. So I hid my ideas in thick, strangling metaphor: "Dark birds, sing to me. . . ." blab blah blab. One critique session cured me of that. John and my fellow students called me on my evasiveness: What did I want to write? What was I trying to say? How could I say it simply, clearly? I had come out as a gay man when I was twenty-one. Now, at twenty-seven, I was asked to come out again, as a gay poet.

Over the course of that quarter, I started the process of integrating my everyday life into my work. My poems moved from their tangled morass of metaphor to clearer, simpler observations, sometimes incorporating graphic fact, most often illustrating unapologetically my experiences as a gay man. By the time Christmas 1990 arrived, I wasn't content to listen to anyone, least of all a family member, use the word *faggot* as a derogatory term. I asked my nephew what the term meant; he said it was just a dirty word. I explained the difference.

That scene stayed with me long after the holidays, and as a new quarter of advanced poetry began, I wondered what I wanted to write about. I was registered in "The Poet in the World," a class examining the social and political ramifications of contemporary poetry. I knew that whatever work I did, it had to continue the progress I'd made in the previous months, had to move toward some sort of integration of my sexual self into my writing. As I covered the assigned readings, I mused over the way certain labels for gay men are used in our society as generic "dirty" words: faggot, queer, cocksucker, homo, fairy. I wanted to know (I still want to know) why these words have taken on this generic quality. A person might call another a faggot and not really be questioning his or her sexual orientation at all. The use of gay labels as generic "dirty" words seems to be tied up in the American social structure, in the way the heterosexual patriarchy has claimed dominance over the rest of the world, in the way that the two true sexes are not male and female but (heterosexual) male and not male. It is not usual to use any other stigmatizing minority label as a generic insult; someone with a prejudice against the Japanese (an all-too-popular and frightening trend these days) wouldn't call just anyone a Jap or a Nip. However, I've heard "homo" and "queer" applied randomly to everyone.

The writing project I finally settled on was an exploration of the very labels that had been used to hurt me and my gay brothers all of our lives. With a nod to Judy Grahn, whose *Another Mother Tongue* suggested my own agenda, I called my project "A Faggot's Lexicon." I set out to examine the lexical origins of some derogatory gay labels, to try, as others before me had tried, to reclaim these lost words, to take the weapons used against me and turn them into positive words of power.

The work proceeded rapidly; I wrote the first drafts of ten or eleven poems in under three weeks, and turned in a twenty-four page manuscript at the end of the quarter. What I discovered, as I wrote "Faggot," "Queer," "Invert," and "Fruit," was that these words meant nothing in and of themselves. I had been willing to buy into their meanings as assigned by a homophobic population, willing to carry around all of the garbage that the words as insults implied. I discovered that the words could tell stories, and the stories could be positive, funny, poignant, or angry; that my experiences, no longer obscured through the filters of heavy metaphor, were my best material.

No new ideas here, I realize. Every writer goes through this distillation process at some point. But for gay and lesbian writers, perhaps for writers of any minority, this process is more difficult. Not only are we faced with finding a voice, but we must also struggle to claim our right to that voice. In a society that works consciously and unconsciously every day to erase us, we have to work that much harder to reinscribe ourselves, to be recognized as valuable, authentic voices in the literatures of our world.

I'd like to stop for a moment and meditate on what it means to be a poet in contemporary American society. When I was growing up, I didn't read poetry unless I was forced to, and it was a painful, confusing experience; I had no idea what poetry was, what poems meant. They didn't seem to be in any way connected to the real world. I doubt my experience of poetry was unique. I don't have any statistics on hand but would be willing to bet that most Americans cannot name one living poet, cannot quote even one line from any poem. We are not a poetry-reading society. I won't go into my theories as to why that is so, but I will stop to ask the reader: What do you think of when you think of a poet? What image crops up in most people's minds when they hear the word? I recall watching reruns of *The Ernie Kovacs Show* when I was a teenager; I thought Kovacs was hilarious. He had one character, Percy Dovetonsils, who was a poet. Percy wore a smoking jacket, an ascot, and thick glasses; he smoked cigarettes in a long holder and spoke with a lisp. Percy was a priss. And this, I would argue, is what most people think of when they think of a poet or a gay man. Kovacs' creation material was an all-too-accurate portrait of what his culture thought a poet was. Since the beginning of the nineteenth century, many poets have been sexually suspect: Shelley, Byron, Wilde, Whitman all played with popular notions of masculinity and femininity, all crossed that forbidden boundary between (heterosexual) male and not male. Although some were gay, some bisexual, and some heterosexual, all were labeled homosexual because of their choice of vocation. *Poet*, like *faggot*, became a dirty word.

We're a practical nation, demanding that everyone and everything earn its keep, justify its existence. Where does poetry fit in? To the extent that children are taught poetry at all, it's nineteenth (and perhaps early twentieth) century poetry. According to my public-school teachers, poetry stopped with Carl Sandburg, and he and all poets were celibate, and nothing they wrote really had anything to do with the world at large; we only read them because they were in the curriculum. For myself, for many Americans, a poet was Percy Dovetonsils, a man who wasn't a man, a man who didn't fit in, who had nothing practical to contribute.

In the same sense, a gay man was a misfit, refusing to adhere to the heterosexual constructs of the social majority, not adding to the growth and wealth of the population by reproducing. Since I grew up knowing I was gay, afraid to let that secret out, I couldn't read or write poetry; that would doubly implicate me, make me twice as displaced. In a sense, I had to come out as a poet, long after I came out as a gay man, and claim my place in a long line of American misfits.

Poetic silence is a craft I've learned from each of my teachers, from the poems I've read since I rediscovered poetry in 1990. The simple adage that showing is better than telling rings truer each time I sit down to write. Readers must discover for themselves the heart of the poem, and the best any writer can do is take the readers on a journey into the work and hope that they find their way out again. Sometimes, what's excluded is more important than what's included, because without a little mystery, a poem falls flat; truth is necessary in poetry, and then there is dogma. But at some point, poetic silence collides with what I like to call personal silence. Most people in our society are taught to control their emotions, keep quiet about their feelings and ideas, stay neat and proper, and this is personal silence: the learned, repressive behavior that dictates how and whether people express themselves. A problem arises when we, as gay and lesbian writers, must mediate the difference between personal and poetic silence. In a society which often denies us the most basic human rights, which routinely tries to deny our existence, where do we draw the line between poetic craft and personal freedom? Certainly, we want our poetry to be as well crafted, as eloquent, as the work of writers in the social/sexual/literary mainstream, but we must also be constantly claiming our place in that social/sexual/literary mainstream, breaking the silence that has obscured us for too long. Our right to speak and write about ourselves is not guaranteed, so that what many heterosexual writers can afford to take for granted—the things they can leave unsaid—we cannot. (A poet who accomplishes the difficult task of mixing the mundane with metaphor, who achieves the balance between personal and private silence, is Paul Monette in *Love Alone: 18 Elegies for Rog.*) A great many people would rather not think or read about homosexuality. Being a gay poet means learning to balance subtlety and sledgehammers, obscurity and clarity, honesty and deceit, the literal and the figurative; what is at stake for gay writers is our very existence, in a literary, and perhaps a literal, sense.

Some time ago, I returned from the Second Annual Gay and Lesbian Graduate Student Conference in Urbana, Illinois. (I'm currently completing my PhD in English.) The conference, entitled "Making It Perfectly Queer," focused primarily on theoretical, academic concerns, and seemed to have an unofficial, if not unspoken, agenda: mending the rift between theory and practice. This split is not new; feminism has been struggling with the problem since the inception of the women's movement. But for gay men, negotiating the differences seems particularly urgent; in the age of AIDS, when our brothers are dying by the thousands, we cannot sit back and simply theorize, or we will theorize ourselves right out of existence. Action is demanded. But neither can we be content simply to act, for activism requires a great deal of intelligence, a theoretical foundation from which to proceed. My own questions arising out of the conference focused on my work as a poet: Who am I to sit back and write poems while people die? How can my poems, any poems, make a difference? I found myself falling back into the old habit of considering poets and poetry in the manner of many Americans: Poets do nothing, they add nothing, they don't help. Fortunately, I took the time to remind myself that there are poets all over the world whose work does contribute to our understanding of what it means to be human. I remembered the work of poet Kenny Fries, whose *The Healing Notebooks* deals so honestly, so powerfully, with the loss of a lover to AIDS: "Sarah says, People with AIDS need drugs / not fiction about AIDS. There I use / the name in someone else's name. / Not one of my poems ever saved / one Jew. And still I sit all day as if / choosing the right word could save your life."

If we are to overcome public ignorance and governmental apathy, the theorists have to act and the activists have to theorize until their understanding of the world is as tough as their grip on it. And we each have to use the tools at our disposal. I am a poet; I use poetry to the best of my ability to help readers consider, if even for a moment, whether or not poetry can make a difference, what words can and do mean, what it is to be a gay man in our society, and what it is to be a poet in our unpoetic world.

Cuddling up with the Self-Censor

KATHLEEN NORRIS

It seems to me that the self-censor, that inner voice of the critic which speaks harshly to the writer as he or she happily churns out verbiage, has been getting too much bad press. As a sometime writing teacher, I know the value and necessity of encouraging people to "let the writing come," and find William Stafford's metaphor of lazily fishing for words a good one. Sooner or later there's a nibble; *something*, even if it's not the *right* thing, comes along, and it's better to catch it on the page than reject it out of hand. I agree with Stafford that most writer's block comes from taking ourselves too seriously, and not being willing to, as he puts it, occasionally "lower our standards."

But writing, like much that is important in life, is a matter of attentiveness, and I've learned to pay close attention to the way that my inner voices—the critic (the arguer, modifier, and reviser) as well as the advocate that wants to simply let the words flow—are necessary complements. Each is a valued component of the writing process, and the trick is not to reject one in favor of the other but to keep them in balance.

As one who writes poetry and personal narrative (frequently on spiritual themes), I walk a well-mined valley, using the word "mined" in two senses. The self-critic can become a tyrant here, calling me both audacious and ridiculous for assuming that I can come up with something new under the sun. It reminds me that self-indulgence is a danger in each of my genres, and that the temptation to allow undigested journaling to invade my writing is always there. If I need an object lesson, my own work serves me well. Many of my early poems read like code: Like many young writers, I was writing more to express myself than to communicate with others. Now even *I* can't tell what the hell they're about.

Writing encourages me precisely because it's not a young person's game. Compared to mathematics, writing has few prodigies, few people capable of turning out masterworks in their teens and early twenties. Many top-notch mathematicians are obsolete at thirty, but writing is a more sustainable activity, and this pleases me. But I must also acknowledge that writing well means agreeing to always be a student, young at heart. Long ago I realized that I'd never get it right the first time, and I learned to listen to the self-censor. And a little over a year ago I had to listen, horrified, as another critic (my editor at Ticknor & Fields) suggested that my well-worked manuscript for *Dakota*, then about 325 pages, would benefit from major cuts, maybe as much as a hundred pages. I never thought I'd say this, but working it out—I ended up with ninety-nine fewer pages—was one of the best things I've ever done as a writer. The book is now in its tenth printing and has engendered nearly a thousand letters from strangers all over the country, largely because my self-censor and I cuddled up for a week or so and removed the bilge.

A few years ago, I heard Galway Kinnell give a lecture in Minneapolis in which he made a valuable distinction between writing that is "merely personal," containing too much that is of interest only to the writer (and possibly the writer's close friends) and that which is "truly personal," more open, more hospitable to the reader. My rule of thumb when writing, reading, and reviewing poetry and prose is that detailed accounts of dreams or journal entries fall into the former category. I am looking for resonance, which occurs when the writer, as E.M. Forster said, manages to "only connect," and thus transforms what could be a banal detail into a telling one. I am looking for stories in which the self-absorption needed by any writer in order to write has been transcended, making room for the reader to make his or her own interpretations.

I am looking for humble speech rather than ether; I much prefer language that is grounded in and that evokes the five senses to airhead prose. Abstraction, jargon, and code for the initiated, whether it's sociological, theological, or New Age, is the enemy of good writing. It refuses to let true language through. Ironically, it also refuses to let writing be truly personal—self-revelatory in any meaningful way. The best poetry and personal narrative has an individual, human voice; not a voice that is the center (much less the hero) of every story, but one that reflects ordinary human doubts and weakness. The goal—one that the self-censor is uniquely suited to help us reach—is writing that is self-revelatory without being self-indulgent or self-aggrandizing. It takes a lot of work, and scary time spent listening to the downside of one's soul, but it's worth it.

Negotiating the Boundaries between Catharsis and Literature

CHERI REGISTER

Ten years ago, I completed an account of my experience with chronic illness and sent out the manuscript. The most memorable line in my collection of rejection letters was one that began, "Maybe if you were somebody famous. . . ." At the time, I was offended by the implication that only voyeurs could care about so private an ordeal as illness. My point, after all, was to bring this experience to public consciousness, to make people care about the psychological impact and the social consequences of being interminably ill.

I am thankful now for that rejection letter. It saved me from exposing my still-inadequate narrative voice: a glib, heroic persona who hoped that readers, as they learned about illness, would also notice how well she was doing. I had to think a lot harder about what makes an account of personal suffering worth reading, and I went on to publish a much better book than that manuscript would have become. The rejection forced me to ask myself some fundamental questions: Why write about suffering in the first place? Who cares about blood and guts and sobbing and quaking?

We are usually advised to set such censorial questions aside: Write for yourself, we're told; don't worry about audience. Indeed, writing for catharsis has enough lifesaving value for the writer to make the reader irrelevant. A writer who expects to transform catharsis into literature, however, has to involve the reader in a negotiation of boundaries. If the work merely invites the reader in to witness the catharsis, it may come across as a tedious display of the writer's endurance. Lauded by a Minneapolis audience for her courage in surviving imprisonment and torture, Nien Cheng, author of *Life and Death in Shanghai*, retorted, "There is no virtue in enduring hardship." Nor is there immediate literary value.

I have come to believe, however, that all writing about suffering—
or any emotionally charged personal experience—must initially be cathartic. The first draft has to be an emptying out of all truths, some so
closely held that we can't see them until we get them down on paper. If
we don't do this, uncontrollable revelatory outbursts or the tension of
secrecy itself will impede the work. This doesn't mean we are obligated
to tell all to everyone, but that we cannot select the truths worth telling or find the best form in which to convey them until we've done an
honest and careful self-examination.

Writing it out also helps to contain the experience of suffering, to
give it form and coherence. When I'm lying in bed with a high fever, I
often tell myself the story of what's happening to me, narrating it moment by moment. When the fever borders on hallucinatory, these stories
can become quite imaginative. Sometimes I think about recreating them
as short stories, but once I've recovered the momentum is gone. They
have served their purpose, and I need some other motivation to make
them public, which was provided one time in a Loft fiction class.

Given the assignment to describe, with attention to detail, a character engaged in an action, I decided to try turning one of these fever
narratives into a literary piece. I showed a woman coming out of a
faint on her kitchen floor, picking herself up and getting back upstairs.
The response from the other class members was encouraging, but one
question gave me pause: "Did this really happen to you?" Although
I believe it arose out of genuine interest in my welfare, it made me a
little uneasy. Was my writing so compelling that the story had to be
true, or so raw that it could only be personal experience?

Making suffering coherent does not by itself turn it into literature.
To move it from the private to the cosmic realm, we also have to find
the meaning in it, to turn the cloud inside out and expose the ragged or
silver lining. Natalie Kusz wrote in this publication (September 1991)
that it is "not so much what happened" that matters to an audience,
but "what we know because of what happened." The point of commu-
nicating this to others, Kusz says, is "to enlighten the real world" and
"to help move it forward."

My experience in the Loft class reminded me that moving others to understand and respond in a compassionate way requires more

than literal detail. One reader asked me why I had the character go downstairs for aspirin when she could have kept it in the bathroom medicine cabinet, and why she dragged herself upstairs to vomit when she could have thrown up in the kitchen sink. I was savvy enough to know that "because that's how it happened" was the wrong answer, but I was reluctant to change these details just to keep readers from puzzling over them. I knew they had something to do with sacred space, with controlling danger, with what uncomprehending people call denial. Keeping medicine close at hand is, for me, a concession to illness, like keeping the telephone next to the bed. Unless I am immobilized, my phone sits across the room on a dresser, and jumping up to answer it is an affirmation of health. How much space I allow illness to inhabit in my house helps determine how much of my life it occupies. I will store IV bags in the refrigerator and hang them from the dining-room chandelier, but I will never, never defile my kitchen sink. If I ever do get around to turning that class assignment into a short story, I will need to create a character who manages her life in those ways, for those reasons. What the reader needs to know is not what I do, but what chronic illness does to daily life. In this case, the readers' puzzled responses helped me discover that behavior I had thought natural and unremarkable was actually motivated by the chronic aspect of my illness.

"Because that's how it happened" is, nevertheless, a legitimate motive for writing about suffering. Personal suffering may be the primary raw material life offers us, along with the landscapes we inhabit, the characters we encounter. Much like ethnicity, what we have suffered will probably inform all that we write in some way. I suspect that a raft trip down the Mississippi narrated from Jim's point of view would carry a sharper consciousness of race than Huck's voice could give it. Likewise, if Ahab were the narrator of *Moby Dick,* the novel would probably convey a more intimate sensitivity to the absence of that leg.

Having an experience of suffering in our supply of memories, plots, and images does not obligate us to write about it, however. Choosing what use to make of it gets us into some tricky boundary negotiations. Even those of us who accept disability or illness as the normal condition of our lives have trouble writing about it in that way. If we send a character limping, wheeling, or wheezing along the ordinary course of life, we can expect an outcry from curious readers: "Hey! What's wrong with her?" There are few writers who assert the normality of disability as boldly as Anne Finger, whose short stories feature a protagonist with crutches and leg braces going through adolescence, having her first love affair, becoming a political activist. When she first sent her work out for publication, editors objected that the stories were not really about disability. Readers were presumably not ready to accept a disabled character as anything but the victim of whatever misfortune had left her in that state.

Two incidents in another Loft class illustrate the hazards of using an experience of suffering as enlightening information about a character rather than central subject matter. They show how the reader's preconceptions about a certain form of suffering might illumine or obscure the meaning of the work. I cite these examples with some trepidation, having followed the debate in the *View* about classroom critiques. I want to emphasize that I have no complaints about the class, the teacher, or the participants. There was no violation of ethics. The issue would be difficult and sensitive in any context.

In the first case, a member of the class submitted for comment a personal essay about her experience of a particular landscape. Midway through the essay, she informed the reader, very briefly, that her child had died in this landscape. That piece of information became the focus of our discussion. Some people wanted her to say more: to tell about the child, about the death, about her feelings at the time. Others felt that she had let us know, in a stunning economy of language, that the death of her child was a cataclysm that altered her relation to the landscape and her perception of nature itself, which was what the essay was about. I asked her later how she felt about the comments. She agreed with the suggestion that a portrait of her child might strengthen the essay, but felt that describing her feelings would be stating the obvious and would trivialize the meaning that surviving the loss of a child has for a parent.

I sensed in the discussion of her essay, as she did, that some of the comments were intended more to show sympathy than to polish the writing. The request for a description of her feelings sounded a little like permission to give way to the catharsis that this worst sorrow imaginable surely warrants. But expecting her to do that right there, in front of us all, in an essay about something else, ignores the boundaries she had established between her private experience of suffering and her public, literary expression of it.

The second incident is an illustrative contrast to the first. Another participant handed around a memoir describing a little girl's sense of security in her family and neighborhood. A dim aura of danger around the edges highlighted this theme. Toward the end of the memoir, there was a critical scene in which the girl's father reminded her, in a situation that was menacing for other reasons, that she had better not tell "our secret." The discussion of this piece focused on formal matters: the effectiveness of the images, the need for more descriptive detail here and there. The passage in which the sense of security was undermined was cited and praised. But no one ever mentioned the word "incest." No one ever asked, "Did this really happen to you?" or said, "Tell us more about the secret."

What is the difference between the two cases? Both had presented shocking personal information in a skillfully compact form. This information was not the core subject matter in either case, but had a profound impact on the meaning of the piece. Were we more restrained by taboo in the second instance, or could it be that incest is now codified in our literary vocabulary, so that we understand immediately that a secret between a father and a daughter is not about Mom's birthday present? If we accept a passing reference as sufficient to denote the suffering of children violated by parents, why do we ask for lamentations from parents who have lost children?

Ultimately, these examples have to do with comfort level. Loft members are, for the most part, nice people who want to support each other as writers and as human beings. When some of us write about or make reference to distressing experiences, we blur the boundaries between catharsis and literature and test the rules of critical etiquette. I felt that my boundaries were safely in place when someone in the fiction class said to me, "I really like your writing. I wish you didn't have to go through the experience, but I love what you do with it." It is just as proper to say, "What happened to you was awful, but your telling of it would flow better if you left out that long explanatory passage on page three."

This is by no means an us-and-them issue. Writers are readers, too, and we all feel some curiosity when the anomalous goes unexplained. Suffering one trauma out of the many life offers does not confer membership in an omnicompassionate elite. I have struggled to maintain the boundaries between catharsis and literature mostly as one who writes about suffering. I recently became conscious of my role as reader in this endeavor after being asked to comment on some poems-in-progress by a friend who writes very candidly about personal suffering. The poems that had to do with physical illness posed no problems. I could excise words and move lines without wincing at gory images or praising his courage or asking to know more about how pain feels. Critiquing poems about his mother's death, however, was a more sensitive matter. How could I tell someone who was grieving, without feeling crass about it, whether his metaphors for grief worked? The difference is that I am still a stranger to this experience. I am the passerby watching the funeral from across the street. I have to remind myself that my business as a friendly critic *is* inherently respectful: A direct, cathartic cry of sorrow calls for consolation, but a poem offered for critique deserves to be read as a poem.

Fiction, Nonfiction, and the Woods

RICK BASS

The hunting season is when I lay in my meat for the winter and the rest of the coming year and, to a large part, when I lay in my dream-time; when I carve out some space in my imagination. I wander the woods, think, and observe. I never notice things quite as sharply as when I am hunting. Time seems to stop; perhaps, for brief moments, it really does stop and I'm able to notice this phenomenon. It is like a dream, only better: it is real, even hyperreal. I'm glad hunting season doesn't last all year. I couldn't stand it. Just two or three months is enough to charge my battery—the core of my self—for the rest of the year. It's a cycle, a rhythm, which is critical to me as a writer. I don't think of it so much as taking a deer (or elk or grouse) from the woods as I think of it as a giving of myself over to the woods: an immersion into the hunt as if I were plunging off a cliff. Doing what I love, for the love of it—and respecting my quarry and its life, and my life, as one respects one's garden, or one's art.

As I get older, I baby myself more and more as a writer. I work less than ever, it seems, at structuring what lies ahead in my work, and in-stead only plan my days, my external life, around the notion of staying in a rhythm or cycle of unknowingness. This, of course, wreaks havoc on my ability to function in the so-called real world—phone calls are an agony—but as anyone knows who's ever had the good fortune to be able to structure their life around their writing, whether for two weeks, two months, a year, or a lifetime, it lets me position my work so I can hit it at pretty much the same time and place every day. It makes it that much easier to enter into the depths of the subconscious and occasionally even the unconscious. Travel, in this regard, though frequently a good and necessary stimulant, can also be a debilitating interruption, a distraction from the rhythm and cycle of writing, and of being a writer.

So often now, my days—my good days—are filled with a rested, content kind of peace (I hesitate to use the word laziness), in which, upon finishing the last sentence of the day's work, I begin the movement in the cycle toward tomorrow's work. It feels like the moon's orbit to me. I don't stew or mull over what will come next, though I do try to leave each day's work at a point of beginning, a scene or moment of energy that will serve as a jumpstart for the next day's work, to try to bury any seam or sign of transition, to try to keep the cycle and rhythm whole.

Now I am free to play with my family, and to address myself to the demands and chores of paperwork; to fool with plumbing, firewood, repairs of this or that, and hiking, and reading, and hunting, and journalism, and to begin also, in my mind, resting immediately, trying, in that unnameable, immeasurable, daydreamy way, to stay close to the story I'm working on without really thinking about it. The effort is more of a negative direction than a positive one; it doesn't even so much involve trying to get or stay close to the meat and essence and possibility of the story as it involves simply trying to hold one's position—to keep from drifting or skewing too far afield. The feeling or image I sometimes get is that it is like lounging on an inflatable air mattress, a raft out in the gulf. Even though you're lolling on that raft, shades on, half-lulled by the sound of waves and seagulls, some small part of you, some knot deep within, is somehow trying to tense and hold that air mattress more or less in place—to keep it from floating too far out on the tide, but also to keep it from riding back into shore until it is time to write again.

Silly stuff, but real; that's how it feels. It's like the deer in November, the bucks who've laid down their scrapes and rubs with their antlers, rubbing the bark off small trees along the approximate edges of their territory—in the writer's case, the story's rough boundaries. The deer then bed down and rest, never too far from these signposts, and wait, and watch, and listen for all manner of things: intruders, predators, rival deer, or, best of all, one must imagine, for receptive does, ready to be bred, ready for new life to be created.

Write what you know is one of the most ancient writing dictums, but it's one I think about a lot, and one to which a simple corollary might be added: *Know something.* Once again, in the vein of rhythms, it's good to have a model within your brain, a grid of logic, which the direction (and logic) of your story can then follow and imitate, in order to be as lifelike, as realistic—as creative—as possible. For a while I used to get bummed when I realized that in talking to students I often compared writing not so much to great acts of art but to earthier, more elemental processes: football (an offensive line firing off the ball; the desire to move the ball downfield); hunting (the tracking and searching for an unseen thing ahead of you); and geology (the layers of sediment laid down one upon the other, even in the midst of erosive forces, fault shiftings, earth thrusts, etc.). Even sawing and splitting firewood and building rock walls, when you are in the rhythm, can become a model for your writing. New-Age words such as synergy, harmony, and resonance come to mind, but just because these words are sometimes abused and sold six-for-a-dollar does not make them any less valid or powerful when you encounter them in their real incarnation.

Knowledge of a system—any system—enables one to work more authoritatively, more confidently, with perhaps the greatest artistic tool, the power of metaphor; how one thing, perhaps thought previously different, is understood now to be like or similar to another thing. *Discovery*, epiphany. Or, conversely, how two or more things previously thought to be alike or similar are found now to be different—rifted, broken apart.

I think about the notion of nature writing a lot because, I suppose, I do it a lot. My greatest passion is the writing of fiction, but because the American wilderness—a system of great beauty, complexity, grace, and logic—is being fractured and gouged and sold on the cheap, stolen from both the present and the future, I find myself spending, of necessity, most of my time writing environmental nonfiction, to try to help save the last corners and pockets of the last truly wild (and truly healthy and truly creative) places.

It makes me feel like Dr. Jekyll and Mr. Hyde. Sometimes when I am in the woods, hiking or hunting, I worry that my nature writing is in direct opposition to my fiction writing: that one of the things I do in nature writing (and in hiking and hunting) is notice as many elements as possible, both great and small, and strive to understand their relationships to one another—to weave the knowledge and observations together toward a greater whole, from and amongst infinite parts. And in doing this, whether in the observing or the writing, a harmony is achieved.

But sometimes I worry that the power of fiction is the power of conflict, not the power of harmony; that the driving force in fiction is things at odds, not the incredible interdependence seen in nature, as one sinks deeper and deeper into it. I worry that my mind might turn to mush with regard to fiction—that I might lose the edge of conflict and dissent, and the love of it—from loving nature.

I know there is a huge flaw somewhere in the logic of this fear, as there is in so many fears. But it is one I am thinking about and wrestling with right now. It's hard to do both fiction writing and nature writing. Sometimes it feels as if the earth has two moons. You look up in the sky and see one moon, and respond to its pull, and its rhythms, but then, over your shoulder, you sense or catch sight of a second, conflicting moon.

It's hard enough to learn, and stay positioned within, the cycles of one rhythm. I get really pissed off at the business interests—the extractive industries that are devastating (with the help of federal subsidies) the public lands. The woods, and the wilderness—the landscape around us, as well as the landscapes within—are my way of being in the world. It pisses me off to see the wilderness, and the power it has to give us imagination and story, being vandalized. What's going on in the West, back in the forests, is far more brutal than the slashing of any painting in an art museum.

Anger can be a great help to an artist, but history has rarely, if ever, shown it to be nurturing of growth. Perhaps it is better to write, in the long run, out of love rather than hate, to keep from becoming brittle with cynicism.

But still, the sons of bitches keep coming. Still they are cutting the last wild places into halves and then quarters and then eighths, and smaller still, so that wildness, and imagination, are disappearing completely.

Writing is like football, like music, like grouse hunting, like drilling for oil, like gutting and cleaning an elk, like building a house, like giving birth. It is like everything that is alive. It is about giving more than taking, and it is and always has been about noticing things that do not always get easily noticed.

It is about feeling alive. My best advice to a writer would be to hold on desperately to the things (besides writing) that make you feel alive, that stir the senses. They will keep you supple and growing. They will give you vigor and energy to attempt to push beyond the boundaries— to create new boundaries and metaphors, and new understandings. To create, rather than diminish or destroy.

Tesoros

I came to writing late. I was thirty-nine before I gathered enough courage to begin. When I hear other writers talk about writing, or read what they have to say about their art, I am amazed by those who say they always knew they had to write. When I was a girl, I never wanted to do it. It was a doctor I dreamed of being, but I frequently had a book in my lap, and so I was linked, even then, to writing and to the spell that stories cast. My favorite book was *One Thousand and One Nights*, the tale of Scheherazade, whose stories, night after night, kept the executioner's scimitar in its scabbard and away from her dewy neck. Oh, the power explicit in this: Stories can save our lives. Is it any wonder that I did not burn to write? I compared my stories to Scheherazade's, and mine seemed paltry and contrived. No question, making comparisons is the first step on the road to writer's block.

But time passes, and if our love for the written word has been constant, the want to write, the need to tell stories, may beckon. Sometimes we cannot resist.

Let me tell you a few stories.

It is 1967. I am twenty-six and living in Saint Louis. I have two sons under the age of five. One of the things I like to do when I have time and extra money is shop for antiques. Right now, I have a mission. I am searching for a trunk, the flattop kind. I want to use it for a coffee table. This is something I have seen in magazines: You take an old trunk, clean it up, top it with glass.

One day, I am in an antique store, and I am discouraged because for a long time I have not found the trunk I want. I have seen numerous humpbacked trunks, and even some flattops, but these have been too weathered to redo. This time, however, I spot just the one. The shopkeeper is in sight, so I stifle a shriek of delight. The trunk is flat, all right, and well preserved. Brass fittings hug the corners, leather straps hang at the sides. The wood appears to be oak. Canvas stretches under the strips and forms rectangles over the trunk's surface. The canvas is soiled but looks scrubbable.

"How much for that one?" I ask, too excited to play the I'm-just-looking game.

The shopkeeper scratches his head. "There's a little problem with that one," he says. "It's locked and there's no key."

I give the trunk a close inspection. A brass key plate shaped like a fat exclamation point is fitted into the front of the trunk. There is a hole in the plate for a key to slip in.

"No key?" I say.

"No key," he says.

It takes me a moment to grasp what this means. "So how much?" I ask, trying not to think that the trunk might be filled. I try not to picture coins, jewels, priceless oils. *Tesoros.* I fear he might look into my head and see the treasures too.

"Forty bucks," he says, "but since there's no key, give me thirty and it's yours."

This time I pretend to think it over, but then I say "okay," and soon the man and I are duck-walking my find out to the car.

That the heft of the trunk is less than I had hoped is not lost on me, but I smile brightly at the man as I lower the car's hatchback. "Enjoy," the man says. He gives a wave and I drive off. I feel that somehow I've been had.

It takes me a week to pick the lock.

I am careful because the key plate is scrolled and I don't want to mar the design. Into the place where a key would fit, I introduce the tip of a knife, a screwdriver, a hairpin. I worm these around, holding my breath, waiting for the little click that will tell me it's done. My children watch the lock picking with an eagerness of their own, but toward week's end their interest droops. Down in the basement where I've set up shop, they ride their trikes, circling me and the trunk. Christopher, the oldest, pedals by. He says, "Mom is a burglar." "Burglar," Jonathon, the little one, repeats.

Between lock pickings, I scrub the canvas, sand and revarnish the oak. I saddle-soap the leather, paint the canvas the color of oyster shells, polish the brass until it gleams. From time to time I raise the trunk on end, hoping to catch the sound loot makes as it rolls from side to side, but there is silence each time I raise it. It is then I picture bills, of the one-hundred kind, stacked so tightly they cannot be moved.

In the end, it is a metal nail file that does the job.

It is 1951. I am ten. I am living in San Salvador, El Salvador. Dad and I are in his Ford pickup. We bounce over a gravel road that leads up the side of an inactive volcano to the place where Dad's gladiolus grow. Dad harvests flowers and has hired Chema and his family to oversee the crop. Dad maneuvers the truck up the rutty path, and the landscape around us is lush and green. We drive up into mists and around *campesinos* trudging evanescently up and down the mountain. I am thrilled to be with Dad. In the cab of the truck, the smell of cedar and sweat commingle, and this excites me too. I feel like Dad's assistant, like maybe for a moment I will share a life with him.

We come up over the lip of the volcano and stop to look out over the crest of San Salvador, lying way off beyond the fringe of trees and scrub. San Salvador is an ochre and saffron quilt thrown, it seems, almost carelessly across the lap of the valley below us. Dad's gladiolus patch is small. When we drive up, I take it in at one glance. Orderly rows of knife-edged stalks rise up, dark green and defiant, like the hue and stance of *Guardia* who post themselves on street corners in the harsh sun and deep shadowy doorways up and down city blocks.

Dad brakes to a stop, and Chema comes running. He is a small man but solidly built. He runs agilely despite the encumbrance of sandals with square soles cut from rubber tires. I jump out and call "*hola*," but Chema says nothing to me. Dad and he go off, and I stay near the truck.

I have been here before, but today a stillness comes over me. I feel strangely disconnected, as if somehow I am floating up and over the volcano and can look down at myself, a small, slight girl, hair parted severely down the middle and gathered in two braids at the sides. I am walking toward the men when a child, three years old or so, steps out from behind a hut set at the edge of the flower patch. The child is naked, and I see she is a girl. Her belly is huge and distended. She stops short when she sees me, but I walk slowly over.

I am only ten, but I feel a rush of new emotion that later, when I have my own sons, I will recognize as that sheltering kind of mother-love. I want to scoop the girl up. Though her face is smudged and her nostrils caked, I want to hold her close.

A woman emerges from the hut and calls the girl's names. The girl turns and runs off and only once looks back at me. She and her mother disappear into the hut, and I am left, longing to follow after, to go into the hut and penetrate the secret reality of their lives.

It is 1956. I am fifteen and living in Unionville, Missouri, on the farm of my paternal grandparents. The farmhouse, built around the time of the Civil War, is two-storied and narrow. Its façade is rough to the touch and is the color of pigeon wings.

Sometimes, when Grandma has gone to town and Grandpa is farming the fields, I lift aside the length of fabric that curtains their bedroom and step inside. I rummage through their dresser, fishing past underwear and the stiff squares of never-used hankies until my hand falls on the dresser set put away in the third drawer. I take out the oval hand mirror. It is edged in mother-of-pearl and has a silver handle, and it is just the size to reflect only my face. It is my twin's face that I pretend to see—my sister, identical to me. "Hello, Susana," I say to the mirror. "If you were alive, this is how you'd look." After a time, I look away, across the room and through the window to the pasture and the puff of smoke rising up from Grandpa's Farmall traveling slowly across his land. I look back into the mirror. I think, "if that is you, Susana, then who am I?"

The trunk. When I pick the lock, I discover this: burnt-wood boxes for scarves and gloves; hand-embroidered handkerchiefs, lace blouses, a silky slip; a small leather purse, a beaded bag. There are letters with two-cent stamps and postcards with one-centers, all postmarked in the 1920s. There are dozens of valentines, some from Ina and Imogene, some from Wilson and Carl, all addressed to Helen Miller. One card has scalloped edges and features an accordion-folded heart that pops out when opened and is, most sincerely, from Tashido Sonada. In addition, there are granny glasses and a lorgnette. A collection of thimbles.

Seed packets of alyssum, dwarf petunias, blue-nosed peppers, regal pink larkspur. Wrapped in yellowed tissue is a square of silk, an inky background sprinkled with red and blue flowers. Helen Miller's treasures. For twenty-five years I have held them close because fragments of her story are contained in them, and I have honored that.

I think of my family. Objects passed from hand to hand. Stories told, others not talked about but known. Dear friends and acquaintances recount stories of their own. In public places, behind walls and doors, voices rise. Stories float up and are deposited into the trunk of our collective unconscious. We have only to pick a lock to set our stories free.

When I write, I touch the core of the girl I've always been, and with this heart I try to access mythic stories. When I write, I allow my mind to travel. Crossing time and space, I stand once again on the threshold of a Salvadoran hut. In my stories, I do not hold back. I step inside a simple hut and am surprised by *tesoros*.

For a long time I forgot the tale of my flattop trunk, but one day I showed up at a friend's house wearing a silk scarf with an inky background and red and blue flowers. She remarked on how striking the scarf was. I unlocked my memory and told the story of Helen Miller's trunk.

In *Crow and Weasel*, Barry Lopez says, "Sometimes a person needs a story more than food to stay alive."

These days, I stay alive by placing fragments of my story into other people's memories. I do it by writing.

Writing stories is the mirror that tells me who I am.

Guarding Voice

SUSAN POWER

As a working writer who has published stories, poems, a handful of essays, and a novel, I have been asked from time to time to share my creative process with readers. It remains a mysterious activity to me, even after years of practice, and I resist scrutiny I consider to be too careful or intrusive. I'm as reluctant to discuss the alchemy of process as I would be to pin a butterfly to the wall. I have always protected the writer in me—protected her voice, learning to snatch paper and pencil when she speaks, becoming adept at getting out of her way. I look in the direction she urges me to look. I record what we see. I am loyal.

When I was twelve years old, my English teacher asked if I would consider writing a poem in celebration of my hometown, Chicago. The city was sponsoring a poetry contest, open to grade-school students, to be judged by Gwendolyn Brooks. I was new to the school, quiet, shy, but my teachers had already noted how I sparked to life on the page, talking to them on paper the way I dreamed of talking in my spoken voice. I agreed and tried my hand at the project several times before inspiration came to me through a record I had borrowed from the library. I was listening to Shakespeare's plays, a volume of his complete works open in my lap so my eyes could fasten on the phrases I was greedy for, that extravagant necklace of words I longed to loop around and around me like great lengths of pearls.

"I'm dying, Egypt, dying," Cleopatra told me in *Antony and Cleopatra*, and the queen's words became my own lament. At twelve years old, I ended up doing what I have always done: I listened to myself and wrote what I heard. *I love my city; there, you see, I always claim it for my own even though it belongs to no one but itself and perhaps Lake Michigan, its moody partner.* But the Chicago I claimed as my own, a city of libraries and museums and long stretches of beach, was not the only one. I knew others.

"I'm dying, Chicago, dying," I wrote, as I listed the grievances of the urban Indian ghetto. I was thinking of Lizzie Wells, immobilized by a crippling arthritis but raising two cheerful granddaughters in a basement apartment infested with the largest rats I have ever seen. I was thinking of all my crushes, young men who joined the Latin Kings because there were no Indian gangs, their hands flashing signals as potent as Indian Sign Language. I named the Indian bars: the Tipi, the Reservation, the Crazy Horse, dark places I'd only glimpsed from the sidewalk, smoky, splintered with fights, an Ojibwe dwarf passed out on a table, hoisted from the floor where her friends were afraid she'd be crushed. She was so small, they said. I claimed the winos for my poem: Big Tom, Albert, Mabel, the Spanish Flea. All of them were buried within the year.

When I was twelve, I didn't know I would become a writer. I thought everyone survived this life by scratching their thoughts onto the page. I thought everyone told the truth, whether lived or imagined. I could have written a celebration of Chicago as surely as I could have written my address or phone number. I could have tried to please my English teacher, attempted to win the contest, put words together in pleasing ways that would have made everyone smile. Instead, I tracked the voice inspired by Shakespeare's dying queen and let her sing out a ballad of betrayal and loss. My poem chanted a story of relocation, the Native migration from homelands to cities. Somehow I understood that I could love my city and my experience of her and still reveal her flaws, unveil her secrets, confess that she wore many faces and was not always beautiful.

After reworking the document several times, I was pleased with my poem and confidently handed it to my teacher. She read it through, standing there before me, and read it through again.

"Isn't this a little—well, grim?" she finally asked.

I shrugged my shoulders.

"You did understand the assignment, didn't you?"

I nodded, mute as ever.

"I just want you to submit your best work, that's all, because I think you have a real chance of winning, or placing. You're a good writer."

She meant to be kind. She was kind. She took a special interest in a student who was a little different from the others, "less aggressive," as many teachers would complain to my mother. But she annoyed me that day. With all the courage I could summon, I insisted, "This is my entry. This is it."

"You know you won't win?" she told me gently.

"I know. But it's my poem. It's the one I want to give you."

This was a small moment in my life, yet I remember the exchange vividly as a kind of test. Beginning writers often ask published authors for advice, for the secret blueprint that will launch their success. I wish I could introduce them to that painfully shy little girl, swooning in the attic over Shakespeare, immortalizing winos, cracking Chicago's lovely (clean, white, smooth) shell, tipping out the syrup of yolk. Writers can be taught technique, guided in forming their intentions more skillfully, but writers cannot be given a voice. What we see and hear, what we value, what we remember, these are the small stones we collect and spill, collect and spill. These are the threads that weave a voice. "My ribbon is strong," I would have told the teacher if I could have named what I was feeling. "My ribbon is iron, and it is mine. It isn't yours, so you may not like it. You don't have to like it. Because it is mine."

I am a visual writer, so images form in my head before I can find the words to describe what I am seeing. When I think of myself as a writer, I am always a child; that child is what I see. Her fists are clenched at her sides, her mouth is a firm line. She isn't angry or unfriendly, although she cries easily. She is simply guarded, careful. Her words may not be unusually eloquent or profound, but they are hers. She thinks of this activity, this vocation, as a series of choices. She closes her eyes before she lifts the pen so she can better see the pictures rise, so she can clearly hear the voice and chart its song. She can be fierce in her choosing. She wants to tell the truth as she knows it. She wants to get it right.

Writing

TOPICS COVERED:

Phone Book Roulette

The Smell of Valerian Root

The Second Emotion

Resisting Faithful Ugliness

Wishing Harder

The Power of Whoosh! Plop! and BAM!

Mortician's Shoe Glue

Writing What You Don't Know

Throwing Sequence to the Rabid Wolves

The Wave Function in Poetry

Formal Pleasure

Mistrusting Ingenious Transitions

"Damned Esoterism"

Drinking Coffee Like a Fiend

Being More Interesting

In Favor of Uncertainty

MARK DOTY

I believe that writing poetry is a process of inquiry, an act of investigation. It's more usual to think of the poet's work as self-expression, a pouring out of feeling, which suggests that a poem is a vessel for emotions and ideas which already exist. Of course this is partly true, but I suspect that the part of poetry which is most alive, most energetic, comes into being during the writing process itself. The live, growing edge always lies with the understandings or questions that are forged there, in the process of intellectual and emotional discovery which takes place when we bring experience into focus under the lens of language. At its most active, the writing process is the place where we enter more deeply into experience than we can in other ways, coming to what Hart Crane called "new latitudes, unknotting."

This means, I think, that the practice of poetry has more to do with our questions than our certainties—more to do with what we don't know than what we do. It isn't always easy to remember that, in any process of inquiry, our uncertainty is our ally; it's a good thing for a poet, being in a state of not-knowing. During the process of generating a poem, during deep revision, the longer we can stay in the state of uncertainty, of unfolding possibility, the better.

Here a notion from physics might be useful. I like the idea of the wave function, which is a term for the multiplicity of things which might happen. Studying a traveling particle, one might plot all the places where the little thing might land; as possible landing sites increase, the wave function expands. When the particle comes to rest somewhere—that is, when any event takes place—the wave function collapses. As we work on a new draft, we're expanding the wave function, opening out the range of things which might occur, of ways our poem might be developed. When we choose a direction, a central metaphor, an ending, we collapse the wave function; out of all the things this poem could be, it will be this.

Staying uncertain, keeping the possibilities for discovery open—sounds easy enough. But everyone who writes knows how difficult this really is to do. Don't we all find ourselves beginning a draft, seeing a possible direction for it, then pursuing that direction swiftly to an ending—only, later, to find what we've done slight or unsatisfying? I often see poems in workshops which seem to behave like trains; the poem establishes a direction, makes some tracks for itself, and then proceeds to travel down those tracks. I imagine that most of us have the experience of thinking, partway through working on a draft, "Oh, here's a great ending line!" I think this is an impulse to be resisted, even if the ending we've imagined is great; this will-to-closure too often packages the poem neatly, closing it down before we've done the work of investigation.

It's that work—the work of uncovering, questioning, pushing into the material to see what it might yield—which makes the difference between a slight poem and a poem of substance. Haven't you looked at a draft you've written only to find it sealed off, too limited, the depth or intensity you felt when you were writing it somehow unavailable on the page? This is a sure sign that the realms of possibility, the charged complexities lying within your poem, haven't been investigated yet.

My own writing process always seems to begin in ignorance; early on, I literally don't know what it is I'm talking about. I just know that something compels me, seems to demand my attention. Usually it's an image, something I've observed, so I'll begin in description, trying to capture something of the nature of that point of interest. For instance, a couple of years ago I found a beautiful little crab shell on the beach, one which had been recently hollowed out by a predatory gull. Very recently, because the inside of the shell was a startlingly deep blue I'd never seen before. When I brought the shell home, the color rapidly faded to a more familiar lavender. But I found I kept thinking about that color; it gave me that familiar feeling of a nagging tug at my imagination: something there, something to investigate.

But what? I began just trying to say what I saw, to honor the physical through description. This endeavor leads inevitably to metaphor, and soon I found I'd compared the crab to a bronze sculpture, to a suit of armor, and (through a little joke echoing a translator's phrasing) to the headless torso of a god Rilke describes in his famous poem "Archaic Torso of Apollo." Then, describing the fate of the crab, I arrived at a description of that startling blue which had triggered my interest in the first place.

And there my poem stalled for a while. Having begun in description, trying to evoke an image, I found myself saying, "So what? Why, or how, does this matter?" In other words, to what meaning, what complex of emotions, does this image point? I suspect if I wrote a poem about this crab shell at different times in my life, I might write quite different poems; images are vessels into which we pour the moment's constellations of thought and feeling. The clue to what the crab shell meant to me came with the metaphor which presented itself next:

> Though it smells
> of seaweed and ruin,

> this little traveling case
> comes with such lavish lining!

The proximity of beauty and ruin which these lines suggest brought me toward what was, for me, the heart of the matter; I began to understand that what I was writing about was what death might reveal about us, an understanding which becomes overt when the poem poses a question: "What color is / the underside of skin?" This poem was written six months after the death of my partner, Wally Roberts. In all the writing I did at this time, I was trying desperately to make some psychic accommodation to the fact of his dying. The poem's an attempt to see, in mortality, a coming to knowledge, a joyful revelation of the fact of our belonging to the world—that we carry, in ourselves, sky, and that we might have to die to know this.

I could never have told you this was where my poem was going when I began to describe that crab; I was only aware of my attraction to that haunting blue. If I'd known at first where the poem was headed, I probably wouldn't have been able to write it. I was one groping my way toward an understanding of why this visual image compelled me;

I only understood toward the end of the process just how much that little shell held, along with its emptiness. My process was full of missteps, experimental assertions, questions which haven't remained in the final poem; a poem is an enactment of a process of knowing, not the process itself! The real process is messy, tentative, private; poetry, I am glad to say, is more orderly than that. But I like poems which embody their search for the reader, which involve us in a replication of the writer's struggle of coming to understand.

I offer this example because it seems to be a poem that could have stopped sooner—to its diminishment. The poem could have quit after describing shell and gull and blue. Or it could have stopped after the image of the fancy suitcase (in early drafts, it probably did). But to my mind it's the imaginative entry into the body of the crab, and the concomitant thinking about how we're like this creature, that makes the poem matter; I think those last nine lines reveal what's been pressuring the description so far, what is responsible for (I hope) a sense of urgency beneath the surface of the description.

If there were one sweeping, general statement I'd make about developing writers, that would be it: they tend to stop too early on in the process, to reach for resolution before it's time. This, of course, is only human. A blank page is a dauntingly large place, and so when we see a direction it is natural for us to seize it, in order to safely limit what we're doing and rule out all the other possible paths. To write is always to court feeling, and to invite onto the page messy, ambiguous, challenging emotional states which may threaten to swamp our craft, taxing our ability to control what we're writing, to shape tone, structure, narrative.

In other words, we're always simplifying, editing out complexities, difficulties, contradictions, trying to give shape to what we write—and of course that impulse to order is our ally, too, just as our uncertainty is. The problem is, the impulse to order tends to win out, too often, over the disruptive and deepening forces of complication.

Not very comforting advice for an artist: invite complication, court the disruptive, get messier! Challenge your craft, allow more uncertainty into the poem! Question your assertions, shake up your structures! Perhaps I can make my call for complexity and doubt a little friendlier by offering some particular suggestions as to how to go about trying out this advice. Here then, are some ideas.

1. Take a draft of something in progress and decide not to bring it to closure for a while. In other words, when you feel interested in working on that draft again, add more to it; pick up on a phrase you've used and vary it, make another assertion about the same thing and go from there. Try the *more is more* approach: more language, more imagery, more material to work with means you're more likely to get at what is essential in this draft. You can collapse the wave function later, editing out what doesn't seem essential. As an experiment, try setting some arbitrary time limit; try, say, adding to the draft for two weeks, not allowing yourself to cut it back until that time has passed. Or say, "I'm going to write two hundred lines beginning from this material, even if the two hundred lines don't seem to belong." See where it takes you. (Keats used this sort of approach for "Endymion," and became a poet of far greater reach in the process.)

You might think of the poem architecturally, as a house with many rooms. Succeeding drafts may explore different areas. Perhaps they won't all be part of the final poem, but the final poem will be enriched, pressurized, by your knowledge of the other rooms.

2. After you've written a draft of a poem-in-progress, set yourself an exercise to extend that draft. For example:

Go through the piece you've written and see where you can generate a question or questions. If you write down all the questions you can come up with in relation to this text, you're likely to pose some that you will want to investigate.

Alternatively, try formulating a question which encapsulates what you've written. How would you pose the question at the poem's heart, what it's trying to understand? (You don't have to answer it; we probably want literature to inhabit questions, as Rilke put it, more than we want literature to provide us with answers. But you certainly need to know what your poem's question is.)

Rewrite the draft in another point of view. If you've written in first person, see what you say differently, how your poem changes if you recast it in third person.

Change the tense. What do you say or know differently from a different vantage point in time?

Shift to another, related scene, something that's happened before or after the moment represented in your draft. Can your poem-in-progress hold more than one moment?

3. Read your draft closely in search of statements you might challenge, correct, contradict. Where in a poem might you confront yourself, make your thinking dialectical? Imagine stepping into the draft and saying, "No, it wasn't that way at all," or "I'm lying," or "Maybe. . . ." Often when we push ourselves we get to the more charged, urgent material just beneath the surface. I've a private theory, not yet fully articulated, that all poems involve an act of self-questioning, that the energy of poetic language derives, in part, from self-confrontation, which is visible to varying degrees in the final poem. In my crab poem, for instance, isn't there an implicit argument going on about the nature of death? "Not so bad, to die" suggests that the speaker also entertains the opposite notion, that it is very bad indeed.

4. Take two drafts you're not satisfied with and combine them. What if you interweave the two pieces sentence by sentence? What if you jump-cut from one to the other? You may or may not wind up keeping the two poems together, but one is likely to teach you about the other.

These exercises are, of course, mechanical, but often what begins in technique ends in imagination. The important thing, I think, is to surprise ourselves, to pry open our poems so that instead of reinscribing familiar ways of thinking and feeling—the already known patterns of saying who we are—we push toward the new. Because when we say ourselves differently, we aren't merely expressing what's already there, we are becoming. Which is what real writing is, and which invariably communicates its energy and intensity to the reader.

A Green Crab's Shell
Mark Doty

Not, exactly, green:
closer to bronze
preserved in kind brine,

something retrieved
from a Greco-Roman wreck,
patinated and oddly

muscular. We cannot
know what his fantastic
legs were like—

though evidence
suggests eight
complexly folded

scuttling works
of armament, crowned
by the foreclaw's

gesture of menace
and power. A gull's
gobbled the center,

leaving this chamber
—size of a demitasse—
open to reveal
a shocking, Giotto blue.
Though it smells
of seaweed and ruin,

this little traveling case
comes with such lavish lining!
Imagine breathing

surrounded by
the brilliant rinse
of summer's firmament.

What color is
the underside of skin?
Not so bad, to die,

if we could be opened
into this—
if the smallest chambers

of ourselves,
similarly,
revealed some sky.

Working from Experience

LARRY SUTIN

It's fun to hear about what works for other writers, in the same way that it's fun to hear about any private little rituals of other people—how they make coffee, disperse their anger, buy themselves treats when they're depressed.

Anecdotes about other writers—famous ones, or friends of mine who'll be famous in a week or so—are the main things I think about to the extent that I think about "the craft of writing" (as opposed to a particular piece I'm working on) at all.

When I interrupt my writing to make a pot of coffee, it is a great pleasure for me to recall Balzac working by night, fueled by the thick black coffee he drank like a fiend. This fact of his life means more to me than any of his works that I have read.

The "craft of writing. . . ." In order to write well you have to write a great deal. Writing a great deal is a difficult thing to bring oneself to do. By all means, then, one should foster whatever private fantasies and convictions facilitate the writing process. If these fantasies or convictions do not facilitate the writing process, they should be abandoned posthaste. The key thing is to keep writing (never mind why you want to write in the first place). There are times when it is helpful to reflect upon the reasons for the periodic "silences." More often, I think, it's a waste of time. If you truly want to quit smoking, you don't consider the understandable factors that led you to enjoy smoking—you focus upon the knowledge which convinces you that you must quit.

I don't mean to imply that writing is a particularly grim business. It is no more or less difficult to write well than to do anything else of value well. The "role" of the writer is to write well on the subjects that fascinate him, and attempting to write well on such subjects suits me just fine as an activity.

But to write well you cannot rely upon being "in the mood." I am never in the mood to write until I am actually writing. Thinking about

writing in advance, I am usually appalled. Do what you have to do to
get to that desk. Kafka is a great source of bouncy, inspirational work
tips like this one:

"10 o'clock, November 15. I will not let myself become tired. I'll
jump into my story even though it should cut my face to pieces."

The "first thought best thought" approach can be a useful spur so
long as "first thought" is not equated with the first draft. You must
trust and love your initial impetus to write a particular story. That impetus is "germinal," meaning that it needs time and attention in order
to grow. Think of the sheets you crumple up and throw away as forming a nutritive compost heap. Dostoyevsky:

> One ought not to hurry, my friend; one must try to do noth-
> ing but what is good. . . . Believe me, in all things labor is
> necessary—gigantic labor. . . . You evidently confuse the in-
> spiration, that is, the first instantaneous vision, or emotion in
> the artist's soul (which is always present), with the *work*. I, for
> example, write every scene down at once, just as it first comes
> to me, and rejoice in it; then I work at it for months and years.
> I let it inspire me, in that form, more than once (for I love it
> thus); here I add, there I take away; believe me that the scene
> always gains by it. One must *have* the inspiration; without
> inspiration one can't of course begin anything.

Henry Miller is hard for some people to take, but when he sings, he
sings: a joyful, expansive acceptance of life that no one in Am Lit
101 except Whitman possesses. The selected correspondence between
Miller and Lawrence Durrell is the most fun and useful book on writing I've ever read.

The two men loved each other—and each other's work. But when
Sexus was published in 1949, Durrell was appalled, and said so in a
terse telegram: "*Sexus* disgracefully bad will completely ruin reputation
unless withdrawn revised Larry." After he sent off that telegram and
had a little time to think, Durrell grew miserable: had he irreparably
damaged the dearest friendship of his life? A few days later he fired off

a second, apologetic telegram. Before that arrived, however, Miller had already sent Durrell his response, which went, in part:

> I know you'd feel better if I did get angry with you, but I can't. . . . To judge one's own work is impossible. Maybe you're right—maybe I'm finished. But I don't feel that way, not even if the whole world condemns the book. . . .
>
> What I want to tell you is this—I said it before and I repeat it solemnly: I am writing exactly what I want to write and the way I want to do it. . . . "Life's traces," wrote Goethe, speaking of *Wilhelm Meister,* I think. I read that in my teens, that phrase, and it sank deep. I want this book to contain "life's traces." Whether it is in good taste, moral or immoral, literature or document, a creation or a fiasco doesn't matter. . . .
>
> The "considered opinion" about this letter is that you are to feel at liberty to baste hell out of me to all and sundry. I will understand that you are doing it out of love for me. I would be a fool if I thought otherwise.

I realize that the above quote can be dismissed, by certain temperaments, as egotistic bohemianism, so I will add a quote from another Miller letter—to an acquaintance who asked for Miller's comments on a magazine piece he'd done—which will, I hope, help clarify that what Miller is speaking of is not the right to babble wildly in defiance of the reader's tastes and expectations, but of the inescapable task for the committed writer of facing up to his own inner dictates:

> As I see it, what you have done is to "write about." *To write (punkt!)* is another matter. You then become involved—and *responsible* in a different way. Responsible, perhaps, to God, let us say. You invite defeat, humiliation, rejection, misunderstanding. You speak solely as the "unique" being you are, not as a member of society. Do I make sense? Am I answering as you wish me to? "The Paper" itself, while interesting enough, is of no great consequence. It serves to feed the various egos

involved. Once seriously engaged, the ego falls away. You are
happy—and blessed—just to be an instrument.

Being "seriously engaged" is often enough an uncomfortable state of
being. Bob Kearney pointed out to me an observation by Joan Didion
in her preface to *Slouching Towards Bethlehem:*

"My only advantage as a reporter is that I am so physically small,
so temperamentally unobtrusive, and so neurotically inarticulate that
people tend to forget that my presence runs counter to their best
interests. And it always does. That is one last thing to remember: *writers are always selling somebody out.*"

But we mean well, and art is important, so it's okay as long as you
state clearly at the front of your book that any resemblance between
your characters and actual persons living or dead surprises you as
much as it does them. Besides, the act of writing can be so magisterial
and redemptive at once. Balzac: "I cast my life into the crucible as the
alchemist casts his gold."

The image of the crucible is important to me because it recognizes
that memories must be transformed into new structures called stories
before they achieve lasting value. To tell a story is far different from
recollecting and retelling, although memory is always the primary
source of material. Stories must entertain: that much, at least, most of
us think we know about the hidden structure that good stories must
embody. Erskine Caldwell: "A writer is not a great mind, he's not a
great thinker, he's not a great philosopher, he's a story-teller."

It is no accident that all religious traditions give a prominent place
to homilies, parables, legends. Stories, precisely because they do captivate the reader, are the most durable wisdom vehicles which we hu-
mans possess. Folklorists and anthropologists are forever refining their
crossover lists of a tale's structure in, say, Japanese, Scottish, and gypsy
traditions. If you are, even temporarily, a master of a particular structure, your stories can be exceedingly short and penetrating at once.
Idries Shah's collections of Sufi tales provide telling examples of this.

Chekhov was obsessed with the question of what makes a story
a story. In his letters you can find brilliant statements on the writer's
craft by merely flipping pages at random. Younger Russian writers

were always sending him their pieces for judgment, and gentle as his responses were they packed a wallop:

> Your story is a good, charming, clever thing. But the action is, as always, slow, and therefore the story seems in some places to drag. Imagine a great pond out of which flows a slender current of water; imagine on the surface of the pond a number of things:—chips of wood, boards, empty barrels,—all of them, because of the slow flowing of the water, seeming to be stationary and heaped up at the mouth of the stream. This is what occurs in your story,—no movement, and a multitude of details that pile up into a great heap.

My fantasy of what Chekhov must have been like is, thankfully, bolstered by Gorky's recollections of him:

> All his life Chekhov lived on his own soul; he was always himself, inwardly free, and he never troubled about what some people expected and others—coarser people—demanded of Anton Chekhov. He did not like conversations about deep questions, conversation with which our dear Russians so assiduously comfort themselves, forgetting that it is ridiculous, and not at all amusing, to argue about velvet costumes in the future when in the present one has not even a decent pair of trousers.

Jack Kerouac compiled a "Belief & Technique for Modern Prose: List of Essentials" that is full of good sense. Too bad the Time-Life bullshit reportage of the Beat movement still keeps so many people at a distance from Kerouac's writing. Some of his maxims: "No fear or shame in the dignity of your experience, language & knowledge." "No time for poetry but exactly what is." "Don't think of words when you stop but to see the picture better."

To really pick you up when you're having a bad writing day, there's always St. Thomas Aquinas' deathbed observation: "All that I have written now seems to me as straw."

Here's my own list of handy tips. I've broken each one of them too many times to count—but never to my profit:

1. A good story should convince the reader that you know and care a great deal about persons other than yourself.

2. Life is short. Write what you want to write while you're still alive. Fight off "silences" with every ounce of will you possess.

3. Your best ideas come while you are actually writing.

4. Never create a character for the sole purpose of justifying or vilifying yourself or anyone else.

5. A good story must know more than you do. If you are writing a story in order to express your fixed opinion on something, then you are writing an essay and you shouldn't bother with characters at all, since they won't be alive by the time you're through anyway.

6. Never lie to a writer about his writing. In most cases even overly harsh criticism is less destructive than false praise. If you feel that you are about to be forced into a situation in which you will be compelled (for the sake of maintaining the all-too-tenuous "social fabric") to break this rule, then lie to get out of that situation.

A final quote, from Shab-Parak, a Sufi: "O man! If you only knew how many of the false fantasies of the imagination were nearer to the Truth than the careful conclusions of the cautious. And how these truths are of no service until the imaginer, having done his work with the imagination, has become less imaginative."

If I understand Shab-Parak at all, he is confirming the value of good stories and of the effort necessarily involved in learning to write them.

(Quotations taken from: *World Tales*, ed. Idries Shah; *Balzac*, Stefan Zweig; *New American Story*, Robert Creeley and Donald M. Allen; *Wisdom of the Idiots*, Idries Shah; *Storytellers and Their Art*, ed. Georgianne Trask and Charles Burkhart; *Lawrence Durrell and Henry Miller: A Private Correspondence*, ed. George Wickes; *Letters on the Short Story, the Drama, and Other Literary Topics*, Anton Chekhov.)

Twenty-five in an Infinite Series of Numbers

JIM MOORE

Much has been written about what separates poetry from creative nonfiction, but relatively little about the ways in which these two genres reinforce and feed each other.

1.   *Those who can never live anywhere except their façades*
     those who are never absentminded
     those who never open the wrong door and catch a glimpse of the
        Unidentified One
     Walk past them!
     —Tomas Tranströmer, from "Golden Wasp"

2. Too often writers of essays are afraid to open the wrong door or to be absentminded, to drift and waver between choices, to second-guess themselves.

3. Arbitrarily pick one page of a personal essay from one collection of essays and one page of a more factual essay from another collection of essays. Write a paragraph that serves as a transition between the two randomly chosen pages—that serves to connect them. Inspiration loves finding its way between two arbitrary points.

4. Many of the great poets of the twentieth century have thrived on finding themselves in exile—arbitrary fates, whether forced on them or self-imposed: Vallejo, Rilke, Neruda, Eliot, Pound, Lawrence, Milosz. The essayists, however, have made a point of staying home. Is this one reason that essayists in the twentieth century have, by and large, been less interesting, less inspired, and less important than the poets?

5. Mistrust all transitions, especially ingenious ones.

6. Ingenuity is the mother of glibness.

7. An essay that speaks with great clarity is one thing. An essay that speaks with great certainty is another. The former I trust.

8. Serious literature is a way to think, a model of how the mind works. If an essay leaves out—or isn't inspired by—what is given, it feels flat and forced. What are the givens, the sources of inspiration? They're the same ones we've had for centuries: birth, death, war, sex, race, class, age, geography, the seasons. Great essays often are about finding the transition between one aspect of what is arbitrary in our fates and another.

9. What does it mean to think as an adult? It's not about age. By the end of her diary, Anne Frank was thinking as an adult. Thinking as an adult is about not fearing intimacy with one's own mind, about inviting intimacy from the reader, about revealing the mind's complexity and confusion, as well as its passions and momentary certainties.

10. Annie Dillard in *Pilgrim at Tinker Creek*: in spite of the sense of strain that almost all American essayists since Emerson have in their writing—the strain to be right, good, positive, and energetic—one finds here the pleasure of an adult as well as an ardent mind at work, not attempting to show us how easy or correct life will be if only we go along with her. An adult lets her adult readers draw their own conclusions. An adolescent needs to convince you that he or she is right.

11. Bill Holm's "The Music of Failure." An adult essay that finds its subject at the dark and wavering edges of consciousness, where the new and difficult information comes from.

12. Transitions. You can't live with them and you can't live without them.

13. James Wright, in his poetry, took adolescent consciousness—passionate, snarling, naïve, heartbreaking, funny, beautiful with a beauty born of the necessity to shine as purely as possible—as far as it can go. America is still an adolescent country. Of course we love his poetry.

14. Adult poets: David Ignatow, C.K. Williams, Tom McGrath, Josephine Miles, Patricia Goedicke. But most of the adult thinking in

poetry comes to us from other countries: Tomas Tranströmer, Czeslaw Milosz, etc.

15. Carolyn Forché: How long will she appeal to the shaking adolescent in us, the one who has just realized American foreign policy is obscene? I read her work with great care and am shocked and moved. Afterward, I realize that her poems have not challenged me at a deeper level. They have not shown me new paths of the mind, new ways of being in the world, new maps with which to explore the savage wilderness of our century, its inner betrayals and outer ravages. They have the intensity and brittle authority of rallying cries. I long for another sort of authority entirely. I reread her poems because what they are written about matters. Individual poems are amazing. But they leave no room for me to do anything but admire them and assent to them. They are confirmation of what I already believe. This is not enough.

16. Beware of essays that are right rather than true. Truth is not just a specific temperature but the whole weather, the landscape out of which temperature emerges for a moment. Too many essays settle for being right, for giving us the specific temperature rather than the whole weather pattern. These essays can often be identified by a one-note emotional tone: *pissed off.*

17. I, too, love to argue, to be right. But, really, I'd rather read Primo Levi. I'd rather engage with a mind that has been torn apart by circumstances beyond his control, then put together again, slowly and with attention. The kind of attention that cannot afford the luxury of adolescent thinking.

18. Intimacy and distance. First one, then the other. Show me the dialectic: how you get from what is near to what is far and then back again. Show me the route from your soul to the world. But don't forget the return ticket. I want to see what it's like when you get back home again.

19. If I am the writer and you are reader, I never want you to put down my essay after you've finished it and say, "Now I know what I think. I think what he thinks."

20. If I knew what I wanted you to think or feel, maybe I could finish this essay. But no, that's not it at all. If I knew what I wanted you to

think or feel, I wouldn't write the essay to begin with. If I knew what I thought, I wouldn't write it.

21. And so I am back to poetry, another place where it's the writing itself—how I say a thing—that gives me what I need to hear.

22. Many, if not most, of the best poems written today are really disguised essays. You would read them no differently if you read them in paragraphs. The language and rhythms would not be affected by the absence of line breaks. Take your best poems, if you're a poet, and write them out in prose. What is lost? What is gained?

23. I have yet to see an essay that tells me as much about what it means to feel like an outsider in the late twentieth century—but an outsider determined to find a way to belong to the world—as the first fifty pages of V.S. Naipaul's *The Enigma of Arrival*. We have all been colonized. We are *all*—some more, some less, but all—victims of this imperialist century. Naipaul gives us a way to think about our situation fearlessly. He is determined to belong to nature, to a neighborhood, to a kind of thinking that makes an honorable life possible. He shows us how to move ever more slowly, ever more truly, through these times. Is it a novel or an essay? A novel, but who cares: It embodies a truth that we need to hear.

24. Take any ten of those first fifty pages from the Naipaul novel. Try breaking them up into lines as if they were poetry. And as far as I'm concerned, they are, since they are more interesting, compelling, rhythmic, and forceful than almost any poetry published during 1987. Maybe the reason so few people seem to like *The Enigma of Arrival* is that it's really poetry in disguise. Maybe if he'd broken it into lines and published it as poetry, he would have won the Nobel in 1987 instead of once again being a runner-up. Or maybe he should have published those pages as a long essay; maybe if they'd been published under the guise of nonfiction, people would have paid more attention to them.

25. And now. . . .

A Mentor's Words
and Words on Her Words

MARILYN CHIN

Grandfather Wong's Fatal Flaw

Grandfather Wong parted his hair
far from the left of his crown
and tried to retrain a cowlick
in the center of his forehead
that stared at us like Gautama's
third eye . . . most of our lives.

The imperfections, man, the flaws.
How he couldn't allow them.
How he never forgave in others
what he abhorred within himself.

How he never blamed the times,
the Republicans or the scions
for robbing the empires blind.
"Advanced social malaise
is the disease of the young."
He pointed his bony finger—
"And all of you are guilty!"

And alas, in his whole clan,
only two are gainfully employed!
My brother as an engineer,
and I, a mere teacher
of English as a second,
third, fourth, language.

Today, see how the clever morticians
have conquered that lick
with ordinary shoe glue,
and he's not even alive
to protest the stink.
                    —Spring 1988

To Pursue the Limitless

To pursue the limitless
With a hair-brained paramour
To chase a dull husband
With a sharp knife

To speak to Rose
About her thorny sisters
Lock the door behind you
The restaurant is on fire

You are named after
Flower and precious metal
You are touched
By mercury

Your birth-name is dawning
Your milk-name is twilight
Your betrothed name is dusk

To speak in dainty aphorisms
To dither
In monosyllables
Binomes copulating in mid air

To teach English as a second
Third, fourth language

You were faithful to the original
You were married to the Chinese paradox

美言不信　信言不美
Beautiful words are not truthful
The truth is not beautiful

You have translated bitter as melon
Fruit as willful absence

You were mum as an egg
He was brutal as an embryo
Blood-soup will congeal in the refrigerator

You are both naturalized citizens
You have the right to a little ecstasy

To (二) err is human
To (五) woo is woman

Maí mā *Buried mother*
Maí mā *Sold hemp*
Maí mā *Bought horse*
No, not the tones but the tomes

You said My name is *Zhuang Mei Sturdy Beauty*
But he thought you said *Shuang Mei Frosty Plum*

He brandished his arc of black hair like a coxcomb
He said *Meet me at the airport travelator*
His backdoor is lovelier than his front door

A smear of bile on your dress
Proved his existence

Commentary

I wrote "Grandfather Wong's Fatal Flaw" in my late twenties. It was one of those obligatory Chinese American "grandparent" poems. I remember writing this poem a week after my grandfather's funeral. I felt guilty that my first book was filled with mother and grandmother poems and wanted to write a serious elegy for him. What I ended up with was something very off-key. His cowlick transformed into Gautama's third eye, and finally ended up in the last stanza "conquered"

by the mortician's "shoe glue." The poem didn't behave itself and became more surreal than I expected. Although I was fond of the poem,
I didn't include it in either *Dwarf Bamboo* or *The Phoenix Gone, The
Terrace Empty*. It ended up in my back drawer. Any poem that ends up
there gets dismembered and scavenged. Good images and lines would
get salvaged and get absorbed into future poems. Henceforth, "To
teach English as a second, third, fourth language"—which I think is
a subtle and clever line—got recycled into "To Pursue the Limitless."

The autobiographical information is "coded" in "To Pursue the
Limitless." The poem was written shortly after my mother's death. The
narrative is given via an array of disjunctive images. That personal, fa-
milial lexicon is all there and I believe is decipherable: "Rose" is my
mother's adopted English name, "restaurant" and various foodstuff
refer to my father's business, etc. . . . Formally, the poem is structured
around what I call "parallel Chinese couplets." Sometimes, the couplets are interrupted by a pun or an aside; sometimes I insert a trip-
let to change the rhythm. I tried to disguise some of the couplets by
breaking them into three-four line stanzas. For instance:

> To pursue the limitless with a hair-brained paramour
> To chase a dull husband with a sharp knife

I reformulated the lines into a quatrain to soften the "didactic" sound
of a couplet.—Also the line breaks after "limitless" and "husband" give
the lines following these words added surprise.

> To pursue the limitless
> With a hair-brained paramour
> To chase a dull husband
> With a sharp knife

For fun, I included a proverb in Chinese characters and several puns,
and wedded disparate images together, preferring associative leaps to
narrative coherence. Nonetheless, the constellation of elliptical autobiographical material, e.g.: "buried mother," "He was brutal as an embryo," etc. . . . tells us that there is an undercurrent of sadness and

pathos in this woman protagonist's life. The egghead stuff on language, the puns, the absurd clash of images, the disjunctiveness, the dark humor work against the deep, formidable sadness.

I believe now that the weirdness in both poems is a way for me to cope with death. Many of my more linear poems are autobiographical: they mourn my mother's life, and they blame my father's abandonment as the chief reason for her self-destruction. My mother felt very lonely and alienated in her adopted country. And no doubt, my poetry will be haunted by her sadness for years to come.

I am a poet who likes to vary my strategies. In this poem I was working toward a more surreal and disjunctive edge . . . a controlled randomness. I am interested in this new detour, for now. . . .

The Poem Behind the Poem

MICHAEL DENNIS BROWNE

I once found a definition of melody in a life of Beethoven: "A combination of cadence and surprise." "Cadence" comes from the Latin *cadere*, to fall, and although it means something a little different for the composer than for the poet—it more nearly suggests closure—still, by this definition, we can picture both melody and phrase as something rising a while which then begins to fall, only to be lifted or infused with new life at a point where it begins to drop.

I want to talk about one or two of the sources of that rebirth or renewal, because so many of our poems seem like thrown stones that return too soon to earth. To switch metaphors, they turn for home too soon. The poem behind the poem is the one we usually fail to imagine, the one that fails to get written; the poem must always surprise its writer, both in its particulars and in its overall enterprise, coming as it does unbidden from the pen (or the processor).

Richard Hugo suggests that a poem often has an initial subject and a generated subject, and it's my feeling that most poems fail to generate their true subjects, the subjects often implicit in the poems' opening phrases, even as early as the title. When I'm working with a poem—my own or someone else's—which fails to fire the loaded pistol it began with (to invoke Chekhov), I often suggest going back to the early moments to see how we chose or were invited to begin. The beginning of a poem is seminal in terms of sound, image, rhythm; in terms of putting us on the path, often a very wandering one, to addressing what Allen Grossman calls "the authentic problem." The problem can rarely be anticipated by the poet in advance of the poem. "If I can say it, it's not what I want," some poet—I can't remember who—said, and if a poem can be thought of as the only possible way of saying whatever it says, then it must make its discoveries as it goes—it must generate its surprises.

In Richard Wilbur's poem "The Writer," the poet listens to his daughter upstairs in the family house working on a story at the typewriter, and at the end of five stanzas he wishes her life "a lucky passage." He interprets the pause she makes at this moment as a rejection of this "easy figure"; he then spends five stanzas re-creating the memory of a trapped bird's struggle to escape from that same upstairs room two years ago. After imagining/remembering the bird's final success in "clearing the sill of the world," he returns to his daughter with these three lines, which conclude the poem:

> It is always a matter, my darling,
> Of life or death, as I had forgotten. I wish
> What I wished you before, but harder.

It's not often that we see this mellifluous poet erupt into such plainness or risk of statement; not only does he publicly, within his own poem, call into question the glibness of his own metaphor, but he ends the poem with the kind of large terms—"life or death"—that creative writing instructors talk themselves blue in the face forbidding students to use in their poems. This ending seems to me a clear example of the poem behind the poem, and to see how Wilbur might have made this discovery, I want to go back to where he begins.

The poem's title, "The Writer," already provides some momentum toward the poem's final theme, which has as much to do with the fatherly, as with the fledgling, writer. And then the first three lines:

> In her room at the prow of the house
> Where light breaks, and the windows are tossed with linden,
> My daughter is writing a story.

He doesn't begin with lines such as these:

> In her room at the front end of the house
> Where light shines, and the windows are surrounded by linden,
> My daughter is working on a story.

A lot of our poems begin as palely as this, with as little sense of arousal, and a chief result of our pale word choices is pale associative thought, pale discovery, pale progression, pale resolution. Wilbur's early choices—"prow," "breaks," "tossed"—offer, at the very least, a proposition of sound and image to his ear and his imagination; they propose an initiative of pattern and association which the poem triumphantly follows through to its end.

A poem proceeds on its sound and on its images, proceeds in strides which preclude many minor descriptive steps, descriptive delays, which are finally noncontributory. By this I mean that tendency to cluster descriptions, fattening our poems and causing them to dawdle or mark time while the scent fades. If a phrase can create the right richness the first time, then the poem can move on.

In this poem of Wilbur's, leaving aside such important matters as the poem's metrical beauty and the rhythmical pattern of line endings, which contribute strongly to the poem's effect, we can measure one sequence of strides, mainly through participles and participial adjectives, beginning with "*tossed* with linden," through "from her *shut* door," on to "with a *bunched* clamor of strokes," "I remember the *dazed* starling," "and wait then, *humped* and bloody," and on to the final, "I wish what I *wished* you before, but harder." This recurrence seems to be aroused by the energized nature of the first of these sounds, "tossed," and works as a detectable verbal pulse in the piece. Take a dozen or more colored inks and chart the various patterns of sound and image in this poem; you will create quite a display.

I want to suggest that articulation of the authentic problem surfaces in this poem, insists itself into the final lines, because the poet takes up the proposition of sound that he offers himself, intuitively, at the poem's beginning. Language in poetry, Auden says somewhere, is not the handmaiden but the mother of thought: Words release their energy to other words in poems; they call to and echo each other across the stanzas. The confrontation with turbulence, which Wilbur was avoiding early in this poem with his "easy figure," is sown there at the very beginning, with those first words; the result is that, by the sixth stanza, he becomes capable of dealing with the memory of the starling, "dazed," "humped and bloody" (inevitably we think back to "tossed" in the second line), and so he becomes capable of working through to a much deeper, more empowered awareness of his daughter's situation and some of its meanings for him. He lets it "break" into him. Simply put, he can't deal with it at first, or he deals with it only superficially. But his own charged words propel him toward that confrontation; he rides their sounds to get there. Paler words could not accomplish such a thing—there's no proposition to them.

In *The Psychopathology of Everyday Life,* Freud uses the term "screen memory" to describe either an event in the past that we're drawn to and which leads us, by association, to an event in the present, the one which is really obsessing us but which we can't confront directly, or an event (image, object, and so on) in the present which is screening, but can eventually lead us to, something in the past that we need to come to terms with. Perhaps this corresponds to the generation of the authentic problem out of the initial theme, the sometimes drastic swing of the compass needle which, partway through a poem, points us in a direction that our conscious intention had never considered and might even have backed away from.

Often in dealing with a poem that doesn't seem to be working, I ask, "Where's the *second* emotion?" I find myself saying that it takes two to parent a poem and that many of our poems seem to fail their early potential because we don't manage to generate the second emotion, or subsequent ones. One reason for that failure is the lack of charge in our words. Although the indirection of Wilbur's journey carried no guarantee that it would lead him to his final statement, still he laid himself open to the possibility of such discovery by the energy and arousal of his first words and images—no space here to speak of the monumental prow. In a sense we cast ourselves upon the mercy of our own linguistic and imagistic inventing when we set out into a poem. The results, as in Wilbur's poem, seem to me permanently stirring.

In Sharon Olds's poem "Prayer During a Time My Son Is Having Seizures," an initially weak parent becomes empowered, as Wilbur does, by the poem's end, and rises memorably to an occasion which, at the poem's beginning, provokes feelings of impotence. The poem opens:

Finally, I just lean on the doorframe, a
woman without belief, praying
Please don't let anything happen to him.

And it closes:

I'll change his dark radiant diapers, I'll
scrape the blue mold that collects in the creases of his
elbows,
I will sit with him in his room for the rest of my days,
I will have him on any terms.

How does the weak leaner of the first line straighten to sit stoically, heroically, by poem's end? Less because of this poem's sound, I suspect, although those first lines have a quantity of it, and more because of the ferocity of naming through image, which proceeds from the first "lean," the poet's own stance, through a succession of fearsome pictures in which she imagines her susceptible son falling (four times), darkening, being lopped, being hit, sliding, being pushed off a high wire ("his small, dazzling / brain in spangles," if you can believe it), having his toys (thoughts) ripped away, drooling, and more. This unprecedented stream of visions takes up the imagistic proposition of the first lines in ways that surely overwhelmed the poet herself. What she comes to in her poem, what she generates by entering the arena of her vilest fears, is poetic statement of a resonance that must have been unthinkable before she actually started in on the words. As it does in Wilbur's poem, the screened, authentic problem is transformed into utterance which from now on will be dissolved in the poet, will become a part of who she is and how she sees the world. There is no mistaking the force of such discoveries; they cannot be faked and there is no going back from them.

Claiming Breath

DIANE GLANCY

How do you begin writing poetry? After all these years, I'm not sure. First of all, you read. You have to be aware of what's being written. Poetry is a conversation. Often while reading, I start a poem. An image will set off another image, or I think of something I want to say.

It also helps to know the tradition of poetry, but often there's something about tradition that gets in the way. You strain for a rhyme without thought for the fire, the energy of the poem, the originality of voice.

Contemporary poetry does not rhyme. There are exceptions to that rule also. If I read two poems of equal merit in content, I'm more impressed with the rhyming one, the sonnet or villanelle. But I will still say, don't rhyme at first.

Begin by getting words down. How does the message ride upon them? What have you got to say? Even if you want to remain obscure, there has to be coherence. The poem has to stick together on some cognitive level. If you get your words in order on the first row, you make room for craziness later on, deeper in the poem, in a more important place.

Work with what you have experienced. What idea, impression, image do you want to convey? Again: 1. read, 2. write what you have to say, and 3. read it to someone. Listen to their reaction, their criticism, and write again. Contemporary poetry lets you say what you have to say in whatever way you want to say it. Make sure you have a style, a voice, a certain way of expressing yourself. Where is your uniqueness, your individuality? Your thumbprint is different from other thumbprints. You have a way of seeing and a way of expressing what you see that is also different. Develop that difference. Take chances with unusual words and combinations. Writing is a long process. Reveal what it's like to be you.

It's not easy. Is something bothering you? Get into it. That will save the trouble of writing boring poems.

What is life like for you? That's what you should be writing about. Is there hope for humanity, or is there not? Are you confounded by life, or do you feel confident about it?

Remember imagery, the mental pictures your writing makes, usually through metaphor and simile. Make sure your images haven't been used before. They have to be new. Tell me something in a way I haven't heard it said before. Let an image connect with a thought, sometimes a memory. Juxtapose lines and phrases in a unique way. Get rid of weak verbs: the usual "is's," "ares," and "ings." Watch tenses; make them consistent. See if the active, present tense is possible.

Use detail! A cotton dress printed with crocuses is usually better than "a dress." Look for the right words. The inevitable ones. And though poetry should not always be analyzed, ask what your words mean. We discover ourselves and our world through poetry.

Remember also the richness of language. Make sure there's a lot in your writing. Read your words to yourself. Listen to them on a tape recorder if you want. The way a poem sounds is important. Pay attention to assonance and consonance.

The form a poem takes on the page is integral. Experiment with line breaks, stanzas (short and long, even and irregular), the square— or prose—poem, the words falling over the page.

What central image holds the poem together? What emotion or impression is shared? What stays in your mind after you've heard it? Is it in the form it should be in? Have you said the same thing too many times? Is it clear? Is the reader rewarded for reading it? What conclusion is drawn from it, even if not a logical thought, but an impression? Good poems are simple on at least one level.

Workshop a poem. I was in a small group for many years. I also went to summer writers' conferences in which there were lectures on craft and technique, readings by conference leaders, and round-table readings by students with comments from others on our work. Critiques are usually common sense. Does the poem work? Do you like it? Does it begin at the first stanza, or do you really get into the poem several lines later? Are the stanzas in the order they should be? Do the parts form a whole?

It's also important to think about why you write. Why do you want to capture your thoughts? If you do it once, what keeps you coming back? Writing is also catharsis. Be interested in a lot of things. Be an interesting person; live a responsible life. Start keeping notes.

Letting the Poem or Picture Book Out

SHARON CHMIELARZ

"I see," wrote the poet Robert Lowell in regard to his playwriting, "there's a sea of energy inside one that can't come out in poems and will come out this way." In my experience what can't come out in poetry can often come out in a picture book—in this way, a single personal experience supplies content for two different genres.

A writer's work in choosing a genre for a store of material is akin to the choices a builder makes in deciding the features of a house, temple, or skyscraper—it's a case of form following function. All structures have roofs and floors; it's the use that determines what goes in between. Just so the writer eases the same material into the different genres of poetry, essay, memoir, picture book, or novel. All need beginnings, endings, middles, clarity, style, and voice. The writer, like the builder, has to consider the habits and needs of the voice who will inhabit the structure.

To depict a man in my hometown, I once wrote a poem drawing a parallel between him and his house. The poem was complete in the sense it created by the description of a mood and a place. I had saved "for all time" a memory of one man's life. I thought I was finished. But the man as a character itched for the company of other characters and the process of conflict and resolution. He wanted a different form. So, since I was working for him, and he wouldn't stop pestering me, I wrote him a story. Since the conflict arose from a child's problem, the material evolved into another form—a picture book. I realize a child's problem can engage an adult audience, but that wasn't the direction this story took.

Writers commonly cross genres. Same body, different outfit. Same story, different angle. The choice is never finite. If my character returns again, demanding a different kind of space to live in, I, as his chief builder, will have to provide him with another form. And so it goes!

I am most familiar with the forms of poetry and picture books. They are natural bedfellows, and the line between them blurs readily. Notice how in Wanda Gág's *Millions of Cats* the prose story easily breaks into verse:

> Cats here, cats there,
> Cats and kittens everywhere,
> Hundreds of cats
> Thousands of cats,
> Millions and billions and trillions of cats.

Years after readers and listeners encountered this for the first time, they repeat the refrain with gusto.

And what about the picture books that are poems themselves, such as Audrey Osofsky's *Dreamcatcher*, or Margaret Wise Brown's *Goodnight Moon*?

> In the great green room
> There was a telephone
> And a red balloon
> And a picture of
> The cow jumping over the moon . . .
> Good night room,
> Good night moon
> Good night cow jumping over the moon . . .

Most picture books, however, are not poems but stand out because they nonetheless employ poetic devices. Two of the most common are repetition and pattern. An illustrator might use repetition in illustrations where the text seems to go flat. Repeating a scene or image is equivalent to repeating a line in a ballad. The reader/listener comes to anticipate the repetition. For example, in Peggy Rathmann's *Officer Buckle and Gloria*, the dog Gloria's repetitive reactions to her master's actions carry the story, the humor, the conflict, and the resolution.

In a nonfiction picture book like Lisa Westberg Peters's *The Sun, the Wind and the Rain*, the text proceeds according to a pattern. Throughout

the first twenty-two pages/paragraphs/stanzas, the story shifts alternately between images of the earth's work and play and a child's work
and play. Earth makes a mountain; the yellow-hatted Elizabeth makes
a sand pile. The reader/listener is led to find the universal in the personal, the macrocosm revealed in the microcosm. The effect of this
pattern/play is an elegant clarity that is at once brilliant and endearing in its simplicity. The use of the pattern leads to the writer's goal,
which is the reader's comprehension of a natural process. Incidentally,
"stanza," as I was delighted to learn a few years ago, is the Italian word
for "room." In each room of a poem, something remarkable can happen. Each room is outfitted in itself and in relation to the structure of
the house as a whole.

In a picture book, something that has happened, some moment, is
being noted attentively. As in narrative and especially lyrical poetry,
the urge to record is a desire to stop time, to hold it like a jewel. To
make the NOW eternal or to make the unseen NOW seen. In narrative, characters perform this function; if they are strong, they will
live in memory forever. One lovely example is Donald Hall, who is a
writer who crosses genres. The original fourth stanza of Hall's poem
"Ox Cart Man" reads:

> When the cart is empty he sells the cart.
> When the cart is sold he sells the ox, harness and yoke,
> and walks home,
> his pockets heavy with the year's coin for salt and taxes.

When Hall enlarged the audience for the character of the ox cart man
by writing it as a picture book, he simplified sentence structure and
intensified the repetition of structure and vocabulary that was part of
the poem's charm.

> Then he sold the wooden box he carried the maple sugar in.
> Then he sold the barrel he carried the apples in.
> Then he sold the bag he carried the potatoes in.
> Then he sold his ox cart.
> Then he sold his ox, and kissed him goodbye on his nose.

Then he sold his ox's yoke and harness.
With his pockets full of coins, he walked through
    Portsmouth Market.

In Hall's picture book, the listing is not as musical as the lines of the poem, yet he pushes time and events forward quickly, and what he loses in music he gains in the development of character. A child might relate to the expansive feeling of pockets full of money, but not the pinching necessity of paying taxes. A child's view invites the dreamy silliness of kissing an ox on the nose, which would be sentimental in a poem for adults. What is preserved in both versions is the ox cart man's spareness, evoking the laconic New England proverb "Waste not, want not." "Ox Cart Man" has the simplicity of a good Protestant hymn and of people who hear rather than read their stories.

Both poetry and picture book are rooted in an oral tradition whose aural powers began to erode long ago with the invention of the alphabet. This, however, is no detriment to the participation of a picture-book audience, some of whom may not be able to read. They might also not be able to sit still unless the work captures their attention immediately. It must rouse some emotion within them and leave them feeling, in Muriel Rukeyser's words, like a witness.

This leads to another similarity between the two genres: neither art form leaves space or time to dawdle before getting to the point, which is to record/witness a response to beauty, friendship, conflict, etc. In a picture book, the equivalent of one to five typewritten manuscript pages might sum up an entire life! For example, Margaret Wild's *Old Pig*, which depicts the life and relationship of a woman and her granddaughter, is one and a half single-spaced pages long.

Marion Dane Bauer defines a picture book as a book containing four hundred and fifty to fifteen hundred words, and a storybook as a book with fifteen hundred to three thousand words, yet Eriko Kishida's *Wake Up, Hippo!* is told in 195 words. Two of Shigeo Watanabe's books, *How Do I Put It On?* and *Daddy, Play with Me* total two hundred words. How do you say anything meaningful in one hundred words? How can you portray a well-rounded character in three pages?

Both poetry and picture books must weave a spell. Poetry employs the use of rhyme, metaphor, image, incantation, and list (note how effective Margaret Wise Brown's use of a list is, and how we naturally fall into it and love it). Story weaves a spell with its "once upon a time" or "long ago" or "let's pretend" invitation. Both poetry and picture books use sound. Children love sound in stories—whoosh! Plop! BAM! What power writers and storytellers have! They write or speak and presto! the word's image is mirrored in the listener's brain.

In the lecture "On Three Ways of Writing for Children," C.S. Lewis said:

> With me the process [of writing] is much more like bird-watching than like either talking or building. I see pictures. Some of these pictures have a common flavor, almost a common smell, which groups them together. Keep quiet and watch and they will begin joining themselves up. If you were very lucky, a whole set might join themselves so consistently that there you have a complete story without doing anything yourself. But more often there are gaps. Then at least you have to do some deliberate inventing, have to contrive reasons why these characters should be in these various places doing these various things. I have no idea whether this is the usual way of writing stories, still less whether it is the best. It is the only one I know; images always come first.

The use of an image or metaphor is a gift to any writer from the first poet's bag of tricks. It best captures an audience's ear and makes the strongest impact on their hearts. In a picture book, as in a poem, the writing, as Marion Dane Bauer puts it, "must have resonance. Ten percent of what you say is above surface, ninety percent below . . . the iceberg effect."

Is there a different intensity, one may wonder, when writing in a different genre? Sometimes while writing poetry I have the concentration of a bug circling a stone—I believe in my skin that the stone will reveal itself to me if I can just feel it right with my six legs. In stories, I feel more of the snoopy-neighbor syndrome: I'm the eighty-year-old with a telescope set up behind her living-room curtains, or the twelve-year-old who sneaks looks into the houses she passes—with each glimpse she captures a scene in someone else's life. Poetry and picture books both look easy to write. Who couldn't write one? They're short! A mere whistle instead of a symphony. Ah, the bliss of the innocent and the ignorant! As in longer genres, the process involved in writing a poem or picture book is very much a struggle to get things right. The genre we choose to write in can make the work go more smoothly. We can learn new skills, flex and enforce the old ones. We can revel, after the work is completed, in the experience it's given us: our privileged access to the art of making.

Got Them Poetry Blues?

ADRIAN C. LOUIS

Like many poets I know, I sometimes wonder what the point of poetry is anymore. It's ten at night on these northern plains, and I just came in from staring down some newly planted cedar trees. I don't know why I got them. They're so slow growing, and when they're mature, they're about as ugly as a tree can be. In a neighbor's yard, a group of young studs is drinking beer and laughing loudly. I can hear their boisterous conversation. They aren't talking about current world politics, or how America is becoming a third-world nation, and they sure as hell aren't talking about poetry.

Their voices in the night air speak of the things young, uneducated men speak of: cars, women, fighting, the Chicago Bulls and how many years does Michael Jordan have, and women again. It angers me for a moment. Not because they are young and ignorant, but because they are young and ignorant and I can see it and they can't. In the country of the blind, the one-eyed man goes blind.

Once, when I was young and lusty, I entertained for some years the fantasy of becoming a clairvoyant, a mind reader, so I could walk up to women and curve my actions into their softest thoughts. Well, I never became a mind reader, but I did transmogrify into a poet, and I guess one of my prime motivations was a striving for immortality. I wanted to be preserved in books, like Frost and Eliot, long after my silly flesh had decomposed.

The problem is, now that I am inside the pages of books, poetry has come to be of little consequence to American society at large. Nobody really reads poetry these days except other poets and those failed poets who make their livings as English teachers or critics, and of course college students. These guys down the street guzzling Budweiser don't know me as a poet, but they do know I teach English at the tribal college.

Being a poet of dubious distinction and also a teacher of English composition, I am always struck by the kinships between the two professions which transcend the obvious fact that both pay poorly.

This past semester, I told my freshman composition students that one hundred years ago there was no difference between the sentence and the paragraph. Then I could not recall where I had gleaned that tidbit and whether or not it was apocryphal. Things went from bad to worse, and for the life of me I could not remember why paragraphs should be hinged together by transitions. Running into a dead end, I was reminded of some of my recent poems that ended in disaster, and wished that poetic salvation could come disguised as a grammar primer. Sometimes I wonder if the current death of poetry originated at the time we quit diagramming sentences.

I'd like to diverge from the usual discussion of the nuts and bolts of poetry (object, symbol, image, rhyme, meter, etc.) and deal in superficialities, much in the manner I suppose I deal with my life.

I believe we must view a poem's form as we view the basic structure of any communication. That is to say, a poem has a beginning, a middle, and an ending. Or, to use the oversimplified outline of the basic speech, it has an introduction, a body, and a conclusion.

It is from within the basic framework that any vision springs, and here any triggering device is located. So you start with the body and then insert the motor. And if you believe that one, then you may be able to envision the poem as something akin to the sentence. (And now the hallowed halls of rhyme are hushed. What? Did he actually say the poem and the sentence are the same thing?) No, they are not exactly the same. The difference in function is like the difference between the lightbulb and the candle.

The sentence is a complete unit of thought. It can stand alone and make complete sense. Without any discussion of the main parts (subject, verb, and object or predicate), we see that it also has a beginning, a middle, and an end. If truth be known, in most poems that I write, the reader is invited in, given something, and then provided an exit. It's like a house of ill repute. You enter. Boom! The act is committed, and you leave feeling either rosy or guilt-gloomy, having spent both your seed and your bread.

I believe this same commotion happens when anyone reads the

common sentence, and it is a pattern that makes some of my difficult
poems work. This, in itself, is no earth-shattering news, but it is one
approach I have found to making difficult poems work.

The weakness of this reductionism, in addition to its seemingly in-
artistic oversimplification, is that it disallows incoherency, fragmentation, flatulation, and it most certainly demands closure. I'm sure some
people would say that the very concept limits poetic vision, the freedom to fly in any direction, and it may well, but it seems to me that the
problem with much poetry today lies in its inaccessibility.

Poetry is for the most part inaccessible to the common person,
and so we have sociologists trying to decipher the state of the nation
through the Simple Simon lyrics of rap, rock, and country-and-western
music. Worse yet, we have poets who think they're sociologists.

So much contemporary poetry is so damned esoteric, so intellec-
tualized, and so secondhand that it does a disservice to the true aims
of poetry. I believe those aims are to communicate something new
in a new way, all within the context of simple human sharing, simple
human singing.

Much of the poetry we read today is too demanding and not worth
the effort to decipher. We are codependents in a literary form of denial. Many times we just do not get the meaning of the poem and are
afraid to ask what it means.

The truth, as I see it, is that much of what I read today has no
real meaning other than that many poets masturbate, in public and
much too often. We do not need colossal puzzles of mind-fuck. We
get plenty of those in everyday life. In these days where great hunger is
geared toward fast foods of the mind, we should attempt to make our
poems accessible to our intended audiences.

Good poetry need not be the exclusive bailiwick of the intellectual,
or the artist, or the academy, though it certainly has come to be. The
origins of poetry lie in interaction between the poet and the common
person, and if it is to survive, it must retrace its steps back in that direction. That is why, to me, such current fantasies as language poetry
and the new formalism are doomed to failure. They are hoodoo, purely
conjured visions of fragmentation with no redemptive message, no
medicine for the ailing society.

The concept of using the sentence as a model for the poem raises more questions than it answers, I am sure. Someone, no doubt, will scoff and point, and say that we need not look any further than the haiku to see gaping holes in my concept—and no, I'm not going to launch into an argument on how haiku itself functions the same way as a sentence does, but think about it. It may! Someone else will view these very sentences I write as nothing more than a tired revision of the pearl-in-the-necklace concept. Each pearl (read image, action, meaning, device, etc.) is tied to the string of form and in the end makes a fundamental and united object of adornment. The stars are not important in themselves; it is the embracing backdrop of night sky which gives them meaning.

This relates to collections of poems, too, doesn't it? If we are to assume that a sentence is a complete unit of thought, then we should further assume that within a paragraph or longer piece of writing, some sentences are more important than others. What does this mean to a collection of poems gathered together in manuscript form? The implication is that some poems are stronger than others, and usually this works out to be the case.

Still, it is important to keep in mind that though a single poem extracted from a manuscript may seem weak in its naked self, it gains strength from being part of the collective grouping of poems. This is especially true if the poet intends the manuscript as a form of extended narrative.

Stop me before I move on to the book of poems as a novel and discuss the plotting of poems. But before I finish, let me offer some words of advice to student poets. Believe me, this is a hard thing to do, so take what I say with a shaker of salt, for my wounds as well as yours.

First and foremost, do not elevate your mentors to any position near God. Do not sleep with them, physically or metaphysically. They *are* fallible; many have elevators that do not go all the way to the top, and God does not need any more assistants. Be wary of teachers self-exiled to the ivory towers who have lost touch with the common person and the common language. Be doubly wary of poets entrenched in the middle-aged middle class of middle America! Don't be afraid to seek out the wisdom of multicultural poets.

Enforce a variety of appreciation on your mind. Read all types of poems. Read anything you can get your hands on. Reading is the drug all writers use. Read Jack London. Read Jack Kerouac. Read the *National Enquirer.* Read the zine poets. I give you permission to not read Emily Dickinson, but don't skip Whitman, don't pass by Robert Lowell without a glance. And though it may sound unrelated, never trust a person who has never done manual labor.

Do not be afraid to study literature, literary theory, and literary criticism. Although these subservient industries are the progeny of creative writing, they are the transmission fluid of writers. You can actually learn to write better by reading and studying good writers.

Ignore the jealous words of critics who say, "Creative writing can't be taught." Sit on the gems of your workshop years for a decade or two until wisdom arrives. Your hatchlings, a mixture of rhinestones and dead, rotted embryos, won't be all bad. (You can tell when wisdom arrives. It comes about the time your body starts falling apart.)

Become computer literate. It's a tremendous aid. The motivation of the blank computer screen lies in its gray color: ashes, death is coming, get off your butt and write with the enthusiasm of your first sexual awakenings. This does not apply to poets living monastic lives.

Don't be afraid to talk to God. Don't believe the Stevens dictum about poetry being the dominion one enters after belief in God dies. If you believe in any higher spirit, don't be afraid to let that belief become a part of your work. Human beings yearn for hope.

Automatically apply for all grants and fellowships, because if you win one and apply yourself to writing every day, you'll see how many damn years you wasted. Besides, the worst they can say is "No," and "You have no talent," and "Are you kidding?"

If you purport to be a member of the guild, then support it. If you want a poem published in a certain quarterly, buy a subscription. Buy books of poems by other poets. The real problem is that more of us write poems than read poems. Attend readings by other poets. Ask them for their autographs. Ask them if you can donate your life savings to their quest for art.

Don't use words in your poems that you never use in everyday life. That's why they invented dictionaries. Your job is to communicate with your fellow human beings. Come to accept the fact that words *are* cheap: They are easy to throw away and find again. If you ever get a chance to write for a newspaper, take the job for the invaluable experience it will provide. Don't be an elitist, an *artiste*.

Write within your own experience and within your own culture. If you are a middle-class white man, don't be creating Iceberg Slim who be out scheming to get hisself some poontang. If you have a Cherokee ancestor five generations back, don't label yourself a Native American poet. Stick with what you know. It just may work. Poetry can be therapeutic in that eventually you come to define and refine yourself.

Don't be ashamed to promote yourself. Don't be afraid to be what Salinger labeled a "prostitute writer." How else are you going to get known? You can't dash off rhymes in some garret and hope that they will boomerang back to you loaded with acclaim, fame, and fortune. When you're young, you should be making literary connections to help you in the future.

Don't be ashamed to say you are a poet when someone asks. Just remember to have a crazed look in your eye when you say the dreaded P word. And when they ask you to say a poem, give them "After a Long Silence" by Yeats. Claim it as your own and let it be your credo.

Be a true believer. Once in a while, get on your knees and subscribe to the notion that poetry can transcend the dung heaps created by mankind and elevate the reader and writer to thresholds of beauty, to vistas of enlightenment, to all that we hold as noble, loving, and necessary. Be aware that every poem we write is political.

If you believe you have no talent for writing poems, then don't. If you have talent, it will be recognized and will grow of its own accord. Poetry is one of those endeavors where the rewards are minimal, even if you do reach a stratum of success and acceptance. It is something you do for the love of it, and the pay is pitiful, and yes, we all lie when we say we don't love money.

Finally, disregard all I've said and sit down and write something new and exciting. Write an invoice to God for services rendered.

A Few Cranky Paragraphs
on Form and Content

MARILYN HACKER

I haven't written a sestina since 1986, and I may never write another one. The lovely Provençal form I discovered through Auden and Pound in my teens has been so banalized as an (unmetered) exercise in creative-writing workshops—whose products come across my desk in teetering stacks when I'm working as an editor—that I find myself disinclined to read, much less write, any more of them. Not long ago, at an international feminist book fair, a crewcut, fresh-faced young woman came up to me to say she'd recognized me, and she loved my sestinas. I found myself wishing ungraciously that she'd said (instead, or also): I love the way you write about women's friendships, or convey a sense of urban movement, or mix credibly ordinary speech with imagery. Then I'd have known I'd met a reader, as well as a probable alumna of a creative-writing workshop.

A few days before that, a poet much acclaimed for the stance of witness to contemporary history in her work, whose reading I'd been asked to introduce at a bookshop in Paris, said to me, "I've always liked your villanelles." And I felt she'd merely noticed my occasional use of a form she herself would consider clever but trivial; otherwise, she had not found anything of substance in the poems upon which to comment.

I'm not proud of my reaction to these well-meant remarks, a reaction which may only show how ill at ease I am when people talk to me about my work. But I've become impatient and uneasy about the fact that because I use received forms, that is often all that's discussed in the work—oddly enough, by feminist critics and reviewers in particular. The dominance of so-called open forms in contemporary American (here meaning United States) poetry, especially in the feminist provinces thereof, is so pronounced that use of another mode is cause for comment, taking sides, writing manifestos. In a literary climate where metrics were part of everyone's prosodic vocabulary, the use of such forms wouldn't be remarked upon: The exceptionally brilliant, or maladroit, use of a schema or structure would be instead. I'd like to see more of *that* in book reviews! Instead of which we still have debates about the "New Formalism" and its political ramifications, in which both sets of partisans seem to forget that poets as politically—and formally—diverse as Julia Alvarez, Gwendolyn Brooks, Rafael Campo, Hayden Carruth, Alfred Corn, Thom Gunn, Rachel Hadas, Carolyn Kizer, Derek Walcott, Marilyn Nelson Waniek have frequently or consistently made use of formal/fixed metrical strategies in their work; that the usual suspects, in their thirties and forties, white, affluent, East Coast based and so forth, are only one part of a continuing tradition or conversation.

And yet, and yet. . . . I choose to write metrically/formally: It's neither an imposition nor a philosophical/aesthetic conviction. I do it because it gives me pleasure; because (some have said) I do it well; because it's a challenge, and one I can meet (I've never found myself to have a gift for extended figurative language, for example, could not prolong a metaphor to parallel the central movement of a poem, the way some writers whom I much admire often do). Most of all, I do it because it sometimes takes the poem unexpected places, because language itself then becomes the contrapuntal force, establishes the subtext.

Of course, every poem is "formal": The writer's intention in setting it on the page as such, with (usually) line breaks rather than a right-hand margin, with white space, is that the reader recognize that it has a structure, that it is language somehow condensed, ordered, thought and sculpted to do something beyond or besides conveying a fact, delivering a message. Which is not to say that every group of words or sentences arranged like a poem on a page has successfully undergone that transformation.

What makes a poem transcend wordplay, description, or rhetoric? What makes a poem? This kind of (privileged) question always makes me slightly queasy. Although making poems is one of the things I do, poetry is much less compelling to me as a subject about which to

write, think, or act than, say, the homeless young black woman in army
fatigues with a shaved head, and the homeless young white woman
in jeans with long, unwashed, uncombed black hair, both begging
on Broadway between 101st and 106th streets, both of whom, in the
same clothes but bathed, laundered, shampooed, would be plausible
Columbia University graduate students ten blocks uptown. Perhaps
there's a more pertinent question that connects them to poetry: What
makes a poem relevant to the reader so that she or he does not turn the
page impatiently, thinking, "What's this got to do with me?"—or, "Tell
me something I don't know already!" Political relevance isn't enough.
Last night I shut, in disappointment, a book of poems by a black British
lesbian: poems which made necessary points, reclaiming street life and
street talk, haranguing hypocritical white feminists and hypocritical
black male activists; but the poems themselves were just as predictable as the white North Carolina academic's well-made sonnet about
fishing with his twelve-year-old son, or the Jewish pacifist's free-verse
sequence about visiting her grandmother in a nursing home. Poems
about grandmothers in nursing homes, fishing trips, liberal hypocrisy
aren't *a priori* bad or good any more than ones about unrequited love,
the fear or fascination of death, or devotion to a deity. It's not the predictable subjects that make so much contemporary journeyman poetry
unremarkable, but the predictable language, structure, point of view,
tone. (I make this remark as a once-and-future editor, under no illusion that there was any period in the recent or distant past when most
of what was written *wasn't* predictable or mediocre.)

There's a place for mediocre fiction, as any commercial editor
will affirm, if the subject is timely/original/in the news/something
about which some group of people wants to read. Is there a place for
mediocre poetry? Do we want there to be? (And who is "we"—me,
Richard Wilbur, June Jordan, Miguel Algarín, Helen Vendler?) My
first impulse is to say: No, there's not. Then I recall how much hot-
headed, right-on, and mediocre feminist poetry it took to produce a
climate where a woman poet isn't still Dr. Johnson's dancing dog (not
that she does it well but that she does it at all); how much African-
American verse rhetoric had to be written, read, and processed so that
Yusef Komunyakaa, Rita Dove, Thylias Moss could free themselves

of having to be representative or exemplary, and can write—whatever and however they damn please! As an editor, I'm much more strongly inclined to work through drafts one, four, seven, with a poet until we reach one I'm willing (eager) to publish if the poem deals with events, presents a point of view not yet obvious: the point of view of an HIV-positive woman, a description of open-heart surgery, or a convincing rendering of a jam session. And I'd have the same inclination toward a not-yet-entirely-successful poem in an intriguing/difficult/invented-but-rigorous form. The nursing home and fishing trip poems, though—because they are so numerous—have got to be pretty exemplary on first reading.

Often enough, the formally ambitious poem is also the one where the point of view or narrative thrust is not merely original, but compelling. I remember my excitement upon first reading the deceptively laconic, demotic syllabic quatrains of Hayden Carruth's *Asphalt Georgics*, or the rhetorically expansive, psychologically and historically acute dramatic movements of Muriel Rukeyser's *One Life*. And I've experienced the same sensation of expanded possibilities reading new work by younger poets (an editorial privilege): Rafael Campo's sonnet sequence, "The Distant Moon," limning a first-year medical resident's tentative, erotically tinged interchanges with an AIDS patient; Lynda Hull's long, pyrotechnical "Suite for Emily," juxtaposing delinquent girls in lurid, jeweled cityscapes with Dickinson's verbal rigors—which also happened to be the first AIDS elegy I'd read memorializing a woman.

(I didn't intend specifically to cite two AIDS-related poems, but the subject has imposed itself upon poets across generations. I remember, again, the two separated, gaunt, and obstreperous women panhandling on Broadway, and realize that in mentioning them I also may be writing about AIDS.)

Formal ambition—as my examples may show—needn't mean invention from scratch, any more than breaking out of a metrical pattern which has come to seem overfamiliar implies plugging up one's ears to accentual-syllabic structures. Almost every contemporary American poet has read or heard quoted Ezra Pound's imperative "Break the back of the iambic pentameter!"—including those student poets who have never composed ten lines of iambic pentameter in their lives. Hardly anyone recalls that, in order to "break the back of the iambic pentameter," Pound, who *had* written reams of it, advised young poet Mary Bernard to "write sapphics until they come out of your ears." (Good advice: She became one of our finest translators of Sappho.) That is: Compose metered verse stanzas in American English which were markedly not iambic—a different proposition than discarding fixed meter. And a difficult one: Iambic pentameter is very natural to colloquial English. If you leave out the French and Latin words, you spin it out as easily as prose.

After having written a kind of novel consisting of two-hundred-odd sonnets interleaved with a couple of other, also iambic, forms, Pound's decades-old advice seemed particularly moot to me. I'd hovered around James Wright's difficult, dazzling hendecasyllabics for years, paid tribute to them in a slant-rhymed "Letter from the Alpes-Maritimes" (in *Assumptions*), and paid more attention to the rhythm's demands in "Elevens" (in *Going Back to the River*), a kind of response to Wright's lovely Sapphic/Horatian "Prayer to the Good Poet"—Horace—in *Two Citizens*. Somehow it took that gradual approach for me to finally attempt the real metric template: three lines of *trochee trochee dactyl trochee trochee* followed by a five-syllable *dactyl trochee* line called the Adonic. This is about as close as you can come in English, where syllable stress can be noted, but measures of syllable length are, at best, moot. "A Note Downriver" (in *Winter Numbers*) was the first entirely metrical poem I wrote in Sapphics (James Merrill's elegy for David Kalstone in *The Inner Room* encouraged me).

It interests me that distance—in particular the distance and tension between the two cities, New York and Paris, in which I live, between my two languages/cultures, between a heritage of exile from a Europe which cast out its Jews and a coming-of-age coming back to it from states mostly united in their rejection of feminists, anarchists, artists, and queers—is thematically important in just about all the poems in Sapphic (and Alcaic) stanzas which I've written (now about a dozen). It's as if dislocating my verbal/aural reveries—and I do sometimes think in a meter when I'm deeply engaged in writing it—into a non-iambic meter, less natural to English, were a kind of "Invitation au

Voyage," or one to examine the voyage which my life has been for the last twenty-five years.

Alcaics, even more metrically intricate than Sapphics, tempted me after reading for the tenth time Alfred Corn's graceful "Somerset Alcaics" from his book *The West Door.* (In general, those two Greek meters come to us Anglophones modulated by Latin poets' use of them; they are as Horatian as they are Attic.)

My own first presentable work in Alcaics, the title poem of *Going Back to the River,* began (after days of practice sessions with the meter), as so many others have, where it describes itself, where I'm now sitting writing this page: at my work table three floors up above the rue de Turenne, with the number 96 bus belching at its stop just below, on the way to Belleville and the Porte des Lilas. Bus notwithstanding, the street is narrow enough that the neighbors across the way and I live our lives more or less in view of each other; this decade, in what is one of the oldest neighborhoods in Paris, the specter of what happened in this city, in this *arrondissement,* a mere fifty-odd years ago also lives nearby.

On July 16, 1942, almost thirteen thousand Jews, over four thousand of them children under sixteen, were summarily arrested by the French police. Single adults and childless couples were taken to a concentration camp at Drancy—before, and since, a banal suburb. The children and their parents, more than seven thousand people, were penned up for seven days without sanitation or first aid, starvation rations given them more brutally than they'd have been given to penned animals, in the Velodrome d'Hiver, a sports stadium—from where they, too, were sent to Drancy, and thence, with the others, to Auschwitz. Except for those who escaped, or were rescued before deportation—a minimal number—not one of those 4,051 children returned.

The writer Primo Levi said, when he was asked why he didn't write about the Stalinist gulags as well as about Auschwitz (of which he was a survivor), that he could only bear witness to what he had experienced: He knew no more about the gulags than did his interlocutor. (He said more than that: He went on to elucidate the differences.) I don't think I could write a poem about the Vel d'Hiv (as it's referred to, even in historical accounts of the event). I know less about what happened here that week than do my neighbors in their sixties, seventies, eighties, if they want to remember. But those events are still as present as the seventeenth-century stairwell and the nineteenth-century plumbing, just as the fact of being a Jew is present in my consciousness, even without a fixed cultural or devotional meaning.

It has, in part, the meaning given to it by those events. I was a four-month fetus in my mother's womb that summer, but in the Bronx, not in Paris. (Pregnant women were not exempted, nor were veterans.) Fifty-two years later, I know more about poet and anti-Semite Ezra Pound than about the twenty-seven children, my contemporaries, older sisters and brothers, who were arrested that day with their parents in just one antique tenement, 22 rue des Ecouffes—still standing, five minutes' leisurely walk from where I live.

Is this still about poetry? Poetry itself suffers when it's too pointedly "about poetry." (Writing a poem as subject surfaced more often in those manuscript piles than unrequited love or nursing homes.) It's difficult, though, for a poem not to be, on some level, about language, whether directly or indirectly, as a reflection of the conscious compression, shaping, intense attention-paying which the writer must do, whatever the other subject.

It would be comforting to align poetry with the forces of liberation. Those French police were ordered not to exchange "unnecessary conversation" with the French-speaking Jews (most of them were not yet naturalized citizens, or had been stripped by decree of citizenship awarded after 1928—except the children, citizens by virtue of having been born in France, who were arrested anyway) they were to arrest—official language for: Don't talk to them. Exchanged words may lead to mutual recognition. But there was also the literate German officer who wrote in his journal on July 19, 1942, about a stroll through Père Lachaise Cemetery: a lyrical meditation on the long departed, not on what was happening to those who were—so briefly—still alive. And there was Pound, and there was Eliot, and there was, and is, every writer capable of brilliantly manipulating language and, thus, thought, but not of acknowledging the common humanity of Jews or Africans or Arabs, of communists, Catholics, women, or queers.

Perhaps that's why I permit myself that impatience with readers and apprentice writers who notice or comment on only "sestinas" or "sonnets" or "Sapphics." However modest and circumscribed are my attempts to bear witness, or, less ostentatiously, to say what I've seen for myself, I'd like to think that testimony can be perceived in its integrity, surface and ossature together. Which is the skin, which flesh, which skeleton—form, content—is impossible to discern: They're part of one body in motion.

Toward a Metaphor of Translation

JAY MISKOWIEC

In the beginning was the Word.
—John 1:1

Language is not immaterial. It is a subtle body, but body it is. Words are trapped in all the corporal images which captivate the subject.
—Jacques Lacan, *The Function of Language in Psychoanalysis*

Translation is metaphor.

That is, the etymologies of these two words lead us in the same direction, to the same shifting of sides, the same manners of handing on or carrying over, the same traditions and treasons. Literally, they are different linguistic forms of the same idea.

Metaphor derives from the Greek *metapherein* (to transfer), which combines the prefix *meta* (beyond, over) with *pherein* (to carry).

Translation derives from the Latin *translatus* (to transfer or carry across), which combines the prefix *trans* (across, over, towards) with *latus,* the past participle of *ferre* (to ferry, carry, bear).

Trans stems from the Latin *tradere* (to hand on, to hand over, to deliver), from which come both *traditio* and *traditor*—tradition and traitor. Thus Benedetto Croce cited as the translator's best options either a "faithful ugliness" or a "faithless beauty." What is betrayed, in the act of translating?

Ferre shares its past participle with another verb, *tollere* (to raise or remove), from which come "toll" and "tax." What is the cost of changing the form of the text? What must be given up?

The Greek term for translation is *metaphrasis* (the Anglicized metaphrase has the connotation of word-for-word translation), which combines *meta* with *phrazein* (to speak). In this sense of going beyond speech, we see that translation is always already a kind of supplemental or secondary process.

I have a kind of Romantic view of language, a belief in the individual human voice at the center of creation, but speaking of an absolute or ideal or universal. This perspective has an affinity with Goethe's "world literature," that is, a discourse that blends a vast array of languages and literatures: for my purpose not just European, but one that could extend to Hebrew, Arabic, Hindi, West African, and Native American. (We regularly use terms derived from Nahuatl, the language of the Aztecs—coyote, chocolate, and tomato, from *coyote, xocolatl,* and *tomatl.* And I love the idea that "Minnesota" means the land of waters the color of the sky and that Minneapolis is an Anishanaabe-Greek combination.)

I'm not advocating some kind of monolithic protolanguage that could be created from all those on earth. It's simply a matter of realizing that translation does not move between languages that are homogeneous, hermetic systems, but that nearly every word in every language has a potential multiplicity of meaning. The double bind, the catch-22, is that the translation of a word is always another word. (We may except translation between a verbal and nonverbal language, such as art. In *The Raw and the Cooked,* Claude Levi-Strauss claims music to be superior to verbal language, for it is both understandable and untranslatable, a level of feeling and knowledge which cannot be, or need not be, put into words.)

Metaphor must create a nexus between the idea and the vehicle or signifier used to express it. But rather than adding something extra to an already existing entity—rather than going beyond the word or phrase—translation risks the opposite: the detraction, the subtraction, the diminishing of meaning.

Slang and idiom generally are culture specific. *Desmadre* in Mexican Spanish means a mess, like a messy room, and also what might be called a screwed-up situation. But these English phrases omit completely the literal meaning: something unmothered. How will the reader in translation have even a glimmer of the implications that mother conveys in Mexico, with a history leading from the Aztec earth goddess Cihuacóatl and the Catholic Virgin Mary to La Llorona (the Weeping Woman) and the Virgin of Guadalupe, through the pivotal personage of La Malinche—the indigenous translator, adviser, and lover of Cortes—who is considered the great betrayer of the indigenous people? Women held a much more equal place in Aztec society; with the arrival of the Spanish, their role was diminished. One's own mother remains something sacred, but the mother of the other is devalued and disparaged.

And so mother becomes a trope, a word that gives a specific twist or turn to a phrase. *Poca madre* (less or little mother) means really good and its corresponding superlative (father) means excellent; but the expression may also be employed to insult someone for a kind of lack of mothering: *que poca madre tienes* (what little mother you have) means "What a bastard you are." (The English phrase also shows how metaphor stems from cultural values, in this case being claimed by the father.) There exist as well profanities such as *romper la madre* (to break the mother, or beat the hell out of someone) and *me vale madre.*

Let's look more closely at this last phrase (for there is no more illustrative metaphor than profanity): *me vale madre* (it's worth a mother to me), or I don't give a damn. But the force of the phrase is very, very strong and requires some explication: it's worth a mother to me—not my mother (who is a saint), but your mother (who is a whore). "I don't give a damn" certainly conveys the meaning of "I emphatically don't care," but the original connotations are completely lost or left behind.

Translation is metaphor.

That is, simply a figure of speech, a comparison or implied equivalence.

But equal may not mean same. Last year I had the privilege of interviewing Carlos Fuentes. I told him I had been reading the English translation of his novel *Cristobal Nonato* (*Christopher Unborn*) alongside the Spanish original and found many passages that greatly diverged from each other. Even more, parts of the original don't appear in the translation, such as the chapter *"De aves que hablan nuestro mismo idioma"* ("Of Birds Which Speak Our Own Language"), which concerns in some ways, as does the entire book, the appropriation of language and culture. It begins: "*Hace tiempo (una eternidad para él que crece) Angel mi padre decidió que nadie hablaba español ya; porque creer lo contrario era privarse del deleite máximo de la lengua, que es imentarla porque tenemos la impresión de que se nos muere entre los labios y depende de nosotros resucitarla.*" ("Some time ago [an eternity for he who is growing] my father Angel decided that nobody spoke Spanish any longer; for to believe the contrary was to deny oneself the greatest delight of this language, which is inventing it because we have the impression it dies on our lips and we are the ones who must bring it back to life.")

There are also English sentences from the original that remain so in the translation, but in a slightly altered form. For instance, "YOU DON'T MEAN ME?" becomes

"YOU MEAN LITTLE OLD ME?"

Where does the difference lie between these phrases? I asked. Fuentes replied that as he worked on the translation with Alfred MacAdam, they frequently took liberties.

"Somehow it had to be different," he said. "Somehow it was a different work in another language. You needed to feel that."

George Steiner, one of this century's most lucid and poetic literary theoreticians and author of the seminal work *After Babel: Aspects of Language and Translation,* says that translation in its fullest sense "redefines and makes native to our ground" and that great translators "act as a kind of living mirror. They offer to the original not an equivalence, for there can be none, but a vital counterpoise, an echo, faithful yet autonomous."

But still, it seems, the best translation uses the most literal metaphor. The translator should assume that the particular image or object or idea is deliberate, and I believe one has first—at least in early working drafts—to use the cognate or closest literal term. Steiner also says, "Modesty is the very essence of translation.... Without modesty translation will traduce." The metaphor must be captured as much in its indigenous state as possible. (The idea of speech or discourse as something first living and only secondarily inscribed or put down in writing has a long Western tradition, going back at least to Plato and continuing in the modern era with Condillac, Rousseau, Freud, and Levi-Strauss.)

Translation is a form of exchange between different systems, different properties and proprietors. It changes the wording, replacing one set of signifiers with another in order to arrive at the same set of signifieds. Let us not lose sight of the prefix *trans* and its inherent sense of movement.

Translating Neruda: The Way to Macchu Picchu, John Felstiner's two-hundred-page commentary on his thirty-six-page translation of Pablo Neruda's "Alturas de Macchu Picchu," is an archeology, an epistemology of the translator's craft. Felstiner's project goes right to the etymological heart of the word translation: to undertake "bringing Neruda over into English." He purports to transmit the artistic, biographical, cultural, historical, psychological, and textual considerations made while working on the major section of perhaps, along with Whitman's *Leaves of Grass,* the greatest epic poem in American (of the Americas) literature, *Canto General.* What is the nature of poetry (and we may ask as well, of language), and thus what must be considered in its translation? This study replies, "ideas, imagery, pattern, sound, rhythm, which are specific to their own language."

Is there some kind of Platonic ideal of a translation, or are there innumerable ones for any given text? In *Traducción: literatura y literalidad* (*Translation: Literature and Literality*), Octavio Paz says that beginning as far back as the Renaissance, the world is no longer "an indivisible totality. . . . Plurality of languages and societies: each language is a vision of the world, each civilization is a world." In the modern fragmented era, translation not only shows the lack of similarities between languages, peoples, and nations, but "manifests that those differences are unsurmountable." Steiner says in *After Babel* that the ideal translation would "achieve an equilibrium . . . between two works, two languages, two communities of historical experience and contemporary feeling."

Translation is metaphor.

That is, abstract, creative, inexact, aesthetic.

Does some formula exist by which one may come to the most "accurate" translation? May we look to the work of a great translator, as Steiner says in *After Babel,* for "the prescriptive or purely empirical principles, devices, routines which have controlled his choice of this equivalent rather than that, of one stylistic level in preference to another"?

Paz says in his own treatise, "There isn't nor can there be a science of translation, although it can and should be studied scientifically." I believe translators have a lot to learn from structuralist linguistics—concepts like signifier, signified, chain of signification, metaphor and metonymy, code and message, speech and language, difference and articulation all go to the essence of the translation process. Likewise, the theory of modern psychoanalysis, with its emphasis on the linguistic act, can help unlock some of the paths by which the unconscious generates abstract meanings, and thus perhaps aid the translator in approaching more closely the author's original intention.

In the final analysis, is there a methodology, an organized set of methods and restraints, that may be developed? Or does one just read the word or line in the original and *find* a natural, idiomatic, unforced way of rephrasing it?

Borrowing a line from Robert Fitzgerald's rendering of the *Odyssey,* Steiner suggests in *Language and Silence,* "'Soft as this hand of mist' is not a bad motto for translators."

The metaphor of translation is metaphor.

Some Notes on Negative Capability

KATRINA VANDENBERG

In a recent e-mail to my husband, a fellow writer said:

> Cynthia Ozick criticized teachers [who tell] students to write
> what they know. . . . Instead, she said, encourage students to
> write what they don't know. Make writing an act of discov-
> ery, get writing students out of their worlds and into others;
> force them to understand other lives. I believe in this, and I
> believe with Ozick that seeking understanding of what we
> don't know is a moral act, one that leads to a kind of morality
> based on empathy.

John Keats called this practice of empathy "negative capability" in a
letter he wrote in 1817, saying a poet must be able to be "in uncertain-
ties, Mysteries, doubts, without any irritable reaching after fact and
reason." A friend said Keats could conceive that "a billiard ball . . . may
have a sense of delight from its own roundness, smoothness, volubility
and the rapidity of its motion." Not that the ball would remind him of
an evening with his father, or make him think the ball was a planet and
the player a god—the ball revealed the world to Keats by being itself, a
ball, not a springboard back into the world in Keats's head.

Below is a list of questions I use as one way to help keep myself
on the ground as I write, walking through the physical world toward
Keats's idea of negative capability. All are variations on the question
"What does the object know?"

What is inside the object?

Think of the seeds and pulp and pith inside an orange; the gears
in a clock; the grubs and sap in a tree. When I studied under Pattiann
Rogers, she gave us this assignment: "Write a poem about the inside
of something you are usually outside."

I love "Inside a Gorilla," written by a fifth grader in Arkansas, for its King-Kong–style *booms:* "Breathing. Bones. / Bananas. Water. Lemon. / The gorilla walking." Charles Simic put a more sophisticated spin on entering an object at the end of "Stone": "I have seen sparks fly out / When two stones are rubbed, / So perhaps it is not dark inside after all; / Perhaps there is a moon shining / From somewhere, as though behind a hill— / Just enough light to make out / The strange writings, the star-charts / On the inner walls."

What is physically behind, over, under this object or story or image? Or, if you were to put a frame around what is happening in your poem, what is happening just outside it?

One way to play with this question is to write a poem about a photograph—what can you not see in the picture? Dorianne Laux, in "The Catch," shows her readers film footage of "fistfuls of Marines flung / from a helicopter," then carries us into a dead Marine's breast pocket to see a snapshot of "his girl / in a bikini, her whole body sprawled / across the hood of a new Camaro. / She's wet from the blue pool, shining, / car keys dangling from her teeth like minnows."

What is in your object's past or future?

In the poem "Pit Pony," William Greenway takes his readers into an abandoned mine and asks us to imagine what the world was like for ponies who labored there. At the end of the poem, Greenway talks about the few pit ponies still alive, now torn from the pit. Look at how alien he makes our own world as he contemplates the future of a pony who has only experienced darkness: "The last one, when it / dies in the hills, not quite blind, the mines / closed forever, will it die strangely? Will it / wonder dimly why it was exiled from the rest / of its race, from the dark flanks of the soft / mother, what these timbers are that hold up / nothing but blue? If this is the beginning / of death, this wind, these stars?"

What movements does my object experience, when, and why?

According to Jane Hirshfield, "the exhilaration of the washing is [a button's] wild pleasure." Czeslaw Milosz's poem "Realism" takes the idea a step further: his speaker not only enters a seventeenth-century

Dutch painting, Milosz brings the painting to life, the speaker part of its joyful noise and action: "Rejoice! Give thanks! I raised my voice / To join them in their choral singing / Amid their ruffles, collets, and silk skirts, / One of them already, who vanished long ago. / And our song soared up like smoke from a censer."

What is my object made of? Where did all those materials come from? What did those materials first see, smell, touch?

There is a mindfulness exercise in which you are asked to slowly eat three raisins and consider what went into getting those raisins to your palm. The sun, rain, worms, the boy who picked the raisins, the trucker, the cook who fried the trucker's eggs that morning . . . soon, you realize how much of the world's labor went into your three raisins.

A button made of horn evokes a rhinoceros for Jane Hirshfield at the end of "Button": "Old dreams of passion [do not] disturb it, / though once it wandered the ten thousand grasses with the musk-fragrance caught in its nostrils; / though once it followed—it did, I tell you—that wind for miles."

Any of these questions demands a writer see what William Blake called "a world in a grain of sand." And, when I look for glimmers of negative capability in poems, it surprises me how often they come at the end, in a moment of epiphany, and how the speaker seems at that moment to disappear. You leave an Emily Dickinson poem thinking about death, not about how smart she is, Li-Young Lee once said in an interview; in the end, a good poet lets the reader have the poem.

Naming Names

DAVID HAYNES

I love creating characters. What I hate is giving them names.

Example: I'm sitting at my desk at an art colony, writing away. I've started a new novel—I've tapped right in and the words are flowing as if they were oiled. Along comes a new character, the way they will at times such as this. Just waltzes in, this guy, late twenties, foul mouthed, vain. Though we've just met, I seem to know a lot about him, so I go on for a page or two, words spilling out, images flying faster than my fingers can type them. I get to a place where I have to call his name. Wham. The wall. I sit, fingers curled over the keyboard, frozen, ready. I can't think of a thing. I page through the book of names in my head. There are hundreds of names there, thousands maybe. I turn the pages. It's a bad day for browsing; the only names I see are John and Bill and Steve and Sue and Mary. He is not any of them, and I do not want any of them in *this* novel anyway, not even in cameos.

The thing about names is, they have to be just right. A wrong name in a story can annoy you more than a bad plot twist. A right name is enchanting and as important a detail as the color of an eye or the sparkle of a river in the distance. Some writers are brilliant with names. Robertson Davies is a master when it comes to selecting names, ones which are at once delightful and absurd while also being unobtrusive: Leola Cruikshank and Zadok Hoyle. Names like Sethe and Dorcas seem obscure and exotic when you begin a Toni Morrison novel, but by the end of the book are commonplace and absolutely perfect for the characters who claim them. Jane Smiley and Alice Munro favor short, simple names—Lily, Morris, Flora—old-fashioned, never-too-exotic names, which can evoke a whole context: Iowa near the end of this century, the rural Ontario of several generations past.

I'm a middle-school teacher (which is one of the reasons I know thousands of names), and I will now make an ironic and trashy confession. I change almost all of my students' names. Anna is Velma and Nathan is Larry and, oh dear, I can't think of her real name, but I've been calling her Tina for a couple of years now.

"You know," Larry's mother said, "His father and I like the name Nathan. That's why we called him that."

I tried to explain to her that if they had been paying attention in the hospital they would have seen that this child's name was Larry. It's perfectly obvious to me.

An even more shameful confession: I have been known to give out names such as Kitten and Muffin. Two girls once got into a fight over who would be Princess. (Sue me. It has been pointed out to me that I wouldn't tolerate names such as Sambo and Rastas, so I should knock it off with cutesy names for these young women. I'm reformed. Life is hard in the politically correct nineties. By the way, I had given the boys similar names—Duke, Bud, Guy—but it's not the same thing, really, is it?)

I learned this name changing from my father, where we learn a lot of our most endearing and obnoxious qualities. Giving people pet names was one of his ways of showing affection, and it is mine too. I'm very good at it, if I say so myself. I can pick the perfect new (and I like to believe correct) name for a kid almost on first sight. They like their names, and if they don't they tell me so, and sometimes find a better— no, perfect—one of their own.

Does any of this help me with my writing? I should be so lucky.

For an African American writer, which I am, names can be especially tricky. Do you give your characters names with an Afrocentic feel—names like Kwame and Yaguama? I might. A name like that tells me that these people, or their parents, have a strong tie to their African roots, or else they follow fashion. Some names sound street tough to me: nicknames like Stick and Spike and Speed, initials like T.K. or J.T. (Never any Fs or Ms or vowels in those initials.) On *In Living Color*, they often give the women characters names like Shaniqua or Shaquina. They are having fun with—and I think sometimes sneering at—the way African Americans play with sound and invent beautiful, flowing names, or choose the names of things associated with richness: Larinka, Marquez, Tiffany.

Writing in *The Village Voice*, Lisa Jones calls these the "Watts, Africa" names. A writer has to be careful with them. They can inadvertently signal social class, the same way naming a character Bubba or Billy Bob does. Middle-class blacks do not usually pick such names, and as a matter of fact are likely to give their children the same trendy names the rest of America is using, names like Jason or Michelle, family names like Wilson or Leigh, or whichever names the writers have chosen for the hot characters on the soaps. Some middle-class blacks turn their noses up at the invented names that other—often poorer—blacks use, however magical or appropriate. (Or at names they think are made up; a name like LaQuinta might go way back in some family's tree.)

If you put a Deshawn in your story, you are telling the reader more than the man's name, and I hope that when writers choose such names it is because they fit the characters, and they appreciate their musical sound, not because they are sneering, using some sort of cultural shorthand. Character names are one of the places where writers betray their social and class backgrounds, as well as their prejudices.

The names of American presidents or the names Roscoe, Leroy, Beulah, Ruby, and Sapphire have been used by the media in such a way that they are now a genre of stereotyping unto themselves. I won't give a comprehensive list—it's another of those I-know-them-when-I-read-them things, and besides, I'd rather not perpetuate a stigma that the people whose parents innocently labeled them with these monikers do not deserve. I don't use these names in my writing, and they put me off when I read them, particularly in the work of writers who are not African American. Although the intent isn't necessarily racist—they might be the best choice in a satirical piece or a comedy; they might even be the real names of the people on whom the characters are based—they are like a red flag to me. I wonder, again, if some type of shorthand is being used, or if the writer choosing the name believes all blacks have names like that. In T.R. Pearson's (great name!) books about a small town in North Carolina, there is a cleaning woman named Meemaw Higgins. Although the portrait he creates of her through three books is dignified, there is a part of me that cringes when I read this name. Meemaw? I never met any Meemaws. I cringe because in our culture, which seems to have an innate ability for creating and perpetuating stereotypes, Meemaw somehow seems like just the kind of name one might expect a black maid in a small town in North Carolina to have. That in itself would be enough to make me look for another choice.

Is there a comparable problem in the works of African American writers? That's hard to say. I guess the parallel would be using names like Jethro and Ellie Mae for lower-class whites. Truthfully, though, many black writers today have few or no non-African American characters in their books, and looking through my library, I didn't find any white characters with names more exotic than May Ellen.

But then, don't most names signal some kind of identity? Could I get by with naming my black characters Gunther, Siobhan, TouVue, Anders, Marisol? All names bear some baggage, and even though each of us adds our own experiences to the package, some names are more burdened by our common American culture than others. You couldn't get away with naming a character Cher or Madonna or Schwarzenegger, at least not without taking the three (or four) originals along for the ride.

In my family we have ordinary names: Paul, Denise, Byron, Jean, Susan. I recognize that those may be exotic names to you. In my first novel, *Right by My Side*, I used two family names—my Aunt Lucille gave her name to a character (also an Aunt Lucille), and I borrowed the name of a distant cousin, Annie B. I called the mother Rose, and as it happens my father was briefly married to a Rose, long before I came into the picture. I might have been aware of that in the back of my head somewhere, but that wasn't how my Rose got her name. Mostly I use our family names for minor characters—walk-ons. (Sorry, guys. It's not like these books are about you or anything, and hey, I haven't used my own name yet either.) Many friends, colleagues, and coworkers have also appeared. The principal in my novel is named after the Saint Paul principal who hired me into the district. I'm careful never to use anybody's name if the character resembles them in any way. I try to never use the same name twice, particularly for major characters. I'm working on my fourth book of fiction, and I have to admit that I've run out of easy choices. What's a person to do?

Ever wonder why some of Garrison Keillor's stories resonate as you drive around the streets of the Twin Cities? Look at the street signs. (I didn't notice this myself until someone pointed it out to me. That's the brilliance of a clever strategy and sharp writing.) That doesn't help me right now, though—I am writing at the Virginia Center for the Creative Arts; there are no street signs here, only mountains and trees. The highways are numbered. And so I ask some of the writers at dinner how they get the names for their characters.

It turns out I am not suffering alone. They all struggle with the problem to some extent, and yet no one wants to say. People are oddly silent about it, almost as if there were some big secret involved. I suspect that Bea uses her Ouija board, and that Rachel and Paul shamelessly use the real-life names of the people upon whom the characters are based, but that they don't want to admit this because when they get sued I might be called as a witness and forced to gleefully reveal the truth in court.

Here are some other methods I know.

Phone Book Roulette: Close your eyes, open the book, and point. Or read through it until you come to a name which is perfect. (In Minnesota you'll find an awful lot of Toms and Marys and pages and pages on Johnsons, Andersens, and other -sons and -sens.)

School Days: Get out those high school and college yearbooks and start mining. Pick out all those people who got on your nerves, and libel laws be damned.

The Greatest Story Ever Told: The Bible is chock-full of names, though I would hesitate to call an urban youth Hezekiah, and most of these names carry plenty of baggage of their own. (David! What were my parents thinking?)

The Hunter-Gatherer: Explore mythology, watch old movies, and read everything you can get your hands on. Name your characters after food, flowers, trees, pets, products in the supermarket. Say nonsense syllables until you hit on a combination that pleases your ear.

Iris Murdoch told *The Paris Review* (#115) that her characters have to announce their own names. In the end, that is what usually happens to me—though sometimes they change their names later. Long after completing a complicated story, I realized that the main character's name was Julie, not Meg.

So here I am, back at the computer, sitting and waiting. I look out at the Blue Ridge Mountains to see if I find my character's name there.

I don't. I have to be patient, wait this guy out, and so I space ahead far enough for a ten-letter name and continue writing.

Later that night it comes to me. This guy's a Dexter if there ever was one. By the time I finish, he may be Hector or Methuselah or Antoine, but I go ahead and type in "Dexter," and for now it is perfect. It is like I have known it all along.

One last thing: I would have written, "Call Me Larry." The book would have sold better.

A Recipe for Illusion:
Memory, Imagination, Research

GEORGE RABASA

Look into your favorite novelist's head and you will almost certainly find soup for brains. Sure, a few million brain cells are assembled in a quivering gray mass, but this conventional appearance is deceiving. In contrast, you can assume that the brain of your accountant or rocket scientist is nicely organized. As in a toolbox, there are nooks and slots for the different functions of the intellect.

The creative writer unwittingly manages to make a mess of the ordinary thinking process: memory, imagination, and something approximating objective reality are all mooshed together into a dark, rich stew. This brew has been cooking so long, for a lifetime anyway, that the different ingredients have blended into one savory potage—you can't tell where carrots give way to peas to beans to broccoli to squash and turnips. Furthermore, the fragrant mess is being constantly stirred, the recipe changing, if not hour by hour, certainly from one week to the next: memory agitates, imagination warps, new stuff is learned and enters the mixture all the time.

When the pursuit of new knowledge becomes systematic and purposeful, rather than a random gathering of tidbits, it's called research. And research is serious business in the writing of fiction. So serious, in fact, that most stories of whatever length will require at least a little. Research is as much a part of the process as memory and imagination. When I'm asked what an aspiring writer should study in college, I advise going easy on creative writing and literature, saving time for history, geography, biology, anthropology, Spanish. Dig up courses that teach stuff. Learn the names of trees and flowers and birds. Words like *forsythia, eucalyptus,* and *dove-winged parsifano* are downright poetic. The more stuff a writer learns, the richer the soup.

For me, research and writing are commingled in an adventure of discovery. Just as I sometimes begin a story without knowing exactly where it's going, I often do research with no clear idea of what I'll do with the knowledge. I don't disagree that writers should write what they know. We should also write about what interests us.

In the pursuit of the exotic and the merely curious, I have encountered odd books I otherwise wouldn't have read (*How We Die*, by Sherwin B. Nuland), surfed the Web (www.sephardim.com), and watched embarrassing television (yeah, Springer). I've flown, hitched, hiked, and rafted. I've mined a lode of experience from my parents and my children, old friends and new acquaintances. I've stood awestruck in ancient mosques and cathedrals, prisons, brothels, and markets. I've chatted up cops and robbers, pathologists, shrinks, vets, herbalists, swamis, divas and their voice teachers, the inevitable taxi driver, and my haircutter, Scary Stephie. Not a bad range of conversational encounters for someone shyer than Keillor.

Learning stuff is the easy part. Overloading a piece of writing with new knowledge turns some historical novels (not those by A.S. Byatt or Gabriel García Márquez) into vaguely academicky distractions from story and character. To produce the higher truth that good literature aspires to, the magic of research pays off in the details. More precisely, in the telling detail that rings so true that only someone, be it narrator or character, who had been there at that precise moment, would know—e.g., a soldier's rotting boot, the weight of a bird on your finger, the smell of valerian root.

There is something thrilling about the writer creating the illusion of truth with unquestioned authority. We may know a contemporary writer was not alive during the Middle Ages or the American Civil War or the final game of the 1946 World Series, and yet a character behaves so credibly, a place is rendered so concrete, that doubts vanish; the reader believes. If an untold number of angels can dance on the head of a pin, the angel that dances on a telling detail can endow fiction with a sense of the miraculous. This is not about deception; it's about reaching for the wisdom distilled in the best fiction and poetry.

Sometimes research is done after writing, as a way to verify what has been remembered or imagined. In my novel *Floating Kingdom*, I envisioned an outlaw family living on an island in the Rio Grande, in a

house positioned on a ledge halfway up a limestone canyon high above
the river. This image haunted me for more than a year as I worked on
the initial drafts.

Then, I took a trip along the Rio Grande in order to fine-tune
my sense of the landscape. As my wife, Juanita, and I drove along the
escarpment, there were no signs of human habitation. The actual landscape with the slow muddy river coiling between walls of glistening
stone confirmed what I had imagined. But I despaired of finding anyone who could possibly want to live in such an austere environment.
My novel was set in a particular house turned into an autonomous
kingdom by the family patriarch. It appeared that no such dwelling
could exist here. My whole premise was predicated on an absurdity.
My precious three-hundred pages were being eaten by the dogs of
plausibility.

Then, at a bend in the road, as we climbed higher along the canyon
walls, I saw it! The house, a boxy two-story of gray brick with barred
windows, fronted by a chain-link fence topped by barbed wire, with a
chained and padlocked gate, a black Ford Galaxy on blocks, a shed to
one side festooned with hubcaps, an unfriendly dog. It was all there,
and then some. I was giddy with the power of imagination, the magic
of reality, the mystery of memory. Out of the soup had emerged my
hero's house. I stuck my camera out the window and snapped a picture
before hastily driving off.

My last point is that as much as I value solid research, the novelist
shouldn't let reality get in the way of a good story. Facts are overrated.
A writer's view is necessarily personal. The rivers in the landscape bend
to his or her purpose. The lives of the rich and famous can take delightful turns in the service of fictional mayhem and scandal. On the other
hand, if you're writing about opera singers, death row inmates, crooked
accountants, or native speakers of Catalan, you'd better get it absolutely right. You'll be surprised how many readers you have when the
mail comes in deriding you for inaccuracies in the depiction of brain
surgery, tightrope walking, or murder by gunfire, poison, or pillow.

As creative writers, we bring to our experience of life an intense,
almost privileged perspective. The world around us is livelier than it is
for ordinary mortals. The play and display of nature and the vagaries

of human behavior should be approached with a mixture of reverence and scrutiny. Waiting in the grocery line, interviewing for a job you don't want, sitting for three hours in the middle seat of NWA's flight 199—all these are moments that rise into enriching experiences. The creative writer pays attention. A finer appreciation of the world inevitably brings greater self-knowledge. To know life, even with all its warts and smudges, is to love it. This explains why writers are such interesting people with lots of admiring friends, and why even just-okay writers also make great lovers. This is all true. I've done the research.

The Ten Exhortations for the Literary Researcher

1. Go where no writer has gone before.

2. Don't feel you have to use everything you've learned.

3. You don't even have to use anything you've learned.

4. Keep in mind that someone out there reading your book knows more about your subject than you do.

5. Don't worry too much about that person.

6. Don't confuse facts with details. Facts are stones. Details are wings. The astute researcher smells out the telling detail like a pig rooting after truffles.

7. Hang on to notes, clippings, book titles, photos, souvenirs, postcards, road maps, hotel receipts (good for taxes, if you ever make any money).

8. Whenever you don't know something when you're writing, make it up. You'll be surprised how true it is when you check later.

9. Don't forget to check later.

10. Research does not make the story. The story makes the story.

Nicole Helget

in dialogue with JESSICA DEUTSCH

JESSICA DEUTSCH: You and Nick Healy were both MFA students at Mankato State and Speakeasy Prize winners. What do you think about this coincidence?

NICOLE HELGET: It's not a coincidence. Mankato is bulging at the seams with literary talent these days. I've workshopped in and outside of classes with writers like Nick, so I see great writing all the time. I surround myself with it, and I know Nick does the same here in Mankato. We are constantly challenging each other to write new and better things, to revise old things until they are good enough for publication. This sort of culture lends itself to productivity. The MSU-Mankato creative writing program is directly responsible for fostering these relationships.

J.D.: What was it like to see a colleague win the year after you did?

N.H.: Validating. I've been talking about the writers down here ever since I started writing just a few years ago. I believe that Nick is just the beginning of the other talents Mankatoans, Minnesotans, and the publishing industry are going to start noticing and hearing from.

J.D.: When did you start writing? Was there a memorable moment or person who influenced you?

N.H.: I started writing two years ago, and I didn't know anything about writing at the time, but what I did know was how to read like a writer. So, that made the transition easier, I think. I read and read and read and read. And I always have since I had my first child nine years ago.

Nate LeBoutillier, who has an MFA and is my first and most reliable editor, helped (and helps) me. I was telling him stories, and he showed me how to write them. He painstakingly edited my first story, "The Summer of Ordinary Ways" (the last chapter of the book), filled it with comments and suggestions mostly related to structure, pacing, and plot. Eddie Micus, another Mankato writer and MSU teacher, gave me the second edit. He's got the language and voice angle. I didn't know it at the time, but this process would follow me and the book to its completion.

J.D.: Describe the writing process for your book *The Summer of Ordinary Ways*.

N.H.: Some writers feel compelled to tell their stories, their life story. I don't. I feel compelled to write, and that's why *The Summer of Ordinary Ways* exists. So if all of that is true, why, you might ask, did I write a memoir for crying out loud? It's very simple, really. I am a beginning writer, and I'm still learning the intricacies of this craft. The first rule for beginning writers (especially according to Terry Davis, one of my first teachers in Mankato) is to write what you know. My life just happened to be the thing I knew the most about, so my life became my topic.

J.D.: You have been receiving quite a bit of press lately. I came across a review of your book in *People* magazine. What do you think of all this attention?

N.H.: The *People* gig is bizarre, very appreciated, but kind of creepy, too. It seems a paradox for me to say that I am really an intensely private person considering I've just written a memoir, but it's true. I enjoy no place more than my own home with the windows closed and phones turned off and my children and Nate all piled up on the couch for a night of movies and popcorn. But I'm happy for the book, for my publisher, and for the effect it has on sales, of course, and for the positive attention it brings to writing, to the job of it.

J.D.: What was the best piece of advice you received?

N.H.: Terry Davis told me to (a) write what I know and (b) attack the heart of the reader without being sentimental.

J.D.: Do you have advice for other writers?

N.H.: 1. Get in a workshop or create one, an intimate one. Writers stimulate writers. Find yourself a few (three to four) good people who know you, know your work, and trust them to edit.

2. Say the hardest things. Tell secrets. Expose gossip. Claw at the tidy hem of convention and tradition and let the emotional truth of people, places, and situations spill out.

3. Filter through the mess and group your stories, chapters, or essays by theme. Chronology sucks. Throw sequence to rabid wolves.

4. Reveal the humanity of every character, the good and the bad of each character. The saints are almost never who convention says they are. True victims are very rare and few. Also, many times, they are literarily boring, so leave them to their silent martyrdom. Real readers like to think and like to be conflicted. They don't want to be cajoled into feeling sympathy for a character who obviously deserves sympathy. This type of writing insults the reader's intelligence. Force the reader to sympathize with the baby-kidnapping politician, the chronic wife beater, or a fallen priest. Then, make the reader feel bad about sympathizing with such obvious scum. Aren't these paradoxes the stuff of life?

5. Be precise. Use the exactly correct word every time. Don't use two adjectives when a strong noun and verb work better.

6. Adjectives and adverbs are junky. Use them sparingly. Nouns and verbs should run the story.

7. Watch pronouns. Every single one needs to have a clear antecedent. Find all of the *its* and *thats* in your story and then replace ninety-nine percent of them.

8. Don't dilute the true meaning of the "to be" verbs by overusing them. Only use *is, are,* or *was* if they are absolutely correct. Then count them up. Do seventy-eight percent of your sentences really warrant the "to be" verb?

9. Other words that suck in excess: *seem, appear, might, maybe.* Do you see how these words attack the authority of the author?

10. Read poetry. Let poetic music and metaphor affect you. Listen to your language. There should be music in your story. There should be metaphor.

11. Never get lazy while in exposition. Exposition is, by its very nature, more boring than scene, but is necessary for the sake of efficiency. A writer has to constantly push the story, even through those expository moments. You still have to create images in exposition.

12. Teach yourself to write by reading. Read what you like. Write what you like.

Critique

TOPICS COVERED:

Guilt-Ridden Narcissism

Embracing the Mythology of Wholeness

Heroism

Creeping Dismalism

Self-Serving Confessionalism

Poetry: Not an Equation

The Preferability of a Soup Over Its List of Ingredients

Little Goody Two-Shoes

Midwestern Sentences

The Long-Suffering Poet

The Sad Epiphany Poem: A Tirade For Two Voices

BRIGITTE FRASE AND ROSEANN LLOYD

Brigitte's Story

It was deep winter, and I was browsing in poetry journals. The poems, with their sing-song rhythms, had a mildly soporific effect; it was like listening to torch songs played in Muzak arrangements, their sadness pleasantly blurred.

I flipped through my pile of *New Yorker*s, looking for the cartoons and the poems; as usual, the cartoons were better. The poems, with their wispy sentiments, their listlessness, their sad-eyed and schmaltzy references to Nature, all ran together. They were short and skinny and hovered uncertainly near one of the margins; at least they had sense enough to be self-effacing.

When I got to the February 6, 1984, issue, I had a shock in the form of a two-page poem by Charles Wright, called "Italian Days." With apologies to the admirers of Wright, I must confess that this poem sent me over the edge. Perhaps it was "the olive leaves as they turn and tick," or "the fog sliding in" as cautiously as a bride, or "you . . . whistling in the dogs of mold." Most certainly it had to do with the waitress admonishing Manzolin, "*Non si taglia la pasta.*" "Who the hell is Manzolin and why should I care about his noodles?" I sputtered.

My diffused boredom and dissatisfaction suddenly became focused. Mentally I sat up, blinked, cursed, and then started laughing. I was no longer "tranquillized by sweet sadness," to quote from a recent poem by Patricia Goedicke, "Mea Culpa," in *The New Yorker.* (I can be big about this; sometimes I do find a poem I like.)

I reread "Italian Days." It was so portentous, so enigmatic in its allusions to names and places (I began to feel guilty, as if I were reading a letter addressed to someone else), so unhappy about time and snow;

it made such large, vague motions in the direction of philosophy, murmuring about nothingness, that I half-suspected a put-on.

I hoped against hope that it was a parody and called Roseann Lloyd to read her some parts of it. She confirmed my fears: This was a real poem, and it was very sad. She had more bad news: the current *American Poetry Review* was full of sad poems by sad people who seemed to have consulted the same writing manual. (Details follow in due course.) She read me a few samples, and we became slightly hysterical. "Let's start keeping a list of the most common words in these sad, boring poems," we said, and we were off. We found *luminous bones, opaque fog, stained snow, fish rising and falling, biting or not biting,* and *thin disappointments* (no kidding, I saw it in the *APR*).

Roseann's Story

From this beginning, we expanded to a series of parodies, some of which follow. Their production became an obsession for both of us. While Brigitte worked on a Wright parody, I went off on a tirade against *fog,* as in "What needs to be said is fog" (actual line from a published poem). Of all the things that can be said in this (my) fabulous, terrible, problematic world, *fog* is not one of them. It doesn't even make my top-forty list.

We wanted these and the other parodies to ward off the dread disease, Creeping Dismalism. But we were afraid that the truth of the matter was and is the scientific theorem: Creatures who are *in* a system have difficulty describing that system. We could be swallowed by Creeping Dismalism and not even know it.

Both Voices in Chorus

As a way out of the system, we tried to define it in more detail.

Sadness in these poems is the fundamental Given, switched on at the outset like the rhythm button of an electric organ. We wanted to bark at the writers, like disenchanted City Room editors, WHOWHATWHENWHEREWHY?? Give us some reason to believe you!

In these sad poems, people other than the poet are faded outlines or ghosts. They represent separation, lack or breakdown of communication, mystery, or death. The poet takes advantage of their rhetorical absence to take center stage and commune with the universe about Relationships. Nobody ever gets a high, much less an epiphany, from talking *to* someone who is made substantial and palpable in the poem. Further, nobody has an epiphany in Kmart; nobody gets high in the woods!

Now you may ask, Dear Reader, what is the exact nature of this genre to which we are objecting? Can we, in fact, be specific about *our* vague lack of ease? Here, then, is what we have christened the Sad Epiphany Poem:

1. The poet is alone in a sad place, bedroom, study, tree, or town.

2. The poet moves into another sad place and stays sad. The poet is unable to name the cause of sadness—whether it's loss of childhood, sanity, fertility, life or limb.

3. In a moment that is momentous with silence, the poet realizes that the universe is:

a. sad (under the weight of Time and History)

b. at peace in its oneness but snubbing the poet

c. not at peace in its fragmentariness and confiding its woes to the poet

4. Consequently (and/or Nevertheless), the poet remains sad. The poet never connects personal anguish to the larger social order or disorder.

5. (Optional) In a variation called the Travelog, the poet repeats the first four steps fourteen times. The poet sends postcards full of sadness, "Wish you could be as sensitive as I."

Ironically, the *APR* has published essays that rail against the very poetry that dominates its pages. In "Inflation and Poetry" *APR*, July/August, 1983, Eric Torgersen writes:

"We've all known—if we haven't *been*—student poets who spend their lives in the library, the Union, and the bar, yet write poems that give the impression that they live high in the Sierras and rarely see another human being."

Brigitte's Polemic

These poems depend heavily on a "fog of atmosphere words." (Torgersen, again, page 9.) Emotions seem to be worked up for show; they induce superficial excitement, followed by boredom. Perhaps the complacency follows from the poet's confidence in looking his/her best in the current poetic style.

Melancholy trembling presents itself as the infallible mark of deep feeling, correct observation, and profound thought about Nature or History or Relationship. The poet sighs as he/she turns to us, poor lumpish readers, and says, "It is such a burden to have the universe single me out for a confidante."

Brigitte's Apologia

I've written my share of sad nouns and verbs and, yes, traveled to sad places to validate my poetic sensibility. I hope that from now on I'll think twice, and twenty times if necessary, before I summon up tenuous iridescences, misty bruises, the scrimshaw of memory, and the rest of the wares from the poetry boutique. Writing parodies is one way—perverse, one of my friends charges—of being hard on my writing.

But I must admit that committing parodies is delicious fun. May laughter free me from the Sad Epiphany!

Roseann's Conclusion

It should be clear by now that we don't want to write Sad Epiphanies. But perhaps they do have a place in the community of writers. We must all be free to write in our own voice—some in the soaring lyrical, some in the raging political, some voices pushing programmatic -isms, others speaking as true disbelievers, and some, yes, in the sad epiphanic voice. At different times in our lives we need to write, and to feel free to write, in any of the available voices.

And so what we are protesting with our parodies is not any one writer or the right to wax vague and wane vague. We are protesting the publishing biz, the current fad for printing primarily poems of the Sad Epiphany School, as if one part were to define the whole. Synecdoche is rampant in the poetry press. (Do they believe ecstasy has been co-opted by rock 'n' roll?)

My immersion in parody, unfortunately, has left me with a hang-over. It's hard to read poetry without cynicism.

The antidote, like the antidote to any fit of jealously, is simply to find the love in my heart to start writing my own stuff again, to read my favorite authors for inspiration—the poems I love passionately, the ones that have life and energy, the ones that say, "Sad Epiphany, goodbye."

A Partial Vocabulary Sheet

Dumb Verbs

wake up	flicker	sit
look	blink	recall
long for	stand	
stare	not doin' nothin'	

Melancholic Nouns

love	loss
thin disappointments	sadnesses
life	innocence

Nouns of Philosophical Angst,
or Oh, How the World Changes & We Face the Big One

shadow/light	blood	beauty
body	gesture	silence
dark, the	dread	death
opacity	bone	nothing
somewhere	God/guilt	heart

Animal Verbs

live	breath	sleep
dream	hum	hiss
piss	skitter	spawn

Sensitive Adjectives

misty	abandoned	wan
bleak	stained	empty
tiny	ancient	luminous
deep	strange	pale

Sad Nouns

fog	rose
lace	window
grandmother	rain, ruin, & snow
teacup	silk
bars	wine
towns (in Montana: cars)	

Anatomical Words

salt	vein	body
spine	eyelid	nerves
membrane	bone	
blood	synapse	

Violent Verbs

twitch	shatter	bruise
hurtle	sluice	scream
knife	shriek	

Verbs of Import

tell	know	matter
see	call	settle

Nature Nouns

fog	stone	moon
dew	lee	flame
rain, ruin, & snow	air	grove
hills	wind	landscape
sun	forest	
(double bonus for archaic nouns, i.e., *copse*)		

Word Nobody Knows
  immiscible

Specifics
  ANY animal, specifically named
  ALSO lousy birds, specifically named
  ANY geographical location, the more obscure the better
  ANY tree and plant, specifically named
  ANY term from backpack books
  ANY classical God/dess
  ANY foreign phrase
  ANY color, specifically named
  ANY reference to classical music (NOT rock 'n' roll)

Notes on Syntax: What Every Poem Should Contain
  "I see the _____, how it _____"
  "Imagine ___*(excessive metaphor)*___"
  "Remember how you ___*(vignette)*___"
  "_____, you said, _____."
  Something in nature is compared to something ugly.
  The line with the most sad nouns is repeated.

The 5-Minute Nature Poem
  by Roseann Lloyd
Sometimes ___*(melancholic noun)*___ is afraid
To ___*(violent verb)*___ the body.
It hovers like ___*(a sad noun)*___
in the branches of ___*(any tree, growing at the timberline in
  the Rockies)*___
Mornings, ___*(any bird, specifically named)*___could
  ___*(animal verb)*___ on me
___*(sensitive adjective)*___ as I am.
The landscape is cluttered with poets like me, who
  ___*(dumb verb)*___ half-naked in
___*(archaic nature noun)*___,
each leaning toward some bright ___*(chemical element)*___
which is ___*(animal verbing)*___ . ___*(Number)*___

___(sad nouns)___ fill the ___(singular noun from fishing book)___
and it
longs to fall.
Even without the ___(nature noun)___ in ___(geographical
location, any, specifically named)___
The ___(any color)___ ___(noun of philosophical angst)___
will dry up, my hands gesture
toward the least ___(sensitive adjective)___ winged thing.

The 5-Minute Image Poem
by Roseann Lloyd

1. First, pick an object (you may consult the list and choose one from the Sad Nouns or the Nouns of Philosophical Angst).

2. Write it down.

3. Now, ask yourself these questions:
What is it made of?
Can you turn it inside out? (Of course you can.) What color is it?
What can it do?
Why does it make you sad?

4. Repeat the above questions in their negative form, as in, What can it not do? Example: *Lace cannot lie on the wingèd sill.*

5. Lift your weary shoulders from your work and look about you. Find a detail—irrelevant—from the room and write it down.

6. Now read your list and circle the lines that you like the most—preferably those that are incomprehensible.

7. Arrange the lines on the page in the most unusual order possible and break the lines for no reason, i.e., make
jarring
line
breaks.

8. Throw in a noun, like "innocence," and personify it so that it can talk about (oops, that is, speak of) your object (Sad Noun or Noun of Philosophical Angst).

9. Stop.

10. Write a sentence that has absolutely nothing to do with 1–9. Example: *And I also want to mention aluminum.* That is your last line. (Heavy.)

I'm Incredibly Sad But I Won't Tell Why
   by Brigitte Frase

My strategy is to stay afloat in the
promiscuous air, egregious
as a barren star stumbling over its
pointy toes.

Walking by the river, I weave muddied
dreams into the branches of the basswood
(a.k.a. the American linden). My childhood gets
tangled up in there like coral reefs
through which grandmothers smile with crooked
teeth, stained
with betel nut. Again the afternoon's tufted
gestures tickle me
lightly as I lean into the bloodfall of
memory. How its droppings
curtain the tiny tongue from unspeakable
messages! How lubriciously it
castigates!

When we left Silicon Valley for the
last time, thinking
the day would make significant progress, smoothing
under our bods like the Posturepedic mattresses of
rendezvous hotels, we did not know yet that pain is
the pea under the box spring, the hard nut to crack (though
we leaped up and down in inexplicable furies)
in Cairo, Pittsburgh, or that little
Mexican town near the border—
Barrionada I think it was, or Empesina

where we ate guacamole. The nachos
crackled in our wan mouths and sank like stones
into the dark caverns of our bellies. And
our love was like that, water coagulating,
leading nowhere. Our lips
were bruised with bad wine. Our
hearts banged together like the stripped bones of desire,
carcasses picked over by
time.
Mist sifted over the veranda at Chihuahua. We
shivered and let the wind, ghost of dead selves,
blow out our cigarillos. My *joie de vivre* had
thinned to a trickle. It was the refrain of the old song,
La Vie en Rose et Pourpre et Orange et Vert et Bleu
et Jaune et Gris et Noir . . .

Dogs waddled in the alleys, littered with
the remains of the good days. *Dolce far niente.*
But that was much later, in Sicily, under
the gibbous, chattering moon. Guglielmo turned to us,
in that way he had, his bulging eyes
full of reticulated bleaknesses, and said
Bon Giorno
before the sudsy white tides swallowed his breath
and we went on and on and on
but it was not
the same

A Tall White Pine:
Thinking About Prophecy

LEWIS HYDE

When I was young and longed to write, I was much in love with Emerson and Thoreau. I loved the plain declarative sentences and flat statements of belief from which these men built their work. Nature's "laws are the laws of [the scholar's] mind . . ." said Emerson. "So much of nature as he is ignorant of, so much of his own mind does he not yet possess."

Thoreau has the same confident cadence: "I believe that there is a subtle magnetism in Nature, which, if we unconsciously yield to it, will direct us aright. It is not indifferent to us which way we walk. There is a right way. . . ."

I liked that Emerson and Thoreau sort life into the sacred and profane, the important and the unimportant, the living and the dead. Take the first paragraphs of Thoreau's essay "Walking":

> I wish to speak a word for Nature, for absolute freedom and wildness, as contrasted with a freedom and culture merely civil. . . . There are enough champions of civilization: the minister and the school committee and every one of you will take care of that.
>
> I have met with but one or two persons in the course of my life who understood the art of Walking, that is, of taking walks—who had a genius, so to speak, for *sauntering*, which word is beautifully derived from idle people who roved about the country, in the Middle Ages, and asked charity, under pretense of going *a la Sainte Terre*, to the Holy Land, till the children exclaimed, "There goes a *Sainte-Terrer*," a Saunterer, a Holy-Lander.

They who never go the Holy Land in their walks, as they
pretend, are indeed mere idlers and vagabonds; but they who
do go there are saunterers in the good sense, such as I mean.

Emerson and Thoreau draw the line and make a choice. The "merely
civil," the "mere idler"—lowlife surrounds us, but we needn't be a part of
it. That elevated tone I loved, and I loved the demands that followed on it:

> We should go forth on the shortest walk . . . in the spirit of
> undying adventure, never to return—prepared to send back
> our embalmed hearts only as relics to our desolate kingdoms.
> If you are ready to leave father and mother, and brother and
> sister, and wife and child and friends, and never see them
> again—if you have paid your debts, and made your will, and
> settled all your affairs, and are a free man, then you are ready
> for a walk.

I was in my early twenties when I read these essays, and I longed for
someone to tell me what to do. My life was not what I wanted. I had
quit graduate school in a late adolescent huff. I wished to be a writer,
but I wasn't a writer. The country was at war; my best friend in jail. I
was stuck in a bad marriage, having neither the wisdom to improve it
nor the wit to leave. I was terrified of death, convinced my heart might
stop at any minute. I lay in bed unable to sleep, rebuilding in fantasy a
stone wall I had once built in childhood.

And I loitered near the tables where old men were saying, "I believe . . ." and "There is a right way," and "Each age must write its own
books." "Believe," "is," "must"—what beautiful, simple verbs! I wanted
to talk like that; I wanted a heroic voice.

I didn't know it then, but the voice that attracted me to these essays is
rightly called "prophetic." We have a tradition of prophetic literature
that goes back to the Old Testament, of course, and, though it is hardly
the popular style in the modern age, one sometimes still finds prophetic
poems, even prophetic novels. Whitman has this voice: He makes us feel
we may be one of the immortals, large-mannered, spanning continents.

As for novels, E.M. Forster once gave a lecture on prophetic fiction, and his examples were Dostoevsky, Melville, Emily Brontë, and D.H. Lawrence. I would add Flannery O'Connor: prophets offer revelation, and so would O'Connor; she designed her tales to induce in us that second sight by which we see the workings of an invisible world.

Poems and novels are not what concern me here, however. I want here to reflect on the prophetic essay, the kind that Emerson and Thoreau wrote, and others after them (among the essayists who work in this tradition—or try to—I would name Whitman in *Democratic Vistas*, W.B. Yeats, Simone Weil, D.H. Lawrence, James Baldwin, Czeslaw Milosz, Norman Mailer and Barry Lopez). I'm not here going to try to cover this whole field (let alone go back to the Old Testament). I'm going to look at Thoreau and "Walking" as a first stab at a more general description of the prophetic voice in modern prose.

Before I begin, I should say that by "prophetic" I do not mean "telling the future." The prophetic voice has an odd relation to time, but telling the future is the least of it. The prophet does not say that the price of soybeans will go up in October or that Jackie Kennedy will soon remarry. Rather, *the prophet speaks of things that will be true in the future because they are true in all time.* In 1963, when Martin Luther King said that if the "repressed emotions [of African Americans] are not released in nonviolent ways, they will seek expression through violence," he was not predicting the race riots of the later sixties, he was describing the nature of things no matter the decade. Sometimes a prophet's words do come true, of course, but that has more to do with whether or not we've paid attention than it does with any prescience on the prophet's part.

Several things mark the prophetic essay. To begin with, it always has a person in it. The mock-modest demand that Thoreau makes at the beginning of *Walden* states the case well:

> In most books, the *I*, or first person, is omitted; in this it will be retained. . . . It is, after all, always the first person that is speaking. I should not talk so much about myself if there were anybody else whom I knew as well. Unfortunately, I am

> confined to this theme by the narrowness of my experience.
> Moreover, I, on my side, require of every writer, first or last,
> a simple and sincere account of his own life . . . some such
> account as he would send to his kindred from a distant land.

In the prophetic essay, a person comes forward and addresses us. This person is not, however, the proud or glum or obsessed and confined first person who carries on in the journals we keep or the letters we address to estranged lovers. The prophetic first person speaks at the point where the personal touches what is in no way personal. When Dante says, "In the middle of the journey of our life, I found myself in a dark wood," the shift in pronoun lets us know, if we needed the hint, that he is talking both about himself and about every human being. "In Dostoevsky," says Forster, "the characters and situations always stand for more than themselves; infinity attends them . . . Mitya is—all of us. So is Alyosha, so is Smerdyakov." Similarly, in *Walden* Thoreau implicitly claims he's not writing about *his* life but about *the* life, the life each of us would lead were we communicants in the church of Nature. The prophetic voice may give a "simple and sincere account" of its story, but it does so in a way that makes us feel we are reading the story of the race, not the story of one man or woman.

The second thing to say about the prophetic voice is that it asks us to imagine being free of the usual bonds of time and space. In regard to time, the rhetoric of prophecy typically invokes daily and seasonal cycles rather than the straight arrow of chronology. "We had a remarkable sunset one day last November," Thoreau tells us toward the end of "Walking":

> It was such a light as we could not have imagined a moment
> before, and . . . when we reflected that this was not a solitary
> phenomenon, never to happen again, but that it would hap-
> pen forever and ever, an infinite number of evenings . . . it was
> more glorious still.

The conceit is typical: the prophet pushes off with a particular day and a particular year, only to swamp them both in eternity, wiping out large sections of history; one November is all Novembers, each evening all evenings.

The prophetic voice alters space as well, though here the technique is slightly different. An unobtrusive description at the beginning of Isak Dinesen's *Out of Africa* sets a tone for the whole book: "The farm lay at an altitude of over six thousand feet. In the day-time you felt that you had got high up, near to the sun...." Dinesen has a touch of the prophet, and these phrases should alert us to that fact, for the prophetic voice is spoken from high ground. Nothing in Concord stands at six thousand feet, but in "Walking" we find Thoreau climbing up whenever he can. He climbs a tall white pine and finds a flower his townsmen never saw. He climbs a hill and looks down on civilization in miniature:

> The farmers and their works are scarcely more obvious than woodchucks and their burrows. Man and his affairs, church and state and school, trade and commerce, and manufactures and agriculture, even politics.... I am pleased to see how little space they occupy in the landscape. Politics is but a narrow field.... I pass from it as from a beanfield into the forest, and it is forgotten. In one half-hour I can walk off to some portion of the earth's surface where a man does not stand from one year's end to another, and there, consequently, politics are not, for they are but as the cigar smoke of a man.

Spoken from on high, the prophetic voice strips the lowlands of their detail. Republican and Democrat, Sunday and Monday, New York and Concord—distinctions that preoccupy us in the valley are flattened out as if drawn on a commemorative plate. From Thoreau's hill the wood-chuck and the first selectman may as well occupy the same burrow.

This does not mean, however, that the prophet is above it all. He may not be constrained by the place of his birth, but the high alti-tudes have their own, subtler constraints. At one point in "Walking," Thoreau imagines himself higher even than that hill: "The outline which would bound my walks," he says, "would be ... one of those cometary orbits which have been thought to be non-returning curves ... in which my house occupies the place of the sun." We are so high up now that earth's gravity itself has been cancelled. And yet the sun's remains. Solar gravity may be (what?) thinner or more expansive, but it still exerts its pull. "There is a subtle magnetism in Nature," remember, and we cannot feel it until we get up high. There we drop the accidents of time and place and feel only the constraints of what it is to be human. High up, those constraints seem less personal, and therefore less of a burden. At six thousand feet, Denys Finch-Hatton's grave is the grave of all lost lovers. Set in space, Thoreau's house is the temporary dwelling of all of us who will one day die.

Extended thus in space and time, the prophetic voice speaks in declarative sentences. It does not debate nor analyze. It does not say "several options face us," or "only time will tell," or "maybe yes, maybe no," or "studies should be done." The prophetic voice dwells in the verb "to be," from which it draws the simple syntax of belief. "This is the case," it declares, or "I am I," or "I am the Way." Thoreau's sentences are long and shapely, but they are grounded in such simplicity: "The sun is but a morning star." "Every walk is a sort of crusade." "In wildness is the preservation of the world."

In the prophetic essay, declarations of belief appear in the foreground, and this alone makes it different from most essays we now read in magazines. The television show *Dragnet* used to feature a cop named Joe Friday whose interrogations were punctuated with the phrase, "Just the facts, ma'am; just the facts." Joe Friday is the ghostwriter of most of the essays written in my lifetime. Michael Arlen's masterful *New Yorker* series on the making of a television commercial (later published as a book, *Thirty Seconds*) is a good example. Arlen is a genius of photorealist prose. In this case, he took a topic that cries out for ethical reflection and foreswore to engage in it. Such reticence gives the "fact essay" a feel of manliness and sobriety. Like Humphrey Bogart refusing to kiss, there's nothing mushy about the fact essay.

The prophetic essay isn't exactly mushy, but it would never make it through the *New Yorker*'s fact checking department. "In wildness is the preservation of the world." There is no way to check that fact. It certainly does not follow from evidence the way conclusions in an analytical essay follow. And yet that does not mean it is not true. Students are often disappointed to discover that Thoreau used to go into town to eat his meals with the Emersons. It's a fact: Thoreau was not a hermit. But the facts of the case are not the spirit of the case, and sometimes the spirit is primary. Thoreau didn't need to be wholly isolated to describe the solitude of our lives.

The prophet stoops neither to argue nor to cede belief to the facts, and these refusals bring us to the dangers, or at least the limitations, of the prophetic voice. Most of the vices of prophecy follow from its virtues, in particular its appeal to our desire for a unified self and a unified world. All the marks of prophecy that I have touched on so far—the "extended first person" speaking for all humanity, the rise of the particular into the eternal, the declarations of simple belief—imply that the divisions, confusions, and ambiguities marking our lives are illusory. Under the spell of the prophetic voice, we are led to believe that there is a simple unity toward which each of us might travel.

But there are times we cannot or should not make the move toward unity, either in the self or in society.

To begin with a social example, to the degree that the prophetic voice flattens out diversity, it is at odds with pluralism. If democracy begins with the call to "come and reason together," then we will have a problem with prophets, for they are not reasonable. They are particularly dangerous, therefore, when they manage to get political power—witness the prophet Khomeini and the fate of the Baha'i in Iran. The voice of fascism borrows from the voice of prophecy, and in a mass society we are right to be suspicious of it. (I suspect that the proper politics of prophecy will be, therefore, decentralized and nonviolent. Thoreau, at least, made that connection, as did both Gandhi and Martin Luther King.)

Politics is not the only realm in which the mythology of wholeness may simplify or even repress. Not all scientists or philosophers, for example, assume the great underlying harmony that Emerson and Thoreau impute to Nature and to mind. Things now seem more fragmentary, more ambiguous, than they did a hundred years ago. There are those in this century for whom even the laws of physics are only local laws, not constant over time and space. "The real [may be] sporadic, spaces and times with straits and passes . . ." says Michel Serres, a French historian of science. To know the truth in such a world is to navigate, he says, among "fluctuating tatters," and where that is the case, the prophetic voice will not speak the truth.

Confined to the mountaintop, the prophetic voice says nothing of life in the caves and shady valleys. Down in the lowlands, the world is messier than the prophet allows. The valley is, by definition, a "long depression." There we find not death but the shadow of death, and there we find the vale of tears. When we're down in the dumps we're down in the valley, and the dumps are a jumble of all we have cast off, denied, or abandoned. Our failed relatives live in the valley and invite us to visit.

But the valley is also Keats's "vale of soul-making," and, as the phrase implies, gloom is not without its fruit. The prophetic essay leads us on a redemptive journey—about which I shall say more in a minute—but there is a redemption of the valley as well, a redemption that comes from abandoning all hope of getting it together. If you need to come apart you do not need to listen to the prophetic voice. Stop trying to be a hero. There is a time to fall to pieces, to identify with the mess of your life as it is, confined inexorably to your present age and your present apartment. Not the ever-returning sunset, but this particular one with its stringy clouds and its number on the calendar.

D.H. Lawrence had the prophetic voice, but he also had the voice of the valley:

> I know I am nothing.
> Life has gone away, below my low-water mark.
> I am aware I feel nothing, even at dawn . . .
> My whole consciousness is *cliché* and I am null;
> I exist as an organism and a nullus . . .

Thoreau never says "I am nothing." He associates the boggy fens with the Prince of Darkness, and he does no work there. Death is elevated in Thoreau; we know he was depressed by his brother's death, but he wrote no essay about that. His journals fill volumes, but they contain no record of his dreams and their confusion. The prophet has risen above confusion; he cannot therefore lead us to the redemption of giving up, of not gathering one's wits but letting them scatter.

Things in the valley may be messier than prophecy allows, but they are also funnier. E.M. Forster contrasts prophecy with fantasy, and the novel that is his prime example, *Tristram Shandy*, reminds us that the comedy of the valley includes digression, coincidence, and muddle. Hermes rules these lowlands, farting, inventing silly puns, and telling lies that make his father laugh. The prophetic voice has none of the Hermes spirit, of course. Thoreau sometimes makes us smile, to be sure—the line about writing your will before you take a walk is funny, for example—but his humor always has an upward thrust. We laugh at the mundane so as to move toward the eternal. We're not talking Richard Pryor here. Thoreau never jokes about his penis, or about race relations, or about Christians and Jews. He lacks, in short, the humor of pluralism, of the particular, of fluctuating tatters—all those jokes that help us live our inexorable divisions in this body, time, and place.

Be this as it may, I listen up sharply when I hear the prophetic voice, for it offers something we cannot get from humor or analysis or public debate.

I spoke above a sort of redemptive journey in Thoreau's essay. It has several stages. At the beginning, as in fairy tales that open with a wicked king and a famine in the land, all is not well in Concord. "Every walk is a sort of crusade," Thoreau says, ". . . to go forth and re- conquer this Holy Land from the hands of the Infidels." The evil days are apparently upon us. A saunterer's requisite leisure "comes only by the grace of God," and few now have such grace. "Some of my townsmen . . . have described to me . . . walks which they took ten years ago, in which they were so blessed as to lose themselves for half an hour in the woods; but I know very well that they have confined themselves to the highway ever since. . . ." Thoreau himself sometimes "walk(s) a mile into the woods bodily, without getting there in spirit . . . the thought of some work" running constantly through his head.

The essay begins, then, reminding us of our "quiet desperation" in the fallen present. Thoreau wakes our dissatisfaction and uses it to lever us out of the present and into the heights, the second stage of this journey. Here, we see the world below with new eyes. Mircea Eliade once suggested that when evil days are upon us, the sacred survives by camouflaging itself within the profane: To recover it we must develop the eyes—some sort of night vision or hunter's attentiveness—that can discover the shapes of the sacred despite its camouflage. Prophets speak to us at the intersection of time and eternity and, if we join them there, we are given that vision, those eyes. The prophetic voice is apocalyptic: It uncovers what was covered and reveals what was hidden. As we walk, we see common flowers we never saw before.

I suggested at the outset that the prophetic voice is spoken in the extended first person. When we identify with such a speaker, we are led to imagine our lives differently. We have, for a moment, two lives, the one we actually lead and a concurrent imaginary one. The second is not imaginary in the sense of "invented," however. If the prophet is speaking of things which will be true tomorrow because they are true in all time, then that second life is real even if it isn't realized. The prophetic voice juxtaposes today and eternity to make it clear that the latter may inform the former. It sets the mundane against the imaginary so that we might see whether or not they match up. Where they are congruent, we discover the true value hidden in the everyday; where they are incongruent, we discover what we may abandon. In either case there is a reevaluation, a redemption. You look at your work, your loves, your children, parents, politicians, and, as at a funeral or birth, you see what matters and what doesn't.

In the final stage of his essay, Thoreau returns to home ground. He claims at the outset that the walker must be ready to leave home never to return but, nonetheless, in his final pages we find him sauntering home with the sun "like a gentle herdsman" at his back. A true walk changes the walker, not the walker's hometown. We read in books of some distant past when there were giants in the earth, or of some future when they will return. The prophetic voice seeks to have us see that the golden age is not in the past or the future; it is here. We who have been "saunterers in the good sense" return to find the Holy Land in the Concord we left behind. Where before we and all our townspeople looked like infidels, now we see that each might be a hero. "This [is] the heroic age itself, though we know it not."

There is yet another stage to the prophetic journey, though it takes place after the prophet falls silent. The prophetic voice doesn't necessarily push us into action. It is more declarative than imperative, more revelatory than moralizing. In *Moby Dick,* Melville is fascinated by the whiteness of the whale; he doesn't tell us what to do, he sings about the mystery of evil. And yet where revelation succeeds, we suddenly see paths that were obscure before. "It is not indifferent to us which way we walk. There is a right way. . . ." Most of us live in a world of almost paralyzing free choice. In America, at least, it's difficult to buy the right couch, let alone find the right way. But under the spell of the prophetic voice we can, sometimes, sort the true from the false and begin to move.

You quit graduate school, rent a room somewhere, and start to read in earnest. You hunker down in your pointless job and paint at night. You go back to the family farm and begin the fifty-year job of reclaiming the spent land. You leave a hopeless marriage or rededicate yourself to a good one. You resist an immoral war and go to jail. The heroic age will not be with us unless we will be its heroes. Great cold air masses gather on the Canadian shield and slide slowly south. Sometimes in a city at night you get an unexpected whiff of that northern air. You had forgotten that you live in a city on the Great Plains, and now you remember.

On Poetry

YEHUDA AMICHAI

transcription by Jane Katz

"The act of creating a poem is like falling in love with life," the poet Yehuda Amichai told his audience at a Loft Mentor Series workshop. Amichai was Israel's most celebrated poet and the author of several collections of poetry, which he and others have translated into English, and of a novel: *Not of This Time, Not of This Place.* He spoke with humility and humor, in heavily accented English, gesturing frequently for emphasis. He spoke in graphic images of his love affair with poetry and life.

"There is no good or bad poetry. Forget about being a poet. To be a poet is a social fad that means actually nothing. The public wants you to behave in a certain wild way. To grow hair when no one grows it, to be bald when no one is bald, to drink a lot, I don't know what. The same with a lawyer or a stockbroker. We all have our images of what a professional person should be. I, for example, would be very suspicious of a stockbroker with long hair. So there is a social fad.

"In Israel, poetry is tremendously popular outside universities. You don't just look like a poet, you are one. The poet is involved with life. There are no special endowments for poets—you have to make a living, which means that the poet isn't special, isn't spoiled by society. We should be happy that we can write about ourselves, about what is happening to mankind. A lot of people experience death and wars and bad love affairs and can't write about it. Poets not only write about it, they get paid for it. Who ever gets paid for a bad love affair? So we should be very happy we can do it.

"Why should a poet talk about his writing? I think we should do it from time to time, to be aware of what we are doing. Writing poetry is not totally instinctive, but at first it's an intuitive process; after some time, you find your own voice, whatever that means. You see people running around looking for voices, yes? Poetry is a marvelous combination of emotion and intellect, a strange mixture of rational planning and thinking, and totally instinctive feelings. Poems which are only emotional are too sentimental. Others are too intellectual and philosophical. A good poem is a combination of these two.

"I don't like poems on the craft of poetry. That kind of poem makes me nervous. A poem should be. If you write a love poem, it should be like love. Not about it. When I read a poem about the process of writing a poem, it seems to me that is like when you go to a restaurant and you order a marvelous soup, and the chef comes out with a long list of all the ingredients. You just want to eat the soup.

"How can one be a poet in our time, after World War II, Auschwitz, and other disasters? The writer Theodor Adorno said you cannot write any more. Of course he was wrong. People have always gone on writing, no matter what they endured. It's an outlet. It's religious.

"Religion is literature, literature is religion. The Bible was written by a divine spirit, or by human beings—it doesn't matter. Literature is everywhere, just as God is everywhere. You can't separate them. So in a way you write about everything.

"Movies, TV, and word processors, these are the enemies of literature in our time. Now you don't write, you process words. What does this mean? You can write a poem with a computer, but it's cheaper for a university to keep a live poet.

"Poetry is an art form that has survived many thousands of years. A modern love poem is not very different from the Song of Songs. The lover is looking for his beloved. Okay, the images have changed. In biblical times, the lover came on a horse, now he comes in a Jeep or in a car—the images of civilization have changed. Now we have different meters and rhythms, but it's basically the same.

"Poetry remains the only language of the soul we still have. Poetry is like prayers. Prayers are poetry.

"Poetry is the last human retreat. It is the pulse of human beings.

"Poetry is unprofessional. Every child from the age of three is a poet. He uses words to describe reality. He learns the word *table*, he learns that it refers to all tables. That is the beginning of poetry. In paradise, Adam and Eve gave names to all plants and animals. That was the beginning of human culture, the first act of poetry. Poetry should stick to reality.

"Poetry is the ripest and sweetest fruit of human laziness. I think that laziness is a great virtue in our time, because we are all so busy running and running. My students at New York University say, 'You have to write a poem every day.' I think that's wrong. It has to come easily, like falling in love. You can't train for it any more than you can train for falling in love by doing a lot of physical or psychological exercises. A poem actually means to fall in love with the reality around you. The best training is to live with open eyes and open senses . . . and to read a lot of good poetry.

"I am opposed to this modern fad, a performance in which you have a dancer dancing, a singer singing, a painter brushing paint on canvas while reciting poetry—this multimedia entertainment is like a bad orgy. Poetry is the inner language of one person, his own life and experience.

"It's natural for a poet to write a poem. On the other hand, we have difficulty writing a letter to the IRS about our financial situation. But writing a poem, this comes naturally.

"Every human being is like a lonely spaceship, and this is especially true of the poet. You travel through space, you describe whatever hits you: friendly spaceships, loving ships, enemies, you describe whatever comes your way. You put words and images together. There is rhythm—whether inner rhythm or meter, it doesn't matter. It is like showing slides from our adventures. Poetry is a kind of private documentation of our excursions; we choose a few memories to chronicle in concrete images. The crumpled ticket of the metro in Paris brings back more memories than all the photographs we take. That's what poetry does. You take out of life certain things and put them on a shelf. You must be selective.

"The lines of a book of poetry are like the shelves in a museum—let's say an archaeological museum where jars and vessels from the past are displayed. If the ancients were to come to this museum, they would say, 'Look at our jars. We cooked our meals in them. We used them every day.' They would stand there awestricken, with dreamy eyes. So in the same way someone will take our Toastmasters and Mixmasters and put them on a shelf in some museum, and for sure in two thousand years you'll have two or three professors, one from Harvard and one from

Princeton, and they'll have big discussions about this Toastmaster. One will say, 'It was a ritual instrument which they used to sacrifice to their God.' The other will say, 'Toastmaster was the conqueror of the twentieth century,' and there will be a lot of public money donated to help them prove their theories, and there will be articles in the *New York Review of Books* about their findings.

"So again, that's what the poet does. He selects one moment from the past to capture in his poem, and the whole experience comes back.

"Every poem you write is like the last poem you're going to write. You want to sum up your life. You compress your ideas in one poem. It's like the last will. It's like the black box which remains after an air crash—the pilot's last words become important. You want to sum up your life. Last words become important.

"Someone says, 'Do you think the snow will stop tomorrow?' Then this person dies in an accident, and we remember those last words. Snow is not just snow—it is eternity. So every poem is actually the last words.

"Poetry is for people. Some people like to write conceptual poems, abstract poems, to do all sorts of experiments. It's okay. People can do what they want. But I think poetry has to do with human experience. If it does not, it has no meaning.

"I don't believe in poetry for poets. If a poem is good, it's good for everyone. You don't have to be a professor of literature to understand it. Shakespeare and the Bible can be enjoyed by uneducated people as well as by the most sophisticated thinkers. A good poem should be intelligible.

"I believe in the power of poetry to heal. After a love affair ends, after a death, you return to poetry. You express your feelings. It helps you to go on.

"Poetry has a healing function in all cultures. An Israeli mother sings her child to sleep. She sings:

> Sleep my child, sleep.
> Your father has gone to war
> The house is falling apart
> But sleep my child, sleep.

She keeps the child in reality. It would be wrong to sing only of the butterflies and beautiful flowers. You use reality to cure yourself of reality. This is what a poem should do.

"Poetry purifies. It is like recycling sewage water, using it again to water the fields. Poetry is the recycling plant of the language. It is often abused, it is polluted by television, by journalists and politicians. Our language is so cluttered. We overuse certain words. A woman asks a man, "Do you love me?" And he says, "Yes." Then she asks, "Do you really love me, really?" We use words to reinforce lies. Language obscures. The poet should enable words to become what they used to be. He uses words in a context that makes them believable.

"We all have our roles: the chemist, the psychologist, the poet. The chemist observes that when you peel an onion, you cry. The psychologist comments on how we feel when we peel an onion. The poet describes the tears.

"As a poet, you enjoy everything in life twice. It is a kind of double take. You pass something, you say, 'Just a moment. I want to stay here for a moment. I want to stay here for a moment.' The poem takes you back to the experience.

"In a sense, a poet is a traitor. You go through life and use your experience. You don't tape-record a conversation with your lover—that's like spying. But you may publish a beautiful book of love poems after the affair has ended. Then you hope for another affair—how can you go on writing if everything is happy? That's a sort of romantic trap we fall into.

"Imagine a poet sitting in his library, a beautiful young woman comes in and gives him a kiss. He pushes her away saying, 'Please don't disturb me. I'm writing a love poem to you.' Art is always a secondary thing. If we make art the first thing in our lives, we lose both art and life.

"Poetry is discovery. The poet sees something others do not see. What is inspiration? How do we select from our many experiences? We all want to write a minimal poem, to compress everything into two lines. Then there is this other urge in us to describe very broadly in seven-hundred-page novels the whole realm of experience. We are always torn between the two. Actually, poetry should start when

someone says, 'I can't describe it in words. It's beyond words.' But then
of course we reach the end of poetry.

"Remember the first astronaut who made his space walk? All he
said was, 'It is wonderful up here, wonderful.' We should know that
there's a limit to language, just as there's a limit to human beings. We
use the same words over and over. 'I love chocolate chips' and 'I love
you.' That's a great challenge for the poet.

"People say to me, 'You speak so much about God. Are you an
orthodox Jew?' And I say, 'I'm Israeli, but I'm not observant.' Why
shouldn't I say God? Why should I go to the trouble of saying, *the
highest supreme law of nature*? Using the word "God" is poetry. You sum
up everything you'll ever know. A great priest, a rabbi, and a scientist
all would agree that there are things beyond our understanding. We
use the word "God" the way we use the word "father." You don't say *a
genetic machine* or *this man who does things with Mommy*, you simply
say "Father."

"An astrophysicist leaves the laboratory and takes a walk with his
lover, and they see a beautiful red sunset. He doesn't quote Copernicus.
He says, 'Oh look, the sun is sinking into the sea.' So the poet recognizes that there are two truths. There is scientific truth, and there is the
truth of our perceptions. It is the latter which the poet should convey.

"Every good poem is political. The poet lives in the real world, he
speaks out about what he believes in. In Israel, most artists do. It's a
small country, and you can influence the public, the bureaucrats, the
military leaders. I personally must speak out about human values.

"Some people write beautiful, aesthetic poetry. Some conflict arises,
they make a speech, then they return to their university or sabbatical.
I personally can't do it. I find it amoral. Good poetry is something you
do as a part of life, every day."

Ted Kooser

a discussion led by JAMES P. LENFESTEY

On Tuesday, April 12, 2005, after a reading the night before at Plymouth Congregational Church attended by upward of a thousand people, US Poet Laureate Ted Kooser lunched at the Loft with a gaggle of area poets and writers: Sandy Beach, Mark Conway, Rosemary Davis, Nancy Gaschott, Dobby Gibson, Heid Erdrich, Jim Lenfestey, Susan Lenfestey, Leslie Adrienne Miller, Wang Ping, Rohan Preston, Sun Yung Shin, Julia Klatt Singer, and Jennifer Willoughby.

After lunch, Kooser participated in a free-flowing discussion for an hour and a half before leaving for the airport to return to his home near Lincoln, Nebraska, then on to Washington, DC, the next day. This was a busy time for Kooser, who retired in 1999 as vice president of Lincoln Benefit Life. He was recently appointed for a second one-year term as poet laureate. And on April 4, Kooser's tenth collection of poetry, *Delights and Shadows* (Copper Canyon, 2004), won the Pulitzer Prize. His most recent book, *The Poetry Home Repair Manual* (University of Nebraska, 2005), has been praised by the *Star Tribune* as a book "friendly, straightforward and useful as a beginning poet is ever likely to read."

QUESTION: You recently visited the convention of the National Council of Teachers of English, which few if any poet laureates have attended. What attracted you there?

TED KOOSER: It was due to English teachers that I am a poet, showing me poems when I was a little boy. I think if we are ever going to increase the audience for poetry, it's got to be in the hands of those people as much as anybody. They really need to be honored, I think. Teachers there seemed to appreciate my presence. One told me so many English teachers work with all their hearts to get poetry into the hands of their students.

And I'm very interested in how poetry is taught. Because it's been taught so badly for so many years—the idea that a poem is an equation with an answer and that the teacher is the only one with the right answer, and if you don't get the right answer you'll fail. What happens when you're an adult after you've gone through that experience time and again in school, you come upon a poem in a magazine and you say, "I've already passed that quiz. I don't have to read that poem again, and I'm not going to do it." I run into people all the time who have had that experience and say they just gave up on poetry after school. It was too hard for them.

But all the teachers I talked to had good ideas about poetry in the classroom, lively things to do. I'd really like to figure out Web sites where all the good ideas are presented. So you'd punch in "Stopping by Woods" and all these good ideas for teaching that poem would come up. I think maybe in my second term I'll try to work on that. The Academy of American Poets has a really good site called Online Classroom, and I've talked to them about linking in somehow.

Q: It seems the job description for any poet laureate, whether at the national or state level, is to be a really public figure for both poetry and the public, with the understanding that promoting it is good for poetry. But poetry is also a really private, incredibly intimate act between two people. Would it ever be possible, hypothetically, that someone nominated to one of these posts would say poetry is really private and I'm not going to go out?

T. K.: Which is exactly what Louise Glück did. She said, I am taking this as an honor and I'm not going to do any of this other stuff, and she did just the minimum. But in general, the Library of Congress does want poets out there on the hustle doing things. They should have known she is a very introverted person to begin with. She had been the poet laureate of Vermont and acted pretty much the same way in Vermont.

Q: You talked last night about the "communities of poets," vital communities that are fairly separate that are flourishing in their own spheres. Talk about your role in addressing those other communities.

T. K.: I personally try to write the kind of poems that I like to read, and that sets us up for a certain amount of community because we are interacting with poets that we are reading, fitting ourselves into a kind of community with those people. And then I think we all as human beings want to be accepted and liked in a kind of community we pursue for ourselves. If you are a member of the English department at Brandeis University, that is a big part of your community, so it is quite likely you would like poems that engage the members of the English department at Brandeis U. Recently a friend of mine, a lawyer in New York City who is not a sophisticated literary reader, said, "You know, I read these poems all the time and it sounds like a bunch of college professors writing for other college professors." Which in fact a certain kind of poetry is, nothing wrong with that, that's just their community. What *is* wrong is when those college professors say, why aren't these people reading what we are doing over here? Well, their community hasn't embraced others, hasn't opened up to let them in. So you have all these insular communities.

I really like the idea of having a broad popular audience for poetry, and I try really hard to make my poems available to that kind of group. But, I don't want to say that my way is *the* way to do it. That is just my bias. Because it's great fun for me to have people tell me, because of something I have written or shown somebody, that they are now getting interested in poetry.

Q: Your reading last night, where we had possibly a thousand people, was like going to a football game with a raucous crowd, and it was wonderful. I think there were a variety of communities there, including one not often represented—who I think responded to some sense of your Great Plains sensibility—people with roots in Iowa, Nebraska, and the Dakotas, who wanted to hear this guy because he has a broad horizon, literally and metaphorically. Isn't there something in your voice that is open to people?

T. K.: I think everybody—readers or people who work in hardware stores—everybody in this whole area feels the comments about these being the "flyover states"; you know, that we may not be literate people at all. There's a certain number of people possibly rallying around me because I am sort of a native son out here, everybody is trying really hard because they want me to succeed and that's great. People say that we have no culture out here, but there is no group of people in the country more provincial than New Yorkers. There's a lot of people interested in me just because they picked me from out here, which is one of the reasons [the Librarian of Congress] picked me, I think.

Q: If you happened to be visiting a regional literary center, such as this one, in a major northern tier city, which is interested in building an audience for poetry from this base, do you have any suggestions for what a place like this might do?

T.K.: Possibly go in the direction we have been sort of suggesting, trying to bring some of these outer communities into the mix—some spoken-word poets, for example, mix them up with the other poets. I brought John Prine to the Library of Congress in Washington because nobody had worked with the idea of writing folk songs, and I thought of bringing some of the better songwriters into the Library of Congress and just talking with them. At one point John asked me to read a poem on stage and I read one, but most of it was John playing and talking about writing songs. There were people there who were John Prine enthusiasts. One guy who had driven all the way from Indiana said to me, "I liked that poem you read, I'd like to look at some more poems." So I think by mixing these communities together you can maybe generate wider audiences.

Q: I'm wondering if we can do more here, working with good writers and good high-school teachers and creating something out of that. Maybe there's an opportunity here.

T.K.: Just to honor those high-school teachers, recognizing them. They get some recognition from the students and obviously their communities, but not enough.

Q: I was thinking that rather than having a poet laureate of Minnesota, maybe we should have a teacher of English laureate.

T.K.: That would be terrific, honest to God, that would be a wonderful idea. What if distinguished arts organizations like this one gave annual recognition to the teachers in the state who have been outstanding in teaching literary arts?

Q: Any other ideas for broadening the reach of poems?

T. K.: The "Poetry in Motion" project has been tremendously success-ful. People mention that to me all the time and not only when it started in New York, but it has gone elsewhere. Poetry in elevators would be fun, too. Or in places people avert their eyes toward. I've noticed that the etiquette at ATMs is not to look at the guy putting in the code. So if the poem were on the sidewalk . . .

Q: Poetry along trails in the woods. Poetry on sticks at the Minnesota State Fair.

T. K.: Wonderful ideas.

The Memoir as Literature

VIVIAN GORNICK

Beginning with Augustine, memoir writing has given trouble, and readers and writers alike often seem preoccupied with trying to puzzle out the genre: Is it reporting a life or making up a story? Telling the truth or giving the facts? Making art or doing journalism? Inevitably, if the memoir is so good that it "reads like a novel," one hears the confused assertion that, after all, every act of writing is an act of invention, so really autobiography is just another way of making fiction.

Not true. A memoir is a work of nonfiction. The nonfictional "I" functions differently than the fictional "I." It originates in a different part of the creative imagination and, more often than not, employs the gifts of an analytic sensibility rather than an intuitive one.

But it is true that the concerns of the memoirist are the same as those of the novelist. The writer of memoir has a story to tell, a piece of experience to shape, a tradition to enter or break with.

When Edmund Gosse wrote *Father and Son* in 1907 and Colette *My Mother's House* in 1926, each worked in the leisurely manner of the writer for whom memoir writing was on a continuum with Victorian novel-making, and each produced a masterpiece of social biography. But when Mary McCarthy put *Memories of a Catholic Girlhood* together in 1957 and J.R. Ackerley wrote *My Father and Myself* in 1967, they worked more self-consciously, because each knew that the nonfictional "I" was now being used to probe the corruptions of memory. Mary McCarthy intersperses her vivid tales of childhood with italicized afterwords that repeat: *I'm not sure this happened as I'm telling it, or if this is how I felt it happening.* Ackerley also keeps repeating: *This is the story of an unlived relationship; who was my father? Who was I? Why did we keep missing each other?* In the end, honestly groping toward a form neither thought *was* a form, each writer produced one of the great memoirs of the century, as unforgettable as any novel that presses on the heart.

· · ·

In every work of literature, there's a situation and a story. The situation is the context or circumstance, sometimes the plot; the story is the emotional experience that preoccupies the writer. In *An American Tragedy*, the situation is Dreiser's America, the story is the nature of desire. In Edmund Gosse's *Father and Son*, the situation is fundamentalist England in the time of Darwin, the story is the unexpected tenderness between Gosse and his father. In a poem called "In the Waiting Room," Elizabeth Bishop describes herself at seven, during the First World War, sitting in a doctor's office, listening to the muted cries of pain her timid aunt utters from within. That's the situation. The story is the child's first experience of isolation: her own, her aunt's, and that of the world.

The memoirist actually has more in common with the poet than with any novelist. The novelist says, "I see the world, and through my characters I will make sense of it." The poet says, "I see the world, and through my own naked response I will make sense of it."

Augustine's *Confessions* remains something of a model for the memoirist. He tells the tale of his conversion to Christianity; that's the situation. In this tale, he moves from an inchoate sense of being to a coherent sense of being, from an idling existence into a purposeful one, from a state of ignorance to one of truth. That's the story. Inevitably, it's a story of self-discovery and self-definition.

The subject of autobiography is always self-definition, but it cannot be self-definition in the void. The memoirist, like the poet and the novelist, must engage with the world, because engagement makes experience, experience makes wisdom, and finally it's the wisdom that counts.

"Good writing has two characteristics," a gifted teacher of writing once said. "It's alive on the page, and the reader is persuaded the writer is on a voyage of discovery." The poet, the novelist, the memoirist— all must convince the reader that they have wisdom and are writing as honestly as possible to arrive at what they know. Unavoidably, the reader wants to know, "Is this voice speaking truth? Is it honestly going somewhere?"

When a reader asks the first-person narrator of a memoir whether this voice is speaking truth, I do not think the reader means, "Is this work factual?" I think the reader wants to know, "Can I trust this narrator to speak psychological and emotional truth? Is the narrator indulging in self-serving confessionalism here, or is the narrator honestly going to try to get to the bottom of the matter being presented, showing me the widest view and making the deepest sense of what happened?"

These are the questions and concerns of all literature: Do I believe this voice? Am I attracted by this tone? Am I drawn to this persona? And beyond that, does the shape of the writing compel? Is the language expressive? Is the story being told through tone, language, and shape?

The questions in writing are always the same: What is the situation, and what is the story? What is the experience being shaped, the insight being expressed, the self and the world being revealed? These questions are asked of the nonfictional witness as well as of the fictional storyteller.

Power and Powerlessness

C.J. HRIBAL

It's an old story—one becomes what one detests. I have always been leery of people in positions of power; I've been well schooled in the notions that power corrupts and absolute power etc. But as a writer, what am I doing but positing myself in a position of power? Arbiter of words, mediator of plots, creator of order, organizer of chaos, prime mover, and Joycean fingernail parer—*c'est moi.*

Writing is the egoist's fantasy—unfettered control not only of one's self but also of others. I inhabit other people's dreams and lives and pass them off as my own. Or I take my own and pass them off as someone else's. I am dictator of my own small realm, and I am a cruel master. Characters are built up and then humiliated; they're made to fall in and then out of love; they hope and then are disappointed (and I keep them hoping long after any realistic chance for fulfillment or deliverance has passed); they dream and are plagued by nightmares; I ruin their lives, blight their children, choose their level of education, their economic circumstances, even the rhythms and syntax of their speech. If it seems right, I kill them.

What I'm talking about here is power. Writers can talk about healing and community and faith, hope and charity, but what they are really after, even in a limited way, is power. One wishes to heal, one wishes to create community, one wishes to instill faith and hope in others. One desires to remake the world. One wishes, then, to have and exercise power. To write—to manipulate language, to create an order by which the world is rendered recognizable, or to mirror the chaos (but still with some structure, since any mark on the page, even gibberish, still creates a structure)—is to insist that the world fit into one's vision of it. Of course, everyone remakes the world in his or her own vision as a means of getting through the *Sturm und Drang* of everyday life. It is the writer, however, who believes that his or her vision should be immortalized in print—another manifestation of power and superiority.

I overstate my case, of course. If you've been working yourself into a fine angry boil as you've read, know this: I'm a guilt-ridden narcissist. I'm about to drop the proverbial other shoe—the half of my argument which mitigates the first half. Notice I said "mitigates," however, not "erases." The impulse toward power is always present—a sort of I-am-the-maker joy that pushes us along in the first place and often keeps us writing when the narrative itself has seemingly failed us.

What mitigates my argument, what mitigates me as pretender, liar, cheat, and mad king of wobbly constructed prose, is the simple fact that eventually the servant becomes the master. Each word I wrestle into place, each behavioral tic with which I afflict a character, each sensorial and emotional description, each line of dialogue, each frustrated, significant, or meaningless gesture contributes to, represents, and simultaneously erects a fence around the world of the possible. The characters, the plot—language itself—impose their own limits. Once I have started my characters speaking, once I have set them in motion, once I have imbued them with certain recognizable characteristics, with personalities, I am stuck with them. Each word after the first continues the exponential proliferation of limits on what I can do.

I hold the pencil and yet I am powerless.

It's not just what spills out but what burbles up inside me that keeps me so. I listen to the ungendered voice inside my head, the voice with which I speak to myself. I think it's this voice that is the author of all discourse. While writing, have you ever found yourself racing to catch up to sentences that had already occurred in your mind, fully formed but evanescent, but all your attempts to accurately capture them were mere approximations? That ungendered voice dictates the story. It says what seems appropriate, and, if I'm listening carefully, I write it down. Imperfectly, of course. A different word, gleaned from the madly spinning card files of my vocabulary, suggests itself. Is that the right word for this space in the sentence? Is memory satisfied? I work on, an employee of a voice which may or may not be my own, editing, making selections and changes and suggestions. If you keep halving the distance between yourself and a desired point, do you ever reach the goal, or do you become lost in a limbo of infinite approximation? The closer you get to that perceived voice in your head, the more you're said to have a recognizable narrative voice. In my own case, I move forward to statement and qualification. I've done exactly that in this essay; I often find myself (it originally had to be pointed out to me by a friend) doing the same thing in my fiction. I resign myself to the knowledge that this is how I work; I've given myself up to it. The ephemeral fox of language races far ahead of me. I am a panting dog, racing to keep up.

I do not mean to mystify the process of writing. Like any other process one attempts to explain (electricity, for example), it's perfectly ordinary. The difficulty comes about because each choice one makes along the way, even though that choice is not permanent, even though it can be changed, remade, altered (and is, over and over and over), still helps shape, still determines what can come next, what will come next, and thus every word exerts a pressure on the text as a whole. In a way it's like performing that high-school experiment of adding salt to a given volume of water to determine the saturation point. You add more and more words, but you want to keep everything in suspension. The kick is to see how much you can add before the bottom drops out.

In chemistry, of course, rigid physical laws govern the results. In literature, as in life, things are a bit more open-ended. But we crave closure. This paradox of desiring control over the ending while knowing that we really can't control it is what fuels us as writers. What we're aiming for is what Flannery O'Connor talks about in *Mystery and Manners*—that moment, that gesture, that is both "totally right and totally unexpected." Donald Barthelme echoes her in his essay "Not Knowing" when he talks about mystery in fiction, the inevitability of its existence. He assumes more than O'Connor, merely noting the presence of mystery and then moving on; O'Connor argues for the necessity of its presence. In either case, though, I think you end up having to separate the process of writing, which is simply work, from its result, which is mystery. I keep writing, waiting for such moments to show up. They're something else that ultimately I can't control.

Children's Literature

PAMELA HOLT

I'm frequently asked for advice about writing for children. What makes a good story? What will sell? My response is always cautious. I say it's a high calling. If one does not aspire to be a poet, one should not dream of writing for children.

If the person asking for advice tells me, "But I love children, and I've always been a kid at heart," I'm particularly suspicious. The writer who sees children as simpler versions of adults lacks respect for them.

The same standards of excellence that apply to adult literature apply to children's. The essence of children's literature is story and language—the best use of words; clean, clear sentences; honest, compelling characters and stories. Anyone who has read aloud to a two- or three-year-old has heard the child repeat a word or sentence. The child is taking ownership of the word or concept by repeating what he or she has heard or understood for the first time.

Children's literature has traversed a labyrinth of ideas about children and what they should read. Definitions and descriptions of childhood have changed significantly since the eighteenth century when John Newberry opened his London shop, The Bible and the Sun, the first publishing house for children's books. The Age of Reason, the Enlightenment, and the Industrial Revolution neither recognized childhood nor accorded children much freedom. Not until the civil rights and women's movements revolutionized attitudes and perceptions did the child get pulled into citizenship. And now the child has gained a place in the most attentive movement of all, the marketplace.

Early writers of children's literature were pedantic, moralistic, and sentimental. Their work was limited in variety, subject, and intended audience. Wordsworth, Blake, Dickens, Alcott, and Twain all challenged the moralistic tone of the children's literature of their time.

· · ·

The first literary character created for children was Margery Meanwell in the 1765 book *Little Goody Two-Shoes*. Margery, a virtuous and resourceful child, suffers cruelty and triumphs over misfortune in a story filled with sociological lessons. The work, attributed to Oliver Goldsmith, was published by John Newberry. Margery served as a role model for two hundred years before Harriet the Spy, a tough, controversial eleven-year-old, became the first literary character to mirror the conflicts and emotions of real children. Adults protested and resisted Harriet's presence in children's literature. Rather than spoiling society forever, though, Harriet has held her place and paved the way for many characters and subjects previously considered too risky for children.

An abundance of federal funding for schools and libraries during the 1960s promoted nonsexist and multicultural literature. This helped expand the scope of children's literature. Today's marketplace offers writers and publishers a great challenge and a great opportunity. Contemporary theories of child development have changed the way the world views infants, children, and reading. Piaget, Kohlberg, and Erickson developed models for evaluating the stages of growth and learning; the recent search for artificial intelligence has changed what we believe the brain is capable of achieving.

Yet in spite of all we know about learning, the country is crippled by massive illiteracy. The 1983 study *A Nation At Risk* brought national attention to education and reading, galvanizing publishers, booksellers, Congress, libraries, and schools into action. The way children are taught to read is changing, all to the benefit of those who are interested in writing for children.

The California Reading Initiative, the Iowa Whole Language Program, a Minnesota program called Book Nook, and the PBS series *Reading Rainbow* are creative, respectful, and exciting reading programs. *Reading Rainbow* and Book Nook were created by teachers who had successfully experimented with introducing reading through children's literature rather than through basal readers. Twila Liggett created *Reading Rainbow* in 1983. Children loved it, but sponsors and television distributors were slow to provide funding and program time to the children's market. However, when the publishing industry noticed the demand for *Reading Rainbow* titles, the program received the funding it needed to stay on the air.

Book Nook was created by Tunie Munson-Benson. Its principle is that children need a sacred place for sustained silent reading or for listening to books read aloud. The program celebrates books and reading. Children are not given assignments or asked for book reports or unnecessary feedback. They are simply required to get lost in the joy of reading.

The Iowa Whole Language program, like the California Reading Initiative, teaches reading by using trade books. However, no worksheets and assignments are given from the reading. Instead, the children are asked to record their experiences in a daily journal. The teachers and children involved in this remarkable program have been amazed by their own success.

Many major publishers have been purchased by conglomerates, and consolidations have affected children's publishers; however, the industry is still committed to providing a complete range of literature for children. Children's literature is the fastest growing segment of the industry. In the spring of 1988, *Publisher's Weekly* produced the first pull-out best sellers list for children's books. Children's books have been featured on the cover of *Time* and in *New Yorker* articles. Congress declared 1989 the Year of the Young Reader and 1990 the Year of Literacy.

We are at the beginning of what I believe will be the Golden Age of children's literature—a time when the child's mind is respected, from prenatal impressions seamlessly into adult life. Fine books are being produced for every developmental stage and emotional need for both children and the people who care for them, and the love of reading instilled in children will be passed on to future generations.

Children's literature is gaining a place in the body of world literature because children have gained a place as citizens. We are writing for the contemporary child, who needs to integrate computer and visual literacy with a love for language and story. The task is not easy. E.B. White spent two years writing *Charlotte's Web*, and one additional year rewriting the story. Commenting about the writing, White said that his fears were "great—one can so easily slip into a cheap sort of whimsy or cuteness. I don't trust myself in this treacherous field unless I am running a degree of fever."

Writing for children is not easy. Children's writers have an obligation to their audience. Whatever aspect of children's literature they work in—nonfiction, fiction, young adult, or books for young children—the writer has to offer the child literature, which is to say, excellence.

Writing for the World

DAVID MURA

Recently, a friend told me she finally knows that nothing—rejections, jobs, poverty, family—is going to take her away from her poetry, she is always going to write. Now, she said, she faces different fears, and those fears involve a shift in her perspective, an enlargement of her literary consciousness and ambition. She doesn't quite know what this shift entails, but she senses it partially involves addressing issues in her writing that seem important on a worldwide scale.

My friend's new dilemma is one many writers here share. In the past few years, several Minnesota writers have published their first books of poetry or fiction, and an equal or greater number are just about to do so. Generally, most first books are apprentice work, work which may show promise and talent, but which needs to be developed if the writer is to move out of the apprentice stage. Unfortunately, unlike New York, Minnesota does not have a number of writers in their fifties and sixties, writers who have practiced their craft for decades and who have a sense that their writing addresses more than their region. In addition, unlike the grandiosity of New York writers, midwestern writers often suffer from a voice which says, "Stay only with what you know and can do; don't overreach; don't be pretentious or ambitious."

How then is the literary community here to move out of the apprentice stage? This is a complex question, and in such a small space I can only offer hints. One needed step is to see more clearly what Minnesota poetry (and fiction) lacks. Take, for example, these lines by Amy Clampitt which begin her poem "Beethoven, Opus II":

> —Or, conversely, hungers
> for the levitations of the concert hall:
> the hands like rafts of *putti*
> out of a region where the dolorous stars

are fixed in glassy cerements of Art:
the ancien regime's diaphanous plash
athwart the mounting throb of hobnail—

Or these lines by Czeslaw Milosz from "Bells In Winter":

Everything would be fine if language did not deceive us by
finding different names for the same thing in different times
and places . . .
     "He that leadeth into captivity, shall go into captivity";—
thus began my age on the planet Earth. Later on I became
a teacher in a city by a great sea and I had just turned away
from the blackboard in which they could read, scribbled in
my crooked writing: "Maximus the Confessor" and the dates
"580–662".

What do these lines show? In the case of Clampitt, we find a mind
concerned with "high" (European) culture and sophistication, a diction
that cherishes the luxury of Latinate words, a poetry that advertises
its artificiality and art, that derives from a certain sensibility that we
might call mandarin, *New Yorker,* upper-middle-class intellectual, etc.
With Milosz we find a mind intensely philosophic, a mind distrustful
of language and its ability to describe the world. The poet does not
mention the specific city or sea where he is a teacher not only because
he distrusts language, but also because he wants to view his life as an
example, as exemplary of a certain age in history. He chooses the general over the specific, the historic overview instead of the intense momentary awareness of the present. The poetry that results challenges
an American reader with its difficulty of thought, its impersonal tone,
its biblical stance and reference.

     Why does it seem unlikely that any Minnesota poet would write
like these two poets? I would posit that most Minnesota poets distrust
the blatant artificiality of Clampitt's writing and the worldview it implies. Minnesotans speak in short, laconic sentences, in short Anglo-
Saxon words; we want things direct, simple, without pretense, and we
suspect, often rightly so, not only the snobbishness of "high" culture

but also its privilege, frivolity, and cruelty; its distance from the natural world. We frequently react like Whitman to the learned astronomer and prefer the muteness of the stars to the dazzle of verbiage.

Milosz's concerns tend to counter the practical, empirical side of both Minnesotans and Americans. We are a nation of doers, not thinkers. If there is a problem, we solve it, but we don't go looking for unnecessary problems or problems that seem merely tricks of language. We believe, with Pound, that a bird in a poem is first and foremost a bird, that there is a language adequate to the fields around us, their corn stubble and drifting snow. We aren't very much concerned with a broad historical overview; how could we be? A hundred years ago, there was little here but fields and forests, and the sense of history of those who did live here, the Native Americans, has been erased and excluded from our culture. We are still concerned with the newness of this continent, its specific look and feel, the virginal present moment. As Carol Bly has remarked, the texture of Minnesota life is one of the few textures of American culture that has yet to be described.

And yet, I am troubled by what Clampitt and Milosz represent and by what Minnesota poetry excludes. For it is precisely these exclusions that make our poetry often seem flat, naive, provincial, too small and narrow to deal with the larger questions of American culture and with the pressing questions facing the human race as a whole. In a sense, it is a lie to pretend we know nothing of "high" European culture or that such culture can be dismissed as easily as we sometimes pretend. It is a lie to look at the fields around us without a glimmer of the genocide which secured those fields or the ravages of twentieth-century history. It is a lie to pretend we are only a small midwestern state and not part of a huge empire whose technological and military resources are without compare in history. And if we do feel that language is adequate to reality, how can we explain the distortions we know take place in our newspapers and on our television newscasts? Descriptions of a tractor resting like a stranded hulk in a muddy field will not answer this. We may wish to believe we are simple country folk, but the fact remains, we are not. (It may help us to look at the South, the one area where regional literature transcended that label; in writers like Faulkner and O'Connor we find qualities the Midwest tends to deny—a sense of history, a sense of evil and guilt, a sense of pride, a sense of language which ranges from the florid and formal to the backwoods and broken.)

This does not mean I believe we should or can abandon those values or facts of our lives which have prevented us from easily assimilating writing like Clampitt's or Milosz's. As the French philosopher E.M. Cioran has pointed out, spiritual belief is, in part, based on naiveté, on a lack of self-consciousness or sophistication, on a willingness to accept wonder. Spiritual belief is also predicated on humility, a humility which wasn't very present in "high" European culture or the dour and doubting, proudly skeptical philosophical tradition Milosz inherited. While this may seem like a leap, I believe it is precisely those rooted qualities of Minnesota and the Midwest that have allowed some amazing things to happen in this area in the fields of psychology and human services: places like Hazelden or Family Renewal Center or the woman's therapy collective, Sagaris, are perhaps a result of something extraordinarily visionary and healthy in the temper and spirit of our state. In a way, I am calling then for a change in focus: we must begin comparing Minnesota values and language with the rest of the country and the world; we must see what in our culture here can provide answers (or at least questions) for the country and our species. This may mean that we need to expand our poetics to include the language and worldviews represented by Clampitt and Milosz—not because we necessarily subscribe to them but because they are part of the world we must answer to.

Is There Life after Elegy?

JIM MOORE

For the last twenty years or so, the elegy has been at the heart of American poetry. This was underscored for me by an article in the current issue (Spring, 1982) of *Field*, "Eden And My Generation" by Larry Levis. In it he writes of "the connoisseurs of loss" when discussing contemporary poetry. He says, "It is as if the whole tradition [of alienation and isolation] has become, by now, shared, held in common, a *given*—or as if the poems confer the same sort of loss upon all of us, not only upon the privately suffering poet." A young poet visiting the Twin Cities recently said to me, "Whatever happens to my poetry, it will always be elegiac." Of course, there are many other strands in American poetry, but the elegy is the one overriding context out of which all else emerges.

It's interesting that in a country and a culture that has suffered comparatively little (to Eastern Europe, say, or to South and Central America, Ireland), so many middle-class poets find, as their poetic touchstone, the elegy. Certainly this has been true for me during the last ten years. I could most fully give myself to the writing of a poem when it concerned itself with loss or failure, as if the only truly authentic parts of myself were those activated by loss and suffering. Consequently many of my best poems (as well, I think, of many other North Americans during the last twenty years) are elegiac. Most of the current interest in historical personae poems is also elegiac, the sense of loss being transposed to another century and/or culture.

Why is it that the poets of Eastern Europe, to take a particularly glaring example, who have gone through so much over the last forty-five years (famine, genocide, invasion several times over, destruction on an almost unimaginable scale) produce a poetry which, while it includes the elegiac, is by no means limited to it? Even Milosz, perhaps the most elegiac of them all, in his recent poetry seems to be moving away from the poetry of loss. (In any case, his poems of loss are often angry rather than sad, the tone not so much elegiac as a strange mixture of bitterness and remoteness). These poets are funny, joyful, mysterious, ironic. I'm thinking of work as different in tone (not to speak of culture, language, and sex) as Miroslav Holub's, the Czech poet, and Wislawa Szymborska's, the Polish poet. (The *Field* translation series has published two recent books by Holub, and Princeton University Press and *Quarterly Review Of Literature* have published Szymborska.)

The only period in our own country even roughly similar to what Eastern Europe has been through over the last five decades was the Civil War. One of our greatest poets, Walt Whitman, lived and wrote through that period. While many of his poems are elegiac, his overall tone is far more wide ranging—humorous, ecstatic, erotic, political, mysterious—than what most of us are doing today in this country.

Why do we so often feel we are most alive when we are suffering through a loss? Why do our poems often sound trivial, or at least strained and falsely cheerful, when we leave the elegy behind?

One (leftist) political explanation might be that middle-class poets unconsciously sense the end of an era (capitalism/liberal democracy), are afraid of change, sense it as the loss of their values, the destruction of what they believe in.

Another political explanation is that poets sense—some consciously, some unconsciously—that we are heading toward nuclear destruction, and their poetry reflects that loss even in nonpolitical poems.

Another possible explanation: Over the course of the last two centuries, "to suffer" and "to be sensitive/poetic" have been formed into an equation so widely accepted it has become cliché. How dare we poets take our eyes off the sadness and the loss, even if for a moment.

Also: grief and sadness, as expressed through the elegy, imply the putting of something to rest, working through it to put it behind oneself. But joy, happiness, the erotic, mystery imply new beginnings, risk, openness toward the future, rather than a memorializing of the past.

Good poets, thank God, repeatedly get around all this by writing poems that are at once elegiac and open, funny and sad, stark and luxurious. Recent examples of such work (wildly elegiac and wonderfully funny) can be found in abundance in *This Journey* by James Wright (Random House) and Charles Wright's *Southern Cross* (Random House).

In my own work, I feel a new interest in exploring worlds that include the elegiac, but are not limited to it. My wish for my poems is that they will become more inclusive in some of the ways I've described, that they will not satisfy themselves only with grief and sadness, but that they will let themselves be surprised in ways that I can't even imagine.

Publication

TOPICS COVERED:

Book Group as Therapist

Airing the Family Laundry

Slams

Bangladeshi Tinsmiths

Ice-out in Bemidji

Awkward Audience Queries

Misunderstood French

Secret Passageways

Careers in Dental Hygiene

Tear-Soaked Rejections

Quaalude-Inspired Dustjackets

The '87 Toyota Tercel

Run-ins With Meryl Streep

Confessions of a First Novelist

LEWIS BUZBEE

On the morning of June 16, 1989 (Bloomsday, a fact I would, of course, find significant), I received a phone call from Bob Wyatt of Ballantine Books, a call I had been waiting for longer than Bob could have imagined. I was just drinking my first cup of coffee and reading the newspaper and was not expecting any momentous news. The call confused me, and I thought at first it was a fellow sales rep wanting to scam some freebies. Then the information sank in. This was no sales rep; this was an editor, and he was offering to publish my first novel and to pay me for this privilege.

"You're serious, aren't you?" I asked, and he said he was.

"Excuse me," I said, trembling, "but I've got to sit down."

After a long call during which Bob tried to set my mind at rest, and my mind refused to rest, trying to comprehend this strange information, the details of the contract were settled. I was, after years of trying to write a novel, and a year of trying to publish the one I finally managed to write, a novelist. Thirty-one at the time, I was only one year past the goal I had set for myself at fifteen, when I had first read *The Grapes of Wrath*. *Fliegelman's Desire*, *The Grapes of Wrath*; Buzbee, Steinbeck. It all sounded right to me.

I spent the next several days on the phone, allowing my excitement to reach out and touch all of my friends, not to mention several enemies. Let me tell you this, I was mostly cool about it. After all, I knew the business from the inside out. I had managed independent bookstores for over ten years; I had been a house sales rep for three years and attended sales, editorial, and design meetings; I had written book reviews for six years; I had been to ABA. I was seasoned already. I would be realistic. I had to be. I had written a small literary novel that six previous publishers had truly enjoyed and admired (they told me so in their eloquent rejection letters), and which would probably never get to more than a few thousand homes.

But, still, some vain demon in me whispered. Didn't we all know stories of surprising and overnight success, books that overcame all obstacles of their "literary" nature and the hugeness of publishing to establish instant fame and fortune for their authors? *Fliegelman's Desire*, after all, was to be published as a trade paperback original, and didn't that mean that more copies would get advanced than had it been a hardcover? I was well known in the Northern California bookselling community, a literary hotbed if ever there was one, and a couple of strategically placed readings might get me on the *San Francisco Chronicle*'s best seller list for a week or two, just enough to start a groundswell. More and more papers were reviewing original paperbacks, and a good review in the *Times* could really get the action pumping. Hell, maybe Updike would do one of those *New Yorker* pieces that sent intelligent Americans scurrying to their bookstores. Get a great cover, the next thing you know, it's dinner with Richard Ford and all my other peers.

It's been almost two years since *Fliegelman's Desire* hit shelves and display tables all over the world (some sixty-six copies were sold to Europe, my royalty reports tell me), and I am a little more seasoned than I was before, and oddly enough a little more hopeful about the whole publishing process, which, at its best, seems quite random and hapless to me.

It all started out quite well. First, there was the publisher's lunch. Bob Wyatt, an editor whose work I had known about for years, was visiting San Francisco, and he took me to Prego for lunch. It doesn't matter that you don't know what Prego is; it sounds like a ginchy place for a publisher's lunch. Bob assured me that my fictional voice was the most original he'd read in years, and that he was determined to make a strong career for me. He even thought Sontag (just the one name) would love the book and blurb it. The Sontag blurb never really happened. We talked about cover design, me adding my vast experience as bookseller and publisher. The design would be very urban, we agreed; we were on the same wavelength. When Bob paid for lunch (they really do pay), I took a quick upside-down glance at his credit card to make sure he was Bob Wyatt, and not some imposter my friends had hired to shut me up.

The next phase of the publishing process was probably my favorite because it involved actually toying around with words, sentences, and paragraphs—actual writing. Bob edited my novel. There is so much talk these days (has there always been this talk?) that editors are sloppy and careless and too quick, and when they aren't, they are busy trying to forge their own stamp on the work. But Bob Wyatt showed himself to be a superb editor, trimming the work with great care and expertise, making the book a better one, making it the book it wanted to be. And he performed this transformation with only the most minor adjustments, taking out a few three-page sections when necessary. He even said to me at one point, "This is your book, you don't have to change a word." I thought that kind of editing was done with.

The next few months were a glorious coming and going of Federal Express packages and telephone calls—even faxes. I never toted up the cost of this, but it must have been exorbitant. Publishers could probably pay for their ABA booths by forbidding anything but first-class mail. I once asked Bob how publishers and writers functioned before the advent of such speedy marvels.

"We got things done on time," he said.

Then the worst happened. In January, I received bound galleys in the mail, a plain red wrapper with black, finished type. I wish it could have stayed that way. Included with the bound galleys was a proof of the cover. I took one look at it and knew I would have to change my name and move to another country. It was the single worst cover ever devised. There was a concept to the cover that fit the novel, but the execution was off. Way off. I showed it to friends, who tried to be kind, but the best they could muster was, "It's not that bad."

Supposedly peeking out from behind a set of bookshelves was not a woman, but a photograph of a woman, a girl really, sort of sixteenish, who looked as if just after the quaaludes kicked in she'd been stunned with a hammer. I don't blame the designers at Ballantine for this. From my time in-house as a rep, I knew that designers, artists, and production people were the hardest-working people in publishing, people with real jobs. That's why I always give back rubs to the people in the art department. Especially when I need a comp cover from them.

After a frantic phone call to Bob, in which my legal rights were reiterated, I assured myself that a bad cover couldn't stop a good book.

The first reviews came in. *Kirkus* gave it a great review, and *Bookseller* loved it. *PW* wasn't as thrilled, but the reviewer praised my ambition, awarding me degree-of-difficulty points, as in platform diving. The reviews kind of stopped there. The *San Francisco Chronicle*, my hometown paper, reviewed it, but based on space limitations, I'm guessing, cut off the last half of the piece, and it was really difficult to tell the import of the review. A reviewer in Vancouver objected to the book, it seemed, based on my author's bio.

The Ballantine publicity department did a fantastic job. They got me interviews in newspapers, two radio interviews, and one television interview. I thought this quite over the top, especially for such a little book in such a big book world. The publicity department treated me as if I were an "author," and they convinced others to treat me as such.

Then came the readings, several over the summer of 1990, some to big crowds (mostly friends) and some to tiny crowds (still mostly friends), but the bookstores where I read were all anxious to have me there. My first bookstore reading was at Printers Inc. Bookstore in Palo Alto, where I had worked for six of my ten years in bookselling.

During my tenure at Printers, I had for several years run the reading series there, signing up authors, introducing them, providing them with cookies or beer, whichever they needed to get them through. While running the reading series, I had the opportunity to introduce some of my writing heroes: Raymond Carver, Wallace Stegner, Ernest Gaines, and many others. Now I was being introduced, and by the owners of the store where I felt I had grown up. The introduction given me brought me close to tears, I must admit, and also close to a runny nose, but fortunately Printers had provided a tablecloth on which I was surreptitiously able to wipe my embarrassment.

I have always loved reading my work in public, but reading in bookstores for the first time was an odd experience, surrounded by all those books, kind of like bringing a live wildebeest to the Museum of Natural History. Yet at each reading and signing, I signed books for people I did not know and who had never heard of me. A small number, yes, but complete strangers.

There was one moment when I thought the book might break big. I received a phone call from a man who identified himself as a lawyer with the Jewish Anti-Defamation League in San Francisco. My first thought was, "Oh my God, I've offended somebody." My second thought was, "Great, I've offended somebody." If someone were sorely offended by the book, they might try to get it banned or to organize a boycott, and then I would be in the pink. Sales would soar; I might even get in *Rolling Stone*. No such luck. The caller had once worked for a man named Fliegelman and was curious to know where I got the name. I had not been smart enough to write a book that offended.

Then, the brouhaha was over. Stacks of *Fliegelman's Desire* got dusty, and some got returned. My first little season in the sun had ended. Still, wherever I go, I look for *Fliegelman*, and I'm surprised at how often I find it, most times now a single copy, spine out.

The first time I found my novel in a used bookstore, I was at first crushed, assuming, of course, some great failure on my part as a writer that caused one angry customer to trade the book in for a ratty copy of *Middlemarch*, a real novel. But after my wounded ego quickly healed, I discovered I was thrilled to find *Fliegelman's Desire* in a used shop because it meant that something I had written had entered what I can only think of as the continuum. It had become part of a larger world. And when I think back on my first novel, that is what I come away with, a sense of a larger community.

I can, and have, complained about everything during all of this, complained about the wretched cover, the reviewers who didn't review the book, the people who didn't buy the book, Amy Tan and her million devoted readers, a friend whose first novel became a bestseller at the same time as mine was failing, huge and careless advances, all of the things people in publishing complain about all the time, especially writers.

Yet, looking back, I see that an enormous number of very talented people worked very hard to get some three thousand copies of my work into the hands of others. I think of the booksellers, especially those who bought more copies than they should have and tried very hard to sell it. It was an exhilarating time for me, and continues to be. In the middle of an industry that is riddled with inefficiencies at every level, that is beset by real problems and competition, a lot of people decided that my efforts were worth their efforts, the same way they do for thousands and thousands of books every year.

I know this because of the little things. The first time I saw my book in a library binding, I was too happy to live. I hadn't thought of it in a library before then, actually. Four people had checked it out in two months. A copy had been spotted at Shakespeare's in Paris. I got a few fan letters. Parts of *Fliegelman's Desire* take place in a bookstore, and this last year I met a young woman working at a Tower Books in Sacramento. She recognized me when I came in for my sales call, though I had never met her before. She had read my novel, it seems, and was swayed enough by it to take a job in a bookstore. All that work by all those people for that small of a change in the world. Just to get someone to read a book.

Lorna Landvik

in dialogue with FAITH SULLIVAN

FAITH SULLIVAN: The first question that a published novelist is usually asked is, how did you sell your first book? Any advice for the novelists who aren't yet published?

LORNA LANDVIK: I did everything by the book: I wrote a snappy one-page letter to agents and sent it out to dozens whose names I'd found in the *Writer's Market*. Eventually I got an agent, but we weren't a good mix—she'd send the novel to romance publishers who'd write back, "Why are you sending us this? It's not a romance." I'd seethe at home, thinking, "Duh."

After parting ways with that agent, I solicited another slew of agents, and my current agent was intrigued enough by my letter to ask for a hundred pages; after reading them, she took me on.

Patty Jane's House of Curl got about thirty rejections (I've kept them all), and my agent would lessen the pain by writing little notes in the margins—"She's a pill," "He'll rue the day," etc. Finally, after four years of sending the manuscript out, the agent called. A small press wanted to buy *Patty Jane*, although *buy* may be the wrong word, as they didn't offer advances. But they worked very hard for the book, getting me a lot of press, and when the paperback rights were sold to Ballantine, the proverbial ball started rolling.

My advice to unpublished writers is: Never give up. Don't let someone's "no" be your answer. Another agent or editor may just say yes. I know writers who keep their manuscripts hidden away in drawers, too afraid of rejection to send their babies out into the world. To them I say: You're bound to be rejected, but rejection is part of the process. Be in the process, because you'll never be published if you're not.

F. S.: How did you continue to write during the period of rejection, which, for many writers, is debilitating?

L. L.: Rejection didn't bother me that much. I knew that the whole thing was a process, and rejection was part of it. The important thing was having the manuscript out there. Rejection or acceptance is a matter of serendipity, of the right person reading the manuscript at the right time.

Also, a little voice of confidence way deep inside insisted, "It will be published." You have to believe in your own work.

I remember crying once, when an editor whose taste I admired rejected *Patty Jane*. I cried, then let it go and went on to the next.

Maybe it helped that I'd acted a lot and knew audition rejection—a rejection that is very personal and face to face. ("You stink. Get outta here. You don't look anything like what we want.") From editors, thank heaven, I never received a "Have you considered a career in dental hygiene?" letter.

F. S.: About what (from inception to publicity and sales) do you wish that someone had warned you when you were starting out?

L. L.: I had read of other writers' frustrations in the editing process, so I was forewarned—but it is rough. My first novel was 562 typewritten pages and eventually wound up being 292 typeset pages. I fought for what I believed in, winning the war, I think, but losing lots of little skirmishes. I think my editor was right sometimes, and I'm glad I followed her advice/orders, but still, the process of being edited is like handing over your beloved shaggy-haired kid to a glinty-eyed military barber whose specialty is buzz cuts. When it's all over, you get your kid back, but it's a more polished, grown-up kid.

F. S.: Had you taken many, or any, writing classes when you began your first novel? Had these prepared you for the process?

L. L.: My style of learning is not classroom oriented, although I did take a class at the Loft midway through *Patty Jane's House of Curl*. I'm very secretive/superstitious about letting people see my work while I'm writing, but *Patty Jane* was my first novel, and I wanted feedback. The others in the group were writing novels too, and each week we critiqued twenty pages of our classmates' work.

Mainly, though, I think I've learned how to write a novel by reading novels and trying to figure out what moves me as a reader.

F. S.: Could you tell us about steps one, two, and three, so to speak, in your method of beginning a novel? Have these changed since *Patty Jane's House of Curl*?

L. L.: Usually a character or several characters come into my head, and often an accompanying title. I didn't know exactly what a "house of curl" was when I started writing my first novel, didn't know exactly who the main characters, Patty Jane and Harriet, were, but curiosity kept me writing.

In all of the books I've written, it's the characters who come to me and tell me what the story is. I may have some idea of what's going to happen, but the characters frequently disagree and go their own merry ways.

I never outline—it would feel too much like homework. I like to write without a map, and if I get lost, I just back up until I find a recognizable landmark that will help me get where I need to go.

F. S.: What is your approach to character development?

L. L.: My approach is to let the characters be on paper who they are in my head. I don't write a character history or a list of their traits, idiosyncrasies, etc. I just begin writing and in that writing the characters reveal themselves. In *Your Oasis on Flame Lake*, there is a teenage character, Franny, to whom a lot happens. She's important. And people have asked me why I didn't let her speak. I did try, but she didn't want to talk.

When I tell people that, they say, "Why didn't you make her? She's not real!" But, fictitious though Franny is, she's real to me, and I have to respect the truth of her.

F. S.: *Your Oasis on Flame Lake* is a story told by several voices, male and female. Could you speak about the difficulty or lack of difficulty you encountered in writing from a male perspective?

L. L.: My pat answer for "How do you write like a man?" is that I put on some old, dirty underwear, boss my spouse around, and it all comes together. Really, my characters just seem so real in my head that it's not that difficult to transcribe their voices. I'm also of the belief that men and women are more alike than they are different. They may have different means of getting to the same goal, but, male or female, they're just people.

F. S.: You are an actress as well as a writer. Has your acting experience been helpful in writing fiction? How?

L. L.: Just as writers people-watch, so do actors. I think performing has helped my fiction, especially performing comedy. It's made me more aware of timing. Acting is also a great outlet. Writing is solitary, and you have no idea how your work is going to be received until it's out there, whereas the feedback on stage is immediate.

F. S.: In addition to writing novels, you pen comedy sketches. Do these two disciplines grow out of different pots of soil?

L. L.: My comedy material features characters who want an outlet, but not in a book. I love being on stage—I love the rehearsals, the back-stage life, that call of "Five minutes!" and, most of all, I love presenting these odd characters with their little stories to an audience. The commonality in novel writing and stage writing is that I'm trying to create real characters in both.

F. S.: Have you always kept a diary or journal? If so, do you feel that this habit has been helpful in developing fiction? What about writer's notebooks?

L. L.: No! I never keep a journal or notebook. I did when I was in my late teens/early twenties, and I can't bear to read them now. I sound like a psychopath. I always figure if something comes into my head that I want to use in my writing, it'll stay there. And if it doesn't, it wasn't that strong in the first place. I've been burned by this practice a couple times, but what the hey, I just can't be bothered.

F. S.: When you were writing *Patty Jane's House of Curl,* did anything about the novel-writing process surprise you?

L. L.: I was constantly surprised. Characters who I thought were going to be minor became major and vice versa; characters who I thought were going to die decided to live. I felt as if I were the guardian of rambunctious children. I believed that I knew what was best for them, but they frequently felt otherwise and acted in ways that amazed me.

The House of Curl is situated on a real street in Minneapolis, and I often found myself driving along that street, looking for the house, then remembering: It's not real. That was immensely enjoyable—having the characters become so real that I'd look for their nonexistent house.

F. S.: Would you speak about your writing habits? You have a family. How does that affect work?

L. L.: I try to write every day, but some days I try harder than others. When my two daughters, ages eight and fourteen, are in school, I usually write for a couple hours in the morning, when they're home, I write when I can—twenty minutes here, half an hour there. It's very unscheduled, but I think most writers who are mothers have learned to be flexible.

I write in my kitchen, which is certainly not a private space, and I often field questions or engage in conversation with the family while I'm writing. I long for my own office, but once I get one, I'll probably be leaving it constantly to see what's going on in the household. Having a family definitely enhances my work. What I lose in time, I gain in a broader, richer life.

F. S.: Do your daughters take an interest in your writing?

L. L.: Yes, and my older daughter has been a witness to the whole process from the beginning. Witnessing the process has demystified writing for both girls. They see that it's not something which only anointed people get to do. It's for everybody, including their mother.

Both girls are avid readers. Recently, reading passages aloud to me from *The Great Gatsby* and exclaiming about how poetic they were, my older daughter said, "You know, Mom, you're no F. Scott Fitzgerald," hastening to add, "Your characters are okay, and you can tell a story, but you're so—blunt." It was very funny. So funny, it hurt.

F. S.: Do you see the greater consolidation of the business (publishing, distribution, sales) as a threat to the sort of book that you enjoy writing?

L. L.: It seems that everything today is judged on its ability to make money; if quality happens to be part of the equation, great, but it's certainly not necessary. I hate that a celebrity is given huge amounts of money for a kids' book or a tell-all or a ghostwritten novel while a really good writer's work is rejected. As far as my own work goes, I can't worry about consolidation hurting it—I've got enough to worry about as it is.

F. S.: As far as you can tell, is being a female novelist an advantage or disadvantage in today's book business?

L. L.: Hmmm. I don't really know about that. I think women read far more men's books than men read women's books, but I also think women buy more books, so maybe it evens out.

F. S.: In general, have you noticed an appreciable and describable difference between the kinds of novels published in Britain and Canada and those published in the US?

L. L.: It seems to me that both Britain and Canada are less commercial in their publishing tastes than the US, more eclectic. Anita Brookner, Penelope Jones, A. S. Byatt, Martin Amis—they're wildly different and yet widely read.

F. S.: Has anybody offered you a piece of advice about writing or the writing life which you felt was particularly valuable?

L. L.: No, I can't think of anyone. But my sixth-grade teacher, Mr. Spaeth, who is acknowledged at the beginning of *Your Oasis on Flame Lake,* was a big influence. He made me feel that my voice was important enough to be heard. And by often reading aloud to the class, he made us feel that books were a vital part of life.

In my autograph book, he wrote, "Best of luck for a fine literary career." He kept the fire going.

F. S.: Do you think fiction writing is part of a person's DNA?

L. L.: I do. I think you come out into the world as a fairly complete package, with your talents and gifts nestled in your brain or heart, waiting to be tapped. Of course a person has to nurture what she or he is given, and determination and hard work can certainly strengthen a gift, but I think some people are given a facility with words, just as other people are given a musical ear, or hands that feel at home holding a paintbrush or saw.

F. S.: In what ways did your background (family, early experiences, education, etc.) prepare you to be a novelist?

L. L.: I think the best preparation for becoming a novelist is love of reading. I remember being transported as a child by books—the Betsy-Tacy books, *Little Women, Caddie Woodlawn,* books with girl heroes—and in turn wanting to create stories that might transport someone else. In fact, being an author was my earliest career choice, after I dismissed baton twirling as frivolous.

My mother is a big-time reader, and my older brother has probably read more books than anyone I know. Growing up seeing the pleasure they got from reading influenced me as well.

My dad, on the other hand, told stories—funny, laugh-out-loud stories. I think it's from him that I learned about surprise and timing in a story.

F. S.: Is there a question you haven't been asked which you wish someone would ask?

L. L.: Ah, yes. "What year was it that you won the Nobel Prize?"

What's Fiction Got to Do with It?

KAREN TEI YAMASHITA

What's fiction got to do with it? What really happened is this:

The man's body crashed spread-eagle across the small hood of my '87 Toyota Tercel. I had seen the specter of his form above only moments before his plunge, his arms outstretched as if in anticipation of some great embrace. The force of his fall crumbled the safety glass in a dazzling halo around his head, and his face—framed with tiny scratches but surprisingly little blood—looked upon me with incredible calm and even wonderment. It was that odd hour on the freeway when the sun is always below your visor and across your horizon, blinding the way, and traffic is thick with tired people moving in a slow current toward the seven o'clock news.

No time to contemplate braking or even speeding up; nothing could have avoided this diving free fall as my car scooped up the man sailing from his concrete perch on the overpass. I continued to move forward in traffic, frantically trying to see beyond the man's distracting body cradled in the crater that was once my hood and windshield, searching around for help. The people in the cars behind and in front were oblivious to my situation. The BMW beside me scooted forward, its driver most likely on the phone and safely hidden behind tinted windows. "Are you all blind?" I screamed. "This can't be happening!"

"I'mm noot baliindd. Mierrda," the man in my windshield managed with a mushy voice.

"You're alive! Are you all right?" My heart thumped like crazy. "Hang on! Just let me pull over!"

The man's eyes grazed the interior of my Tercel. Clearly there was scorn in his look. My deep feelings of pity and human decency faded. "Missed the Mazzzda," he muttered.

"Mazda?"

"RX-7. Bute. Agghh!" He yelled when he tried to shake his head, his face pressed without exit into its sharp-edged but custom-made opening. "P.O.J.," he added.

"You jumped on purpose!" I jammed on my signal, looking back excitedly, trying to find an opening for a right lane change.

The man's face lit up. "Purpose. Purpose," he repeated until the thought seemed to travel to the back of his mind.

"Are you hurt? What were you trying to do?"

"Merge with beauty. Miscalculated. Wouldn't you know it. P.O.J. Not doing so well yourself. Mergin' I mean."

"Damn!" No one was letting me in the next lane. "You're alive aren't you? What does it matter if it's a lousy Tercel!"

"Alive? Course I'm alive. I said merge with beauty."

"Suicide! This was going to be a suicide! God!" I cut into the next lane with a vengeance.

"Hey! Watch it! This ain't much of a hood to hang on to." The man grabbed at my windshield wipers.

"You're gonna break 'em!" I yelled.

"I'm not loco, you know."

"Yeah, I'm crazy."

"But I'm not. How do I know? Used to be an artist. Painter, see? Conceptual abstract stuff. Very beautiful. Grotesque. Torpid. Intense. Major talent. Critics said that. I was just very neurotic. Then, one day, boom! I'm cured. No more loco. Never painted a damn thing again. Well, you know about these things." He looked me in the eyes. "You're just on the edge. A writer."

"What? How do you know that?" My eyes darted back and forth between the man and traffic.

"Hey, the RX-7's guilt ridden. Woulda buried me in the machine. Swear to God. Course the blood, drippin' on the dash like this. Woulda freaked out the RX. But you, baby, are tough."

"Who are you?"

"Was I right? You are a writer. It's the way you drive. No radio. No sound. Windows rolled up. Lookin' out into the distant traffic. Out there, it's all like a blank piece of paper. Always conjuring. Plotting.

But alone. Rideshare? Out of the question. Got to be alone with your soul, so to speak."

I felt limp in the driver's seat. I grabbed the wheel tightly in one hand and pressed my other forcefully into the stick, hoping to find a tactile reality there. Reality.

He continued, "Rarely change lanes. Lane changers're trying to get somewhere fast, like destiny. You? Plot a course. Put one word after another. One word after the other. Maybe something at the end of it. Maybe not." He paused, trying to see over my dash. "Bet you got some miles on this klunker. Don't make no money neither," he sighed, spying my torn upholstery, the yellow stickies with cryptic notes on the dash, and the overdue library books strewn over the backseat. "*Care and Sport of Homing Pigeons. Migrant Patterns of South American Birds.*" He squinted to read the titles. "Hey, where's the fiction?"

Panic turned to fear and fear to terror, overtaking my desire to be in control, to make responsible decisions in a crisis. And yet I continued to drive. I searched in a manic frenzy for help around me, but it was as he said. I was alone. No one around seemed to notice the man with his sooty face embedded in my windshield—his body sometimes gripping, sometimes flailing wildly on the hood of my car. I saw the sign for my turnoff whizz over my head. "Oh no!" was all I could manage. I wasn't even going home.

"Could use a mirror that side." His eyes pointed to my right side. "Three-hundred-sixty-degree vision. Not many writers have it. Use the one up there the most." His eyes rolled upward. "Always lookin' back. See if you lost any characters 'long the way. Or kill 'em off good and dead before you move on," he spat.

I looked through the rearview mirror. There was a police car behind me. "Thank God." I practiced my speech. "Officer, sir, it was an accident. This homeless man fell on my car."

"Accident?" he protested. "What accident? Call it a coincidence, but not an accident."

The police car swerved around us and sped past. "What?" My mind raced in confusion. Maybe the police car was talking through the windshield to its own visitor. Maybe everyone was. I had this homeless artist, but who knew what else could fall from the sky? NASA astronauts? Communications consultants? Political pollsters? Big Bird? Rock stars? Angels?

"Know what I mean?" my windshield companion continued. "Accident is like you didn't look where you were going. This is different. It's coincidence. We occupy the same space."

"I'm hal-lu-ci-na-ting." I enunciated the syllables out loud in order to hear them myself. "This is a test. This is a test." And was it covered by my insurance?

"Hey. You don't do no drugs. People might read the stuff and think so. *The Weekly* could say as much. Not even cigarettes." He sniffed the air. "Car's old but still got that Santa Maria virgin vinyl smell. Hey, not hard stuff anyway. Espresso will do."

I began to whimper.

"What is it?" he puzzled. "Is this the sad part? Tell me. Nothing like reading a book and crying into the pages."

"I want to go home," I began to blubber miserably. "I missed my turnoff. I've got a crazy, suicidal ex-artist gawking at me through my windshield. And yet, I'm completely and tragically alone in traffic. Is this writer's block?" I wailed on and on.

"Hey. Hey. Listen. Get a hold of yourself. Drive the car," he suggested. "Drive the car," he said again, somewhat hypnotically.

I grabbed around for the Kleenex box and blew my nose. My windshield companion looked upon me with what seemed to me infinite compassion. I took a few more tissues and leaned over the dash, dabbing at the little speckles of blood, brushing away the tiny flecks of broken glass in his bearded stubble. "I got earthquake supplies in the back," I remembered. "First-aid stuff."

"Some earthquake, huh?"

We both managed tentative smiles.

"Forget what I said about the RX-7." He was apologizing. "Beauty. Beauty could be something else. You seem honest enough."

I rubbed the wetness from my eyes and shifted up to fourth gear. Traffic was starting to thin out. We were leaving the city.

"I'm not burying you in my car, you know. I need my car. It's purely a utilitarian thing."

"I'm not dead, yet," he pleaded. "And I'm not homeless. Call me an urban guerrilla," he snorted, adding a bunch of grunts and howls. Then he paused to think about the novelty of it all.

"I've got to let you off somewhere. Extricate your face from my window. Where do you want to go?"

"Couldn't you just drive a while more? I'm getting used to this. Warmer here than newspaper on concrete." He rocked his hips against the hood and chortled, "Ouuu. Maybe you could even speed it up a little. Excitement on the road. Lemme see. Let's go east a bit." He licked his lips. "Course, it's your choice. It is a freeway."

I don't know why, but I took the turnout east. We coasted around the pass. He hung on, squealing in ridiculous delight, his coattails and pants flapping like beautiful wings. When we were due east, he said, "You know, I've had an interesting life. Really. Yeah, have I got a story for you."

The setting sun shone through the back window, filling the front in a curious golden glow, my traveling companion's face a mass of quirky poignancy and endless tales. And yet, for a brief moment, I thought I saw, through the very skin of his face made transparent by the light, a fearful mask of death. "I could hold a knife to your heart," he remarked grimly, "and force you to listen, but it's not necessary. Obviously, you're in this for the long haul."

I saw the treachery of the road, held the terror in my throat, but offered brashly, "And I could invite you in." But he would remain beyond the window, the grime of his weathered touch and the stink of his otherness things of my imagination. His voice would again soften, his lips part in a wise grin. Indeed, I discovered, he loved to talk and I loved to listen. I headed toward the dusky horizon, the empty road before me, following that story and the Cheshire grin.

So I lied.

Leslie Adrienne Miller

in dialogue with HEID E. ERDRICH

Leslie Adrienne Miller was one of two winners of the 1998 McKnight Fellowships Awards of Distinction. She is the author of five collections of poetry and her awards include a National Endowment for the Arts fellowship, a Loft-McKnight Award, and two Minnesota State Arts Board fellowships for poetry. She is a professor of English at the University of Saint Thomas. At the time of this interview, she was living in France.

HEID ERDRICH: In July of 1997, at the beginning of your sabbatical from teaching, you left the country to live and work with other artists in communities in France and Scotland. You have been away a year, and in that time you have written almost all of a new book of poems. Can you give some sense of how living in Europe for such an extended time has influenced your writing?

LESLIE ADRIENNE MILLER: I have been in the south of France for the better part of the last year, and though I've been abroad before, I've never spent this extended a period of time outside my own language and culture. From my previous shorter stints in Germany, Indonesia, France, etc., I knew that the longer I stayed immersed in another place, another language, geography, cultural system, the more I would absorb it as a reality. The shifts, for me, are mainly in terms of language, space, and time. It seems to me that language—words and grammar—contains and conveys as much or more of the different sense of reality as anything else. And though I am typically American in my abysmal ability to gain fluency in any language outside of English, my poems have been infused for a long time with the struggle to enter into other languages and to bring back into English some sense of the differences.

H. E.: Was that interest in language already of concern in *Yesterday Had a Man in It,* your most recent collection?

L. M.: I tried to discover and register some of the differences, via language, with exploration of both German and Indonesian words, and perhaps even more importantly, how I saw German and Indonesian speakers using English words, grammar, ideas. In that book, I was interested in contrasting Eastern and Western notions as they occurred in everyday speech. Listening to the "mistakes" in English made by various nonnative English speakers can tell one as much as listening to the actual other language about the way other people think, the way they process sensory information and assign values.

H. E.: And this past year in France—how did you extend that subject, that interest in speech as it reveals culture?

L. M.: Everything lives in the way we use words: history, moral values, spiritual and ideological convictions. As I try to order and collect the poems I have written in my year here, I begin to see that this negotiation of everyday speech habits has been one of my most constant subjects. I hear the speech habits of nonnative speakers of English all day, every day, from my friends here, and many of these habits have become so familiar to me that not only do I no longer hear them as mistakes, but I find that I have also adjusted my own syntax and pronunciation to theirs. Someone once called the adjustments in my speech a sympathetic accent, which is simply adjusting the rhythms, syntax, and pronunciation of words to match those of the listener. I do this in English, and I have witnessed time and again the fact that if I do not do this—if I speak, for example, with my normal American accent—I am not as well understood, even by those whose English is very good.

For most of my year in France, I was speaking a kind of lingua franca, a mixture of several kinds of English with French and German.

H. E.: You said you have a hard time writing fluently in languages. How did being cut off from spoken English influence your writing?

L. M.: All this has had an enormous effect on the rhythms of my poems. I think differently about word origins because I begin to feel, for example, when I am speaking to a French person, that I can use some of the more sophisticated Latinate words because they are common to French and English, and because French speakers use these words in spoken language, whereas in English, spoken American English, words like *insolence*, for example, are rarely spoken and when spoken are, perhaps, pretentious. Speaking these words liberates them from the page, allows me to understand anew how impoverished spoken American English is. Being among French speakers has liberated some of these words, and along with them a sense of playfulness about language, a love of puns—the *jeux de mots*, the plays on words. Some of the most delightful ones I have heard have been plays on words in French and English.

H.E.: You used the phrase *lingua franca*, which I understand to mean the language of common use. That phrase is also the title of one of your new poems. Can you give us a few lines that illustrate the type of conversation you've been describing?

L.M.: "Lingua Franca" is one of the last poems I wrote in France, an attempt to bring together my thoughts and experiences on the language habits I had acquired within the community of friends I had there, and to speak about the emotional impact and associations of particular languages in which I am not really fluent but which I know well enough to interpret or guess at meaning. Even if I don't know every word, there's a way of listening for tone and rhythm, familiarity, that comes through as some kind of understanding, if not full comprehension. There is recognition and emotional response even without complete comprehension—the way, for example, one with little or no musical training can still listen and respond emotionally to a piece of music. In the poem, I use an answering machine to contain all the languages:

> The answering machine speaks French, *il y a trois messages.*
> One is in English, an invitation for her. One is in French,
> and she listens twice before she knows they are speaking
> also to her. *Pick up your photos when you like.* The other,

the German one, is not for her, but she's awake,
looks up from Tsvetaeva in Berlin, Pasternak's
horsy face, the beautiful eyes of the weak husband,
and listens the way one who loves Chopin but cannot

play the piano listens. Ardently.

H. E.: The connection to music you make in those last lines reinforces the idea I get from several of your poems that language has an emotional message understandable apart from the intellectual one. Still, the experience of being cut off from full understanding sounds dislocating to me, even threatening to what I would call the poetic voice. How did you reconcile your way of speaking with the voice you needed to use to write? Or was it a liberating influence, this shifting through various languages?

L. M.: I have always loved the tendency in twentieth-century American poetry to leap midline from high to low in diction, from the vulgar to the sophisticated. English is such a wonderful mixture of languages to begin with—the simple, crisp Anglo-Saxon words right up against the polysyllabics from Latin and French. Living this year in this fascinating crucible of languages, I often felt as if the whole history of language in the West was being reshaped each day in our mouths. We had to communicate, and we had to do it on all levels. The discussion might shift suddenly from whose dog ran off with the chicken carcass to what Rilke had to say about love to where Minnesota was in relation to California or New York—and this discussion would always, always be in a mixture of languages. Very soon after my arrival, I began to understand that my poems, my own way of speaking and using English, had gone underground, as it were. It existed only in my head, and there it became pure. It was and is my own private landscape, and ways to play with and manipulate the rhythms of it presented themselves to me daily. For example, in French, the word pronunciations favor the accent on the final syllable, so the presence of a stronger iambic rhythm was in my ears all day. The iambs were sometimes so insistent in my head when I tried to write that they afflicted my prose as well as my poems.

H. E.: What do you think you will notice as you return to Minnesota?

L. M.: I know that this heightened awareness of rhythmic differences in spoken English will escape me almost immediately when I get home. The poems that have been born out of it here would not have been possible at home. I will not even remember the subtle differences (and the wonderful hilarity we all found in some of the mistakes). I know this. I will immediately begin to suffer a kind of amnesia. And, of course, this makes me sad. I have felt so linguistically alive in this context, but I also know that if I spent years and years here, this too would become ordinary and unbearable. As it is, I know I can come back to France or to Germany, and I will experience the delight all over again.

There is also some compensation, of course, for this loss upon my return. There will be several weeks, perhaps even a month, if I am lucky, of culture shock, and this will also include a time when I take delight in rediscovering Americanisms—in terms of speech, but also in terms of images, joke references. I will have missed a whole year of culture, and I will feel like a foreigner until I begin to absorb the reality there—the news, the products on the shelves in the grocery store, the signs along the highway. The confusion will be one of imagery as much as of language.

H. E.: Your last collection of poems included settings from Indonesia to Berlin, but in the end, in the last poems, you write your way to Minnesota. Is there a way in which living outside the country and writing about it helps you come home?

L. M.: When I come back to Minnesota, I know that the first place I go will shock me with its oddity, its unfamiliarity. I will see a box of Kellogg's Corn Flakes on the shelf as if I have never seen it before; it will surprise me to see English written on everything, and I will miss seeing, for example, "*Nuit gravement a la sante*" on my cigarette pack.

The last poem in *Yesterday*, "When I Come Home from Asia, We Are All Hungry," makes use of this estrangement. Nothing looked stranger than winter, Burger King, the Minneapolis-Saint Paul airport, after two months in Southeast Asia.

H. E.: Do you travel, then, in the hope of finding those moments of estrangement?

L. M.: The enemy of poetry is familiarity. I travel to evade it, and although it is impossible to evade it permanently, one can evade it over and over again with many goings and comings. Travel keeps the world fresh for me. I know that I will return home to rediscover much I love there, whereas when I left, it was all so familiar I thought I could not abide continuing to live there. It's the old idea of defamiliarization—a term from the Russian writer Victor Shklovsky. The idea that the artist, the Western artist, must find ways to look at the ordinary that make it seem strange. Travel to foreign countries is one of the easier ways to effect this defamiliarization. It freshens one's perceptions, disturbs and disrupts habits. I can only hope that this year has disrupted my poetic habits in interesting ways. I know that the poems I have written here will look very different when I get home, that I will even wonder who it was who wrote them and that many of them will require adjustments for American readers whom I needed to forget for awhile.

H. E.: What about your reader? Your poems strike such an intimate tone that I imagine your reader must seem to you like a constant companion. Are you traveling with your reader, in a sense?

L. M.: No, actually, I'm not, I think, traveling with my reader. In one sense, I know the reader cannot go with me. I leave to escape that reader, but at the same time I cannot escape that reader. I write in English, American English, and out of a specifically American aesthetic in poetry. The reader is like a longtime spouse—someone I love and cannot leave but who is so familiar to me sometimes that I confuse her with myself. Without her I do not even exist, but I have to find ways to distance myself from her, to rediscover where my identity ends and hers begins. So no, she cannot go with me, but later, when I come home, I will tell her, I will try my best to fashion solely for her, the whole of where I was, and like all intimacies, it will be a gift and an apology for my departure and my separateness.

The Writing of *Deadfall in Berlin*

R.D. ZIMMERMAN

In my first four books I wrote about other people's dirty little secrets; I took imaginary crimes and tried to make them seem as real and thrilling as possible. In my most recent book, I turned that all around, focusing on a personal issue and transforming it into a fictional story of suspense. Specifically, *Deadfall in Berlin* was inspired by my efforts to understand what role I played in the fate of my father, who died as the result of alcoholism nearly twenty-three years ago.

Losing someone to any type of chemical dependency is a mystery unto itself, and I still don't fully understand how my father could have drunk himself to death while his friends and family watched. In many ways it was like witnessing a slow suicide, or perhaps a hideously slow murder, and it left me with a series of questions: If someone was killed, who was the responsible party? Who was the murderer? My father himself? Or those around who watched but did nothing, or at best did it all wrong?

That's a gross simplification of a very complicated situation, but when I was fifteen and Dad died, the issue of responsibility seemed just that clear to me. After all, I was the one who kept track of how many gin and tonics he drank, I was the one who kept a steady eye on the road, and I was the one who could get mad and make him stop drinking, at least for a day or two. And because I was often more in control than my father, I learned to believe that my powers in life were in an odd way greater than his. Did that mean it had been up to me to save him? Did my failure to do that somehow make me the guilty party, the one to be charged for his death?

Although I now recognize that this overextended sense of responsibility is common to almost all children of alcoholics, I also know this dilemma, this wound, is why I write. It caused a rupture of some sort in my imagination and sent some huge thing hurtling into the world in search of an answer that was much, much larger than me. Pain often gives birth to creativity in an attempt to heal that trauma, and I tried once before to write about all this. The book I wrote, however, was a rip-off, a thinly veiled recounting of events that didn't push far enough away from me and deeply enough into fiction. A mainstream novel, it was bought and then dropped in one of the early publishing buy-outs and shake-ups.

After that I started writing thrillers, none of which dealt with personal issues, but rather with other people's deathly problems, and this gave me both a lot of pleasure and relief. Then one day several years ago, I realized a remarkable and very sad thing: I had forgotten my father's voice. Although I had photos of him and even a few samples of his handwriting, my memory could no longer bring to life the deep tones of his words, or even his infectious laugh. On the heels of that, everything came rushing back and, within the context of the genre I was working in, my mind started weaving together all the issues surrounding my father. What quickly and rather compulsively started taking shape this time was a suspense novel about a man, Will, who can no longer recall the beautiful voice of his mother, an alcoholic and a former cabaret singer, who'd perished thirty years earlier during the fall of Berlin. Distraught over this, Will uses hypnosis in hopes of loosening his memory and jarring loose a tune or two. Instead of his mother's song, however, he hears an awful screech—her scream—and he realizes not only that his mother was murdered, but also that as a boy he witnessed her death and he alone knows who killed her.

That was how I started developing *Deadfall*, and that's actually how the book begins. For months I pushed and pulled and stretched the original premise, and the novel grew, sometimes on its own, sometimes by force, but always centered around the role children play in their parents' fate. Although the plot doesn't resemble my own life, in many ways the novel is autobiographical because I handed over to Will all the love/hate, guilt/innocence issues I had with my own father. Furthermore, I made Will go back to his mother's murder and forced him to take a cold, awful look at the truth he'd been running from.

I've used hypnosis in writing for almost ten years now—I have a tape made for each book I write, and then listen to that tape before I begin work—and so I gave that tool, that means of exploring the psyche, to Will as well. Under the direction of his therapist, Will uses hypnosis to replay the film of his youth, rewatching the events and interpreting them with adult insight. Hypnosis lets him regress from his present life to his war-ravaged childhood in Berlin; it lets him shed layer after layer, as if he were peeling an onion, to get to the core of truth buried in his memory.

I've often heard it said that there are just two types of novels, one of ideas and one of plot. And while advocates of both camps have long flung accusations at each other (the first claiming the other is shallow, the second believing the first self-absorbed), I wanted *Deadfall* to steer toward a middle ground. Once I decided that it was indeed a thriller, I knew that I had to honor the requirements of the genre: it had to have pace, plot, and clear suspense. But I also wanted it to reach beyond that, to incorporate the ideas—really the anxieties—that fueled it.

This was a difficult book to write. I stumbled, ripped up lots of chapters, and gave up hope many times. It is for me, however, a successful attempt because in plotting Will's search for his mother's murderer, I discovered a fundamental truth in the perceived crime of my own life.

And that thirst to make order out of chaos is, I suspect, why so many of us write.

Michael Cunningham

in dialogue with PATRICIA WEAVER FRANCISCO

Jeopardy format: Michael Cunningham for five hundred.

Answer: "Not in a million years."

Michael Cunningham did not expect to win the Pulitzer Prize for his fourth novel, *The Hours* (Farrar, Straus and Giroux, 1998). An homage to Virginia Woolf's Mrs. Dalloway, structured as parallel days in three women's lives, with suicide and AIDS at its center, it's the kind of "quiet novel" overlooked for the most prestigious of literary prizes. Perhaps the judges were swayed, one might surmise, by the fact that its prose is gorgeous, its characters deeply realized, and its structure masterful and satisfying—the word "perfect" arises to describe its achievement.

Cunningham's other novels include *A Home at the End of the World* (Farrar, Straus and Giroux, 1990), which brought him recognition for its portrayal of a childhood friendship that evolves into an entangled sexual relationship between two men and a woman. His 1996 novel, *Flesh and Blood* (Touchstone), stuns with its empathy for its large and challenging cast of characters. It does for the postwar generation what the great novels of time and place have always done—reimagine generational details to frame the personal in its largest, most revelatory context.

When I spoke with Cunningham in preparation for his visit to the Loft, he seemed invigorated by the fact that, instead of feeling intimidated, the surprise of winning the Pulitzer provided him with a way to walk through the acclaim toward his next work.

MICHAEL CUNNINGHAM: What I, of course, have to battle is this sense of having something to live up to. If I learned anything from the completely unexpected success of *The Hours,* it is that you might as well write what you want because you can't possibly know what the world is going to think.

Maybe the most unambiguously good thing about the way *The Hours* has been received is the implication that there's a sizable body of readers who will go with you. New York has this idea that if it's unorthodox and demands anything of readers—then forget it. Turns out that's not true.

Since the Pulitzer, many younger writers have said to me—not in so many words, but by implication—that they're so happy about the prize because *we* won. This great big machine, which ordinarily doesn't take a certain body of crackpots into its view at all, turned around on its big rusty wheels and saw not just my book but by implication a whole kind of book.

PATRICIA WEAVER FRANCISCO: What has the aftermath been like for you?

M.C.: My life is finally coming back to normal. I wasn't a completely innocent victim. Suddenly people are calling you up, saying, "Do you want to go to Brazil?" I've been a full-time *bon vivant*, and a no-time writer, for the last year.

P.W.F.: Are you working on something new at this point?

M.C.: Yes, I'm at the very beginning. What I can say is that it's made up of three novellas and three dreams. The novellas are subtly linked—past, present, and future, each in a genre: a horror story, a lurid romance, and a science fiction-story.

P.W.F.: Very wild—where did this come from?

M.C.: Who knows? It probably originated in the fact that as a gay man who writes about the biggest world I can, using everything I know, I've dealt with the question of gay books versus regular books for as long as I've been writing. It's made me think about categories, about the fact that some of the most interesting writers working today are people like Ursula Le Guin and, in particular, Samuel Delany, who is not at all known.

I grew up on Ray Bradbury and Robert Heinlein. I learned a great deal from them about magic and the range of possibility and the fact that you don't really need to stick to observable reality. I took that in a different direction, but I've never thought of my books as strictly naturalistic even though they obey observable laws of physics.

P. W. F.: When I was reading *The Hours,* I had absolutely no need for plot. I was a perfectly happy reader, moment to moment. Then it began to work on that level as well. *Flesh and Blood,* in particular, has a story that drives you to stay up all night. You know how to push characters into dramatic corners, which is one of the great pleasures of reading.

M. C.: Absolutely. I probably learned that from Heinlein and Bradbury as much as I learned it from anybody.

P. W. F.: Your characters are so marked by trouble, often not of their own making. It's the deeply human moments and your sensitivity to the shades of inner life that make all the difference for your characters—for their survival.

M. C.: It's something I tell my students—that every character in any novel, no matter how minor, is visiting your novel from a novel of his or her own that is wholly devoted to the passion, comedy, and tragedy of that person, while maybe only in your novel long enough to sell a newspaper.

P. W. F.: Yes, both men and women get their full inner life.

M. C.: The question of being a man and writing convincingly from a woman's point of view is probably the most common question I'm asked. The only honest answer is to kind of look blank, shrug, and say, "I don't know. Beats me."

P. W. F.: That's probably the honest answer, but I bet you have another one.

M. C.: I have a slightly more elaborate version. It's mysterious to me, but there are characters I can get and characters I cannot, and that question doesn't seem to have a great deal to do with gender.

P. W. F.: Can you say which characters you can't get?

M. C.: In terms of larger categories, I can't write about characters who aren't white. I tried and I couldn't do it in a way that didn't feel like the well-intended, well-researched attempts of a white guy. But beyond that there are some people whose desires and lives are sufficiently strange to me that I can't quite tune them in.

P.W.F.: I want to ask you about teaching since that's part of what you'll be doing at the Loft. What do you look for in your work with students?

M.C.: All I'm really trying to do is to help whomever I find in front of me to write the story that only he or she could write—to find what's most magic and strange and unprecedented in him- or herself. I am very much aware that we already have enough stories, more than anybody can read. They're just stacked like cordwood. What we need is a brand-new way of looking at the world that changes it, that advances it.

You would imagine that a beginning writer would be at his or her most fearless. It's almost always the reverse. You're afraid that you're deluding yourself, that you're just a figment of your own imagination, another of the ten million that wanted to write, so you tend to write what you think people will want, to duplicate what you see in front of you. I want my students to emerge a little less fearful—willing to take the risk and write the odd thing.

P.W.F.: Do you remember how you came to that yourself? Was it a process of working your way toward the material that had your name on it?

M.C.: Very much. You can't possibly look back on your life and know whether or not you wasted time. But I suspect I wasted at least some time trying to write a *New Yorker* story—thinking that what I cared about or knew about wasn't sufficiently interesting.

P.W.F.: In *Flesh and Blood*, I felt you were writing my life, generationally.

M.C.: That is one of my wildest hopes—that I can take my particular experience and use it to write about people's lives in a way that wakes them up to larger life. One of the things that has been so satisfying about the success of *The Hours* is that it simply takes the characters' sexuality as a given, and we move on from there. I have to say I could probably go my whole life without reading another coming-out story—unless it was fabulous and transformed—which, of course, somebody is probably writing right this second.

P. W. F.: Well, *you* have written it. You've brought us the coming-of-age story, something that literature has thrived on always, for characters both gay and straight. One final question: Isn't there a movie?

M. C.: Well, are you sitting down? David Hare did the screenplay. Now here's the cast: Meryl Streep as Clarissa, Nicole Kidman as Virginia—an odd choice, but maybe she'll be great. Julianne Moore as Laura Brown, Ed Harris as Richard, Miranda Richardson as Vanessa, Alison Janney—she's playing Sally—and Claire Danes is the daughter.

They shot exteriors in New York a few weeks ago, and—get this—I went and met Meryl, and I'm in it—I've got a cameo. I bump into Meryl on the street, and she says, "Are you coming to my party?" And I say, "I am. I wouldn't miss it."

Memoir: Don't Bite Off
the Whole Elephant at Once

LAURA FLYNN

I always intended to write—novels perhaps, or, after living overseas for five years, a book about that. But never a childhood memoir. My childhood with my mother, who suffers from severe mental illness, felt too dark, too shrouded in secrecy, and just too creepy for me, or potential readers, to face. A door cracked open in my midthirties when I started thinking about the doll games my sisters and I had played when we were children. The stories and the beauty of the imaginative world we'd created to shield ourselves from the chaos around us came back to me in a flood. Suddenly my childhood looked less stark. Just as those stories carried me through childhood, they opened the door to writing about it.

I toyed briefly with the notion of writing a novel, which seemed safer and less restricting. But I quickly realized that it was the process of working with memory itself that interested me—of letting the remembered image unfold into a scene, and finding patterns inherent in real events. Perhaps every writer is pulled between the twin tides of memory and imagination—and some of us end up as memoirists because memory has a stronger hold. Then, too, faced with a difficult personal history, the faithfulness of documentary truth felt important.

Almost as soon as I began to write, I began to fret about how my family would react. Joyce supposedly said to be a writer you have to be willing to kill your own grandmother. I wasn't. No contest. How many of us can actually sustain such ruthless self-importance about our work?

My family's reactions were mixed. My father was excited because he'd always felt I should write. He shared his memories freely with me. But even long after I'd made it clear that I was writing a memoir, he'd end our conversations with a nervous, "But you're fictionalizing some

of this, aren't you?" My younger sister, with characteristic fearless-
ness, sent a letter giving me carte blanche to write anything I wanted.
My stepmother succinctly conveyed her ambivalence by handing me
a *Peanuts* cartoon in which Snoopy is at the typewriter. Lucy walks
up and says, "Don't you dare write about me." In the next frame, she
storms back and adds, "But don't you dare leave me out."

My older sister was the one I most worried about. She's a very
private person, and she's held the events of our childhood close. I de-
layed telling her I was working on a memoir about our childhood for
months, maybe even a year, even though we talked two to three times
a week. It seemed unimaginable then that she would ever accept this
book, and yet I was already fully committed to writing it. Last winter,
as the publication date for the book approached, she was the one col-
lecting bookstore contacts to help me set up readings. How did that
happen?

When I started writing, I was so on fire with the idea I was sure
it would only take me six months to write—it took closer to six years.
The long time frame may have helped. My family had plenty of time
to get used to the idea. We had many conversations about the past,
some occasioned by the fact that I was writing. Also, we all had time
to grow up a little bit more.

I didn't share many early drafts with my family, though. I wanted
to protect myself from that pressure until I was very sure of my words.
Before sending the book to agents, I sent them each the manuscript.
Then I held my breath until I heard back.

They all reported that it was a difficult read—though they whizzed
through it. The early sections of the memoir, which recounted my
parents' courtship, particularly affected my father. I thought of this as
the "happy part" of the book, and I hadn't foreseen how painful the
remembrance of what had been lost would be for him. He reported
with some pride that he'd figured out how to get through it: He read
in front of the television with a football game on mute. "Whenever
it gets to be too much, I just look up and watch the game for a few
minutes."

I was prepared to make changes if any of them truly objected to
something in the memoir. No one did. I have a theory—for which I

have absolutely no proof—that memoirs about families where there was no obvious trouble may ruffle more feathers than the ones about families who have come through the vale. In families where there's been trouble, feathers are already ruffled. No one is carrying a pristine image of the past that might be shattered. The thing I hung on to as I wrote was that they'd already lived through this. Could reading a book about it possibly be worse?

For my sisters, in the end, it was not their own reading of the book but the readings of others that most reassured them. Their husbands both loved it—even found humor in places, something my sisters had a hard time seeing. More than that, the book elicited not horror or disgust at the way we had lived as children, but admiration for the way we survived.

Does that mean that my sisters are glad I wrote it? It may be too soon to say, and in all honesty that's not a question I've yet had the courage to ask.

Bottom line: If you are determined to write about your family, you will probably do it even if they object. My advice is don't bite off the whole elephant at once. Don't imagine that you have to resolve every sticky issue before you begin—any more than you need to know the ending or the structure of the whole before you sit down to write. Some people will say you must banish your loved ones from your thoughts to avoid censoring yourself. That's a nice goal, but more likely you will have to struggle with them on the page in much the same way that you struggle with them in real life. A constant back and forth, a phone call here to check a fact, a white lie there about what you are really up to. But then they know you so well; they will probably call you on your shit. And always, in life and on the page, you'll keep acting out, and struggling against, the roles and patterns you've been etching into each other's brains over a lifetime. In fact, the visceral sense of that struggle is what will make the writing come alive.

Editing the *View*

ELLEN HAWLEY

A friend with a gift for raising uncomfortable and important questions raised the following one with me recently: Do I, in editing *A View from the Loft,* close off free discussion and push contributors and potential contributors away? The question led me to think long and hard about editing, and since I was in the midst of assembling a series of articles on editing and being edited, it also led to this article.

I can't answer the question directly, but I can say a bit about editing in general and editing the *View* specifically, and I can open the question up to you, the *View*'s readers, and hope that you will respond.

Relations between editors and writers are famously uneasy, although Minnesota being what it is, the problem is seldom raised directly. One (non-Minnesota) editor described his ideal writer as a person who dropped off a manuscript and then went out and got hit by a truck; I'm sure the writers he edited could have made some equally clever comments if anyone had asked. But there's more to the relationship than a couple of good laughs and having someone to blame our troubles on—important as those are in our lives. I believe the relationship is valuable—or can be.

Selection is the first step in the editing process. What gets printed in the *View* and why? If you'll turn to page two and read the tiny print on the left side of the page, you'll find a sentence that says the *View* is "a forum for the exchange of information and opinion." I take that policy seriously. I don't have to agree with an article to print it; I don't even have to like it. I do have to be convinced that it makes its point well and that it speaks to some segment of the *View*'s diverse readership, regardless of whether it speaks to entertain, convince, challenge, argue, or inform.

The contents of the *View* break down into several categories, including articles about writing, letters to the editor, book recommendations, and contributions to the ViewPoint column. The last three categories are the easiest places to break into the *View*. I edit them least and demand less in terms of form and style, although I appreciate these when I find them.

I'm more selective about articles. In terms of content, I aim for many kinds of diversity: of race, culture, gender, age, and sexual orientation, but also of genre, experience level, topic, aesthetic, tone—the list goes on. I try to keep the pages of the *View* open to newer writers and at the same time set a standard that will allow it to hold its readers. All of this is a balancing act I never expect to succeed at completely, especially given the limits of the *View*'s size and budget, but I do hope to keep the *View*'s pages open and alive.

I don't receive a lot of unsolicited articles. I assume that's because not as many writers are interested in writing about writing as are interested in writing about the world beyond the limits of the craft. But opening the mail and finding a good piece of writing that I didn't expect to receive is one of the joys of working as an editor. And if it's by someone I've never heard of, the pleasure is even greater—I feel like I've made a discovery.

The most common reason I turn articles down is that they don't move from specific experience (or from lyrical description) to some larger point. They don't move beyond the writer to speak to the reader. A typical one might spend four pages recounting, in exquisite detail, the impact a high-school English teacher had on the writer's development and psyche and then devote two paragraphs to some related issue about writing—how important it is that writers teach in high schools, for example. As a reader, I come away believing that those final (or opening) paragraphs were an afterthought, added long after the body of the essay was written, when the author belatedly asked him- or herself, *Why am I sending this to the* View, *anyway?* The article is, essentially, a bit of memoir with an idea tacked on to justify sending it to me rather than to a magazine that publishes memoir and creative nonfiction.

I don't believe editors serve writers well unless they also serve readers by putting out the best publication they can. That sometimes means turning articles down; it also means challenging writers to do their best work.

Once I accept an article, I edit it and send a copy to the author for his or her approval. This sounds simple, but it's not. It's where the process gets complicated.

What am I trying to do when I make changes in someone else's writing? The easy answer is that I'm trying to make it better, but that only leads to the next question: What do I mean by "better"? Ideally, it means that I'm making the article clearer; pointing out confusing arguments and lapses in its logic; strengthening the language and the flow; showing the writer at his or her best. A writer told me once that his edited article felt like what he'd have written if he'd taken three more days with it. It's the best compliment I ever hope to receive on my editing. In an ideal world, that's what I'd do all the time: immerse myself in the voice and opinions of each writer so thoroughly that the edited copy would read like what the writer would have done if he or she had taken three more days with it.

Do I need to tell you that we don't live in an ideal world? Writers have said less flattering things about what I've done to their work. You'll have to forgive me if I don't quote them.

Many things can get in my way when I try to blend into someone else's voice and opinions. Sometimes it's hard to find the line between making the writer sound better and making the writer sound—well, more like me. Maybe I'm suggesting a contraction here because it improves the rhythm; on the other hand, maybe the rhythm's fine and I want a contraction because I happen to like contractions. Maybe I'm changing this phrase because it's awkward, but maybe my ear (trained in this region, that class, the other ethnic group and set of schools) hasn't learned to hear its particular music.

It's even harder to find that line when the author's voice is obscured by a layer of awkwardness. Some writers aren't in control of their grammar, and some use words that don't carry quite the right meaning. Some writers don't sound quite like themselves when they write. Even if I don't know what they actually sound like, I can tell that what I have in my hand isn't it. So I don't know what I'm trying to blend myself in with.

It's also difficult to edit an article when I disagree with the author or dislike the tone. I have trouble knowing whether I'm looking at a flaw in the argument or am just annoyed by what the writer's saying; whether my attention's wandering because the article's repetitious or because the topic isn't one I care about personally, although I believe some segment of the *View*'s readers will love it. I probably demand less of articles I disagree with; it keeps me from stifling them altogether.

All of this is about power: The editor has power to accept, reject, and change. With that as a foundation, how can writers and editors *not* be uneasy with each other?

I try to be responsible about that power; I'm not the one to judge whether I succeed. I try to remember that being the editor doesn't necessarily make me right, and that even if I'm right about a problem, the solution I propose isn't the only one possible. I invite the writers whose work I edit to let me know if any of the changes I've proposed don't feel right to them, and what they propose in response is often better than my suggestion was.

But I don't believe that abdicating that power entirely would lead writers and readers to a better world. In spite of all the tensions and difficulties, editors have their value.

I'm writing here as an editor, but I've been on both sides of the relationship, and I've seen my writing edited both by good editors and by a few people with tin ears.

The first time anyone edited my work, it came back full of deletions and new punctuation; whole sentences had been inserted, making transitions where I hadn't seen a need for them. Looking at all those marks on my manuscript, I felt incompetent, miserable, and all-around dumb, and it didn't make me any happier to know that the editor—this miserable excuse for a human being—had improved the damned thing. But once I pieced myself back together, I had to admit that the experience had helped me write better. It let me see through someone else's eyes—the eyes of a reader—what I had actually written and what more could be done with it.

And that's why editors exist: because as writers we're often too close to see what we've actually written; we tend to see what we *wanted* to write. An editor can come in as an outsider, with less emotional investment, and can see problems, possibilities, awkward spots, gaps in our logic. I can enter someone else's writing and cut my way through tangles that I'd never be able to see—never mind fix—in my own writing.

Which is why, as the editor and entire staff of the *View*, I make a point of not writing for it: I can't edit my own work well, and I'm the wrong person to judge whether my work should be published or not. This article is an exception, and I asked two writers whose work I've edited in the past to comment on an early draft of it. They weren't in a position to accept or reject it, so the process wasn't the same as submitting it to another publication, but they were able to break the article open for me when the parts became locked into place too early, and they raised questions I hadn't thought to address.

I've never found a way to take the sting out of being edited, and the responses of writers I've worked with run the gamut. Some are interested primarily in putting ideas on the page and love to have someone else involved with the actual words. Some care passionately about the words but appreciate—or at least tolerate—an editor's involvement if the editor has a good ear; they reenter their writing and sift through the proposed changes, accepting some, rejecting others, rewriting where they now see weaknesses, adding an extra page where I hadn't thought to ask for an addition. Others consider editing an affront; they defend every word and comma. I think they lock themselves out of a useful relationship, but the creative process is full of quirks, and maybe they're doing what they need to do to keep themselves writing. I'd prefer to know ahead of time that they won't accept any editing, or will accept only limited editing, so I could consider their work on that basis, but they'd be taking a risk—I'm not sure how many editors would read on if they saw that in a cover letter.

And here we return to the original question. The *View* exists to serve writers, as both readers of and contributors to the magazine. Ideally, its selection and editing processes would also serve writers rather than damage them or lock them out. I would welcome comments on how the *View* has fulfilled its mission, and suggestions on how it could do it better. I'll publish as many of these as possible.

Ten Questions I've Been Asked about Picture Books

JOHN COY

"As I envision the creative process, I do not identify with the mother giving birth but with the child struggling to be born."
—Alice Miller

Why do you write picture books?

Let me answer a question with a question: What books have had the most significant impact on your life? How often have you read them? Now think about your favorite picture books and how many times you read them when you were a child.

Picture books are designed to engage the senses of both adults and children. They explore mood, plot, and character with a minimum of words, blending text and pictures seamlessly to evoke dreamlike images or middle-of-the-day realism.

I am intrigued by the simplicity of picture-book text. I am drawn to the challenge of distilling ideas and emotions to essentials. Remembering the sights, smells, thoughts, and feelings of my childhood provides material, and I can write stories now that I would have liked to hear as a boy.

What ages do you write for?

All ages. Picture books are designed to be read by adults to children. Consequently, the text should engage readers and listeners of all ages. This requires that I write from the adult and child parts of myself, and it is gratifying to make a book that people of different ages can share together. Some adults think that picture books are only for young readers. But in school residencies, I read picture books to students of all ages. Ninth graders are as enchanted as kindergartners.

Do you pick your illustrator?

No, the illustrator is usually selected by the publisher, who decides what art style will work best with the text. An established illustrator is often paired with a new writer. The writer seldom has any direct communication with the illustrator while the book is being created. The thinking is that the illustrator was not involved in the writer's creative process and that the illustrator should have the same freedom. Writers usually see the art toward the end of the process and can then make suggestions on omissions or errors of fact.

Do picture books examine serious subjects?

Yes. The developmental needs of children are serious, and picture books explore many difficult issues. For example, *Sweet Clara and the Freedom Quilt*, by Deborah Hopkinson, illustrated by James Ransome, details a girl's experience of slavery. *Daddy and Me*, photographs and words by Jeanne Moutoussamy-Ashe, describes the relationship between Arthur Ashe and his daughter, Camera, as he lives with AIDS. *Smoky Night*, awarded this year's Caldecott medal, examines what a riot looks like to a young child. Exposure to these issues provides readers with new understanding of the world.

How long does it take to make a picture book?

It varies. My first picture book, *Night Driving*, has taken five years. I started the story in a Loft class and worked on it for two years before sending it to five publishers. In July of 1992, an editor from Henry Holt called to say they wanted to publish it. Various artists were contacted before Peter McConkey agreed to illustrate it. Last fall, I finished text revisions, and the book will be in the stores in the fall of 1996. This is not an unusual time line—picture-book publishing moves at a glacial pace.

Do you write other things?

Yes. Some picture-book writers write exclusively picture books. Others write biographies, poetry, and novels. Implicit in this question can be the belief that writing other things is real writing and writing picture books is not. Again, this says less about picture-book writing than about how we value children and our own childhoods.

How many hours a week do you spend writing?

It depends. Each writer determines his or her process. Some weeks I spend many hours with pen and paper or at the computer. Others I spend very few. In the middle of a story, I am as apt to get an idea when I am playing basketball as when I am sitting at my desk. For me, movement is an essential element of writing. Doing yoga or walking the river provides the calm I need for ideas to emerge. Discovering one's creative process and supporting that process are far more important to me than keeping track of specific hours.

Are you in a writing group?

Yes. I am in a writers' group that concentrates on picture books. We read our stories, listen, and critique. Critiquing honestly and sensitively is as difficult, I think, as writing well. The reactions of people I trust are essential to me when I revise a story. A writing group can be a place to exchange information about editors and publishers and to express fears and celebrate successes.

Do you make a lot of money?

Compared to a tinsmith in Bangladesh, yes. Compared to my daughter's orthodontist, no. First picture books usually have an advance against royalties of two to three thousand. Royalties for the writer are generally five percent of sales. This is doubled if the writer also illustrates. The picture-book writers I know write because they love to write. They have made writing their priority. They find other jobs—like picking strawberries, or sanding floors, or teaching—to support their writing.

I've always wanted to write a picture book. What do I do?

Begin. Explore excellent bookstores. Wander into the picture book section and sit and read and look at pictures. If you are in the Twin Cities, attend the Saturday Children's Corner at The Hungry Mind, where writers and performers read picture books. Visit a store that specializes in picture books. Take a class. Buy a picture book for a child. Buy one for yourself. Start writing your stories. For most of us, picture books were our introduction to the world of literature. Welcome home.

Why YA?

PETE HAUTMAN

Seven years ago I had made a good, solid start in my career as a novelist. I had published two successful crime novels (*Drawing Dead* and *Short Money*) and had three more under contract.

I was about as interested in writing for teens as I was in learning to play the accordion. I did not know what the initials YA stood for, and I had no interest in revisiting my adolescence. I was a grown-up guy with grown-up concerns. Why would I want to write for kids? But things change.

For some years I had been playing around with an idea for a book based on a recurring childhood dream. In the dream, I discovered a small door at the back of a large, cluttered closet in my grandparents' Minneapolis home. The tiny door would lead to forgotten rooms and spaces. I might find myself in a dusty, dead, forgotten world. Or there would be a party going on, a celebration of an anniversary or a birthday. Once in a while I would encounter old friends, lost toys, or dead pets come to life. Most of the dreams were pleasant, but sometimes I would wake up with my heart hammering and cold sweat soaking the sheets.

The story I began to work on was about the adventures of a man who passed through this dream door and found himself transported into the past. It was to be a serious adult sci-fi/fantasy epic. But for some reason, the story wasn't working. I expanded it, I cut it back, I rewrote, I added and deleted characters, but the tale simply did not ring true.

I kept going back to the dream, trying to remember how it felt, trying to recapture some of its magic. Finally, it hit me that the magic I was seeking was magic seen through adolescent eyes. Suddenly I knew who I was writing for, and what I had to do to make the story work. It was a teenage dream. I changed my protagonist, Jack Lund, from a thirty-year-old man into a fifteen-year-old boy—a boy the same age I was when I first had the dream. I wished Jack Lund the best of luck and sent him through the doorway.

Jack's story, I quickly learned, was the story of a boy who is thrust into quasi adulthood by the sudden and brutal death of his mother. It was completely unlike anything I had written previously. It was dark, serious, complex, and tragic. The book, titled *Mr. Was,* was not written for children. Nor for teenagers. Nor for adults.

It was written for the kid I used to be: a boy caught between the Hardy Boys and *The Brothers Karamazov.* I wanted to write a story that was both fantastic and real, false and true, futuristic and historical, complex and fast-paced. The final result turned out to be more violent and intense than I expected.

I was advised by several writer friends to sell *Mr. Was* as an "adult" novel. They said it was too complex for younger readers. But I used to *be* a younger reader, and the way I remember it, complexity was not an issue. I'd pick up any book that promised to take me someplace new. I remember reading novels by Ian Fleming and Ayn Rand and J.R.R. Tolkien and J.D. Salinger and John Steinbeck and Mickey Spillane all in the same summer, and every time thinking I'd just read the greatest book ever written. I knew there were other kids out there who felt the same.

Mr. Was was published in 1996 by Simon and Schuster Books for Young Readers. I had no plans to write another YA book. I figured that *Mr. Was* was a fluke—I'd been forced to use a young protagonist to make my story work, it had been marketed as a YA novel, and that was that.

But I was wrong.

Shortly after *Mr. Was* was published, I began work on another idea, the story of an expert card player who was becoming consumed by his passion for poker. I wanted to write a story about a gambling addict, but not your usual gamble-away-the-family-farm addict. My addict would be a *winner.* The story would be a realistic, gritty inside look at the gambling subculture. It would be about a guy who could not save himself from his addiction because, well, his habit produced a positive cash flow.

After investing a few hundred hours at the poker table, and after writing and discarding several dozen pages, it occurred to me that, if I made my protagonist about thirty years younger. . . . So I gave it a try, and the story came together like magic. I found myself writing another YA novel.

Stone Cold was published in 1998. It's the story of a boy who gets involved in a small-stakes poker game and finds out that he has a natural talent for the game. The more he plays, the more he wins. It's every gambler's fantasy.

By the time I finished *Stone Cold,* I had been thinking a lot about writing for teenagers. What is a YA novel, anyway? *Mr. Was* and *Stone Cold,* on the surface, seemed about as much alike as King Kong and asparagus.

Mr. Was is about a boy whose mother is murdered. The boy must go back through time and relive his entire adult life waiting for the moment to occur when he might be able to prevent her death. It is a sci-fi/mystery/romance/adventure that spans seven decades of its protagonist's life. It employs a labyrinthine plot with enough violence to fill an hour of network TV programming.

Stone Cold is about a boy who is drawn into the weird world of high-stakes gambling and who must literally disguise himself as an adult to pursue his newfound obsession. It's a straightforward, contemporary account of one summer in the life of a fifteen-year-old gambling addict.

But these books *did* have something in common beyond the name of the author. They possessed a quality shared with great books such as *Huckleberry Finn* and lesser books such as the Hardy Boys mysteries: they were stories about adolescents who are suddenly thrust into adult roles.

The YA novel is often defined as a coming-of-age story. But most novels written for younger readers are simple adventure stories or mysteries or horror stories or protracted jokes. (This includes virtually all of the series books, because how many times can the same characters come of age?) But the truly memorable stories, the ones that stick with you for years—*To Kill a Mockingbird, Treasure Island, The Catcher in the Rye, The Chocolate War, A Tree Grows in Brooklyn*—these stories all tell us about a young person crossing a bridge from one set of challenges to another, even more difficult set of problems. They address the greatest mystery of our teenage years, and that is, simply: What does it mean to be an adult?

I won't say that any YA novel can answer that question. They certainly didn't answer all of *my* adolescent questions. But when I think back on the books that really affected me, books that I still remember vividly—where I was when I read them, the names of the characters, the plot, specific scenes—*those* were books I read as a young adult.

Ages nine through sixteen were my personal Golden Age of reading. Each book was an adventure to be embraced, to be entered fully and completely without the self-conscious, hypercritical, and jaded attitudes of the typical adult reader. The more I thought about it, the more I liked the idea of writing for such an audience.

So I decided to write another YA novel. And another. And I'll probably keep writing them for as long as I can remember what it was like to stay up all night reading the greatest book ever written.

A View from a Slam

BAO PHI

What can you do in three minutes? Find your keys and run to the bus stop? Punch your code and all the necessary buttons to get money out of your ATM? Pick a tape to put into your car stereo or Walkman?

As a poet competing in a slam, you have three minutes and a grace period of ten seconds for transcendence.

On the Titanic Lounge stage in Kieran's Irish Pub in downtown Minneapolis, home of Minnesota's official National Poetry Slam team, poets and performers and storytellers yell and whisper, shake their arms and sway, close their eyes and work it work it work it baby until hopefully something like a poem or story comes out. Some have slammed for years. Others have never read a poem to anyone besides maybe a couple of friends. Poets represent South side, North side, Saint Paul, Rochester, Saint Cloud. Poems are carried in the head and the heart, in tasteful self-decorated hand-bound journals, on folded pieces of paper. The audience is filled with artistic boho scenesters, drunk-ass business people, proud mothers, college students, dishwashers. We stack onto each other like stanzas.

The sign-up sheet is first come first serve, up to twenty-five poets per night. The names are then written on small pieces of paper and thrown into a bowl or hat. Five judges, one scorekeeper, and one timekeeper are randomly selected from the audience. The slammaster proceeds to go over the rules and make an ass out of him- or herself in the pathetic attempt to draw laughter from a crowd not yet drunk. Then names are drawn and it's time to shine.

When your name is drawn, you have up to three minutes and a grace period of ten seconds to deliver one original piece. No props, no costumes, no musical accompaniment. The clock starts as soon as you say anything to the audience. You get penalized .5 points for every

ten seconds you go over. The judges then hold aloft a score from 0.0
to 10.0, the highest and lowest scores are dropped, the three remaining scores are added up, time penalties are deducted, and you have a
score.

From Grand Slam Champion of Minnesota to the National Slam

The top fifteen proceed to round two. The top five move on to the
money round. These players also qualify for the Grand Slam, where
the five winners from each of the six regular slams compete for the
big money and the title of Grand Slam Champion of Minnesota.
And the top two from each slam earn a spot to compete in a slam
to decide which five poets will represent Minnesota at the National
Poetry Slam.

The rules at Kieran's strictly follow the guidelines set forth by
National Poetry Slam Inc. However, not every slam you wander into
is guaranteed to be the same, national contender or otherwise. At the
Nuyorican Poets Cafe, for example, there is no one keeping time: you're
just asked to be "reasonable." And there are other slams going on in
Minnesota with their own particularities: Sentwali Entertainment
recently launched its slam, hosted by Edupoetic Enterbrainment, at
Jazzville and Chang O'Hara's. There were a couple of slams organized
by Asian American Renaissance. There's probably a couple of slams
going on right now at various schools and universities. But Kieran's
Season of the Slam, taking place on the second Tuesday of every
month from September to March (except February's Erotica Slam,
which is always on Valentine's Day), is so far the only Minnesota slam
to form a national team.

Think of the National Slam as a magnification of a regular slam,
where teams and individuals from all over America come to compete
and meet. The Nationals take place in a different city each year, voted
on by slammasters who represent each team. Slam 2000 will take place
in Rhode Island, 2001 in Seattle. And it is expected that the dysfunc-
tional and crazy family circus will make its way to Minneapolis/Saint
Paul in 2002. Diego Vásquez, former Minnesota Slammaster, is heading up a coalition to spearhead this mammoth endeavor.

The Places, the People

SlamMN started as a Valentine's Day slam at the Mendota Saloon in 1994. Diego Vásquez, Davida Adedjuoma, Deb Stein, and Jaime Meyer were the original ciphers who agreed to front the prize money if the door didn't bring in enough cream. The event was so successful that people demanded another VD slam. Diego, looking for a venue, met Patrick O'Donnell, artistic director and founder of the Titanic Players, who in turn introduced him to Kieran. After Diego explained to him what a slam was, Kieran immediately agreed to offer the space. He also put it upon himself to cover all the prize money so no one would have to pay to get through the door. But he had one question: "Can't you do more than one of these a year?"

So the Season of the Slam was born, with Diego presiding as slammaster. And in 1998, with help from Tom Borrup of Intermedia Arts, Carolyn Holbrook of SASE, ample coverage by Mary Anne Grossmann of the *Pioneer Press,* and of course organizational work and funding by Diego and Kieran, Minnesota sent a slam team to the Nationals for the first time. Team SlamMN 98 was comprised of Diego Vásquez, Patrick McKinnon, Loren Niemi, Kate Peterson, and me. Last year, the posse, comprised of Diego, Matthew Conley, Megan McInerny, John Troyer, Toby Folwick, and I, made it to the semifinals in Chicago.

Success and the Single Slammer

What makes a successful slammer? Who knows. There have been a lot of theories, griping, whining, and debates about what or who "does well" at a slam. With varying degrees of success, there have been sonnets, spontaneous storytelling, hip-hop-laced parables, sestinas, dramatic monologues, and self-absorbed vocal masturbations about Foucault, sex, sewing machines, lobsters, racial injustice, -isms, love, work, pots and pans, monkeys on crack, traffic. Is there such a thing as a "slam poet" aesthetic? Speaking personally, I have committed to and honed my steezo for the past nine years, long before I knew slams existed. I grew up with hip-hop, listened to the Last Poets and Gil Scott Heron, read and heard Langston and Shange, Troupe and Inada,

Alexie and Okita, Harjo and Perdomo, Hagedorn and Mirikitani, Wong and Whitman.

Written v. Spoken

Do poems performed at a slam belong on the stage and not the page? If I may trespass with metaphor, I see each poem as a person: you can stay cooped up on the page all day, but you'll go crazy if you don't get out and dance once in a while. The written poem is undeniably important, but it is also imperative to recognize that oral traditions of storytelling and poetry predate written literature. Do people write differently or choose specific poems because they know they will do better in front of an audience? Who knows. Who can speak for every-body? I think it's both crazy and soulless to change who you are and what you do in order to succeed in a slam or, ahem, get published in a major literary magazine. But that doesn't mean some people won't go that route.

Perhaps the biggest saving grace of slams is that you can try it for yourself and make your own opinion. You can walk in through those doors, sign up to compete or volunteer to be a judge. You can walk up to a poet who really moved you and buy her or him a beer and a plate of fries. Boo the judges' decisions, eavesdrop on couples who are debating whether or not they like certain poems, vow never to come back again, fall in love. Slams are as messy, complicated, redeeming, confusing, and beautiful as each and every one of us.

On Tour

SHANNON OLSON

$\mathbf{M}$y editor gave me a fabulous piece of advice before I went on tour for my first novel, *Welcome to My Planet*. She told me that people would ask extremely personal questions and that I should pretend I was a presidential candidate and answer questions by not answering them, by talking, instead, about whatever I wanted to talk about.

I wish I had remembered more often to do this.

Perhaps it's the sleep deprivation you experience on tour, or perhaps it's my midwestern upbringing, but I kept feeling a compulsion toward earnestness. Answering questions about the book was further complicated by the fact that I'd given the narrator my name, and I'd used my mother's name, "Flo," for the mother in the book. It was the perfect mom name. I couldn't think of a better one.

The first leg of my tour was on the West Coast. I'd been in Seattle, Portland, and San Francisco the first three days, and had been up at 4 a.m. each day to catch flights. I was dehydrated, sniffling from the cold I was getting, and wearing my glasses when I got off the plane in Los Angeles at 8 a.m. My escort was late picking me up, she explained, because there was a rattlesnake in her home that morning and she was afraid it would eat her cats. As she briskly navigated the freeway traffic, she recounted her youth as a rock 'n' roll groupie (she had once slept with Don Henley), her graduate work in English, and the fight she and her boyfriend had had the night before. "You can ignore me if you need to sleep," she said. "Some authors do that. I'm used to it."

As we pulled into the cable studio's parking lot, she said, "I'm going to drop you off so you can put on some makeup. This is an internationally syndicated show. You do know that, don't you?"

I didn't know that, so I went right to the bathroom, where I slapped on some makeup, stuck in my contacts, and brushed my teeth. Knowing I would be going straight to the studio, I'd worn a black skirt and a black shirt, hoping that if I spilled anything on myself it wouldn't show. I hadn't anticipated toothpaste, which I was rubbing off my shirt when the escort knocked and told me it was almost time to go on the air.

I waited outside the green room, which was filled with a noisy family I'd also run into in Portland. The wife had written a book about establishing healthy family dynamics, and we'd apparently been following each other down the coast on the interview circuit. She'd brought her entire family along for the tour, and here in Los Angeles, as in Portland, they were fighting.

The show's host came in to get me wearing full pancake makeup, and she sat me in a chair on the set. While the technicians adjusted the lights, she pulled out a copy of my book with so many Post-it notes sticking out the edges, it looked like a sailing regatta.

I'd been told that the host carefully chose the books she would cover and that she read each one several times. "So," she said to me, "your narrator had breast reduction surgery. Did you have breast reduction surgery? Because my niece should have it. She's very large. And uneven."

Then we were on the air, and the host kept surprising me with her guerrilla interview tactics. "The narrator makes herself subservient to her ex-boyfriend," she said.

"I hadn't thought of it exactly as subservient," I said. "There's definitely an imbalance of pow—"

"Essentially," she continued—I noticed after a while that she would keep talking if she didn't like my answer—"she is date-raped by him, is that right?"

"Yes," I said.

"That must have been painful," she said, "for you." She was blinking at me intently under the hot lights.

I once heard Joyce Carol Oates say that as a novelist, she's like a bird, taking bits from here and there to build a nest, some material from her life, some from other people's stories. I explained to the host that the ex-boyfriend in the book, whom I hadn't given a name, sort of symbolized the bad choices many women make while dating in their twenties. The kind of bad boy many of us wind up with along the way, and learn to avoid. That he illustrated the narrator's inability to stand up for herself.

"I'd like you to read a selection for me," the host said. And then she asked me to read from a flagged page, a passage in which the narrator looks to the heavens and asks her grandmothers for advice, to send some sign. Was she doing all right? Or was it too late? Had she already made too many mistakes along the way?

When I got done reading, the host looked at me and said, "I think if your grandmothers were here, they'd give you a B plus."

After the interview, my media escort told me not to wear black again. That against the set's black curtain, I had looked like a startled, floating head.

My editor and I had talked about using the interview and postreading questions as a kind of "teachable moment." Writers understand how fine the line between fiction and nonfiction can be—that every piece of writing is in some way autobiographical and in some way fiction, because it's infused by what matters most to the writer and crafted to tell a story a certain way. Memoirists lie all the time without meaning to. Fiction writers, especially first-time novelists, have been drawing from their own experience for years; they've just been making more of an effort to hide it. "By using your own name," my editor said, "you're just putting it out there."

In truth, the act of writing is so different from actually being on tour. I just hadn't thought about what it would be like to represent the book and have to explain my approach to it.

I had started the book in an MFA course in which we spent plenty of time trying to dissect the distinctions between genres. I had been thinking of the book at first as a kind of memoir in vignettes, though I had been taking factual liberties all along and didn't feel that stylistically the piece was memoir.

When the book went up for sale, editors read it as fiction. It was a relief to finally think of it as that. In the process of editing the book for publication, my editor and I cut out about a third of the original manuscript. I rewrote sections and created new characters. It was freeing to open up the manuscript to new possibilities. The end product was based on my experience, but it wasn't exactly my life.

But when people come to a reading, my publicist reminded me, they want to walk away with something more real than the book. When I think about it, that's why I go to readings, too.

Although it was easier for me to invent possibilities for my narrator using my own name, if I could do it all over again I might call her Julie or Dora. I might call Flo "Chardonnay," just for kicks. Audiences invariably ask me what my mom thinks about the book, and I tell them that she's working on her own retaliatory novel, *Get the Bleepity Bleep Off My Planet.*

Here in the Twin Cities, where my mother occasionally comes to my readings, people have asked her to sign their books. One young woman actually got down on her knees before my mother and kissed her on the hand, saying that she wished her own mother had been like Flo.

Someone always asks me if I ever got back together with Michael, the narrator's graduate-school boyfriend, and someone else always wants to know if I ever hooked up again with the kayaking guide. People's faces fall when I tell them that although I have been kayaking, our guide was an alcoholic Vietnam veteran, not the young hottie in the book, and that another woman on our trip had an affair with him while I slept alone in my tent.

When I begin a reading, I often tell the audience that for the next forty minutes, I'll be talking about myself in the third person, just like Bob Dole. Or I'll draw a comparison with one of my favorite episodes of *The Simpsons,* in which Leonard Nimoy guest stars and introduces the show by saying, "The story you are about to hear is true. And by true, I mean false."

But sometimes, after a while, I give up on trying to delineate the distinction between myself and the narrator. Having used my own name seems to draw a certain vulnerability from the audience that to me is really touching. Women my mother's age will talk about the complicated relationships they have with their daughters, and women my age will confess to extravagant shopping trips at Target, a particular vice of the narrator. One woman so identified with the narrator that she brought me a couple of cans of the narrator's favorite beverage—Diet Rite Raspberry soda. One of the cans was for Flo. A lovely middle-aged woman with a heavy smoker's cough told me that after they heard me read in Fort Wayne, Indiana, she and her mother could barely talk to one another. She wished her mother had given her the kind of advice that Flo gives Shannon. Then she told me that she thought I was pretty and she wished me the best of luck.

My publicist recently sent me a little pile of fan mail. One letter was addressed to "Author/Main Character Shannon Olson."

I'm not sure which one of us will write back.

The Book Group Phenomenon

FAITH SULLIVAN

"Literature is the last banquet between minds."
—Edna O'Brien

Where and when was it born, this book group phenomenon that has come galloping across the land? Well, of course, groups like Great Books existed long years ago, bringing a sort of Tupperware mentality to culture. But we're talking contemporary book groups—loosely knit cells of coworkers or neighbors, mothers and daughters, library patrons, church members, or just chums, women mostly, but sometimes men—who meet regularly to discuss a book they have all agreed to read. (Occasionally their commitment is astonishing, as in the case of a Saint Paul group that meets every Friday morning at 7 a.m.)

Today, bookstores, too, are bringing readers together. Even the national media have gotten into the act with the likes of Oprah on CBS television and Ray Suarez on National Public Radio.

Personal bias tells me that the movement began in northern climes, places like Saint Paul and Bangor and Helena, towns and villages where winter nights are long and folks gather around a toasty stove or a warm book.

Living in Southern California in the seventies, I heard no talk of book groups. But in 1982, I was thrilled when an LA friend asked me to join a group she'd organized. "Really?" I dithered ecstatically, as if I were being elected into the ranks of a rarified society of arts and letters.

At the first meeting, I knew only my friend Diane, whose children were schoolmates of my own. And during the next seven years, except for book group events, I rarely saw Madere, Janet, Louise, Anne, Pat, and Ursula (who later moved to Boston). But in 1989, when my husband and I returned to Minnesota to live, I was bereft. Beneath the ground surface of book discussion, our roots had grown entwined. In month after month of discussing novels, mostly, although memoir and biography also found their way onto our list, we had come to know one another nearly as well as sisters.

Discussing fiction may be as revealing as the analyst's couch, maybe more so because the participants have so little sense of self-revelation, so little apprehension about sharing attitudes and observations about what they have read. Closely guarded dreams and secret fears, as well as the moral and ethical principles of group members, had emerged, like lemon-juice writing when it is held to the heat. In moving back to Minnesota, I was leaving behind women whom I had come to love through our passionate discussions.

Back in the Midwest, I found that book groups were as common as creeping charlie. Within weeks of settling into our Minneapolis home, I had joined two.

The young couple from whom my husband and I purchased our home moved to Shorewood, and the wife called me not long afterward to say that she had joined a book group on her new block. They were reading my novel *The Cape Ann,* she explained. Would I consider sitting in at their next meeting?

Since then I have visited with countless groups, outstate and in Wisconsin, as well as in the Twin Cities. I have observed and been told that in groups made up of men, or men and women, more history and biography are read than in groups made up exclusively of women. Women seem to enjoy a book diet heavier on fiction and memoir. Sadly, poetry rarely finds its way onto any of the lists.

And how are selections made? All different ways. Some groups make a list months in advance, providing members an opportunity to read ahead. Others fly by the seat of their pants. Both methods work just fine, thank you, though the second can have its problems: Time and again, women confessed that at the end of the evening, as they gathered up purses and slipped into coats, someone would call out, "Oh m'gosh, what're we reading for next time?"

Most groups read only paperbacks. But one California group reads only hardcovers, afterward donating the books to worthy organizations.

The majority of groups have an official or unofficial record keeper who at year's end prints out a list of what the group has read. There in black-and-white is the evidence: "We didn't read a single biography!" or "No classics?!" With this accounting in hand, members may plan a more varied diet for the coming year. Or not.

Often when I sit in with a book group, I ask if they will share their past lists. What I've discovered is a mix of classics (Jane Austen, Balzac, Hawthorne, or Willa Cather) with contemporary writers (Proulx, McCourt, Tyler, García Márquez, Shields, Rushdie, Morrison, and Atwood).

Likewise groups (at least in the Midwest) support local and regional authors. Southern writers, too, are popular. I hear women, particularly, say, "I love Kaye Gibbons," or Reynolds Price, or Clyde Edgerton.

What have been the most-read books in the years that I've conducted my admittedly informal research? Certainly Zora Neale Hurston's *Their Eyes Were Watching God*, Toni Morrison's *Beloved*, and Gabriel García Márquez's *Love in the Time of Cholera* have ranked high. But I suppose it is the surprises on lists that have delighted me most—Jean Rhys' *Wide Sargasso Sea*, Sigrid Undset's trilogy *Kristin Lavransdatter*, Virginia Woolf's *The Waves*, Elaine Pagels's *The Gnostic Gospels*, James Joyce's *Ulysses*.

Why "surprises"? Perhaps they are only surprises to me. But book groups are often made up of readers with varying degrees of education and widely diverse reading histories. Women have told me that until they joined a book group, their reading was made up entirely of romance novels and detective fiction. That an assorted group of ten or twenty people would agree to read the above books while at the same time raising small children, enduring workplace stress, going through chemotherapy, coping with an elderly parent who must be eased into a nursing facility or a grown child who is divorcing and coming home to live says a good deal about the role of books in our lives. And maybe about the real needs we have as readers. Maybe we need to rethink what we mean by "escape literature."

Many of the choices reading groups make remind us that books have the power to lift us outside our own concerns and into a larger world, offering, if not answers, at least perspective. Surely that is a chief function of literature: to enable us to set our personal world in a larger context and, in so doing, to measure our problems against those of others. In that process, we find relationship to those others and an antidote to the alienation that is so much a part of twentieth-century American life.

The book group itself performs the same function. In sharing our thoughts, interpretations, and observations about literature, we connect deeply with each other. The shared "yes!" as we recognize our own feelings in a fellow reader's words is as healing as prayer.

But the times when we differ with fellow readers are equally valuable. The permission to disagree, which lies at the heart of intellectual respect and growth, is fostered by the book group setting. At its best, a book group nurtures the skills of debate and discussion which are pitifully lacking in other contemporary arenas—political, religious, or cultural.

Discussing a book deepens our experience of the material. The more levels on which we connect with a book, the greater the explosion of ideas it touches off in our own brains: A fellow reader observes, "That foreshadowing in chapter two, using the news broadcast—that was sly, wasn't it?" You hadn't noticed the foreshadowing, but now you see it, and not only do you connect in yet another way with the book, but you also read future books with new awareness. This sort of synergy occurs countless times in a book group.

Where does the publishing world come into all of this? Until Oprah, most of the large Eastern houses seemed unaware of the book group phenomenon and its implications for their industry. Although a number of publishing houses have been printing study guides designed to help readers get the most out of a particular book, the shrinking midlists at major houses have left more and more readers with fewer and fewer choices. Unless, of course, the reader is looking for courtroom dramas, horror stories, romance novels, or celebrity bios, which most book groups aren't.

One has only to look at the records book groups keep to see the truth of this: With regard to contemporary literature, roughly two dozen or so books represent most of the choices made in any given year.

This says one of three things (or all of three things) about the large houses: (1) They haven't a clue what book groups want to read, or (2) they don't recognize how significant the book group market is, or (3) they haven't a notion how to target book groups, beyond printing study guides, in order to create partnership.

Given their tiny staffs, one can understand why small houses may publish new work that groups want to read yet still have difficulty creating that partnership. It's a bit more difficult to understand why large houses have trouble.

The study guides, which come from small houses and large, are varied. Some are a single sheet of questions about the story and its meaning. Others are pamphlets containing, additionally, a brief biography of the author, suggestions for further reading on the same topic or by the same author, an interview with the author, praise for the book, or information regarding what prompted the writing of the book. Normally, the guides are distributed through bookstores, and the stores are responsible for seeing that the material finds its way into the hands of readers.

Are the guides a sales tool? I suppose they can be, but according to book groups with whom I've met, if the guide is intelligent and provocative, it can also be helpful in organizing discussion and providing background information that enhances understanding and enjoyment of the book.

Are there other ways that publishers could target book groups beyond study guides? Well, if a publishing house is doing market research that includes book groups, and if any of their editorial choices are based on that research, they could flag the books they deem book group choices—some word or symbol on a dust jacket could alert a book buyer.

But with or without such tools of partnership between publisher and book group, will the book group phenomenon continue to proliferate and endure? Through the coming decades, will Herb or Mary continue marching into Helen's living room at 7:30, tossing a sweater or purse on the sofa, and complaining, "I thought *The Golden Notebook* was a colossal bore and here's why," or rhapsodizing, "My God, Forster *understands*"?

The late twentieth century has created more and more opportunities for us to communicate from our computer pods with people across

town—or across the Pacific—who face us from their pods. It is communication. That much cannot be argued. And it has its uses. But it
does not satisfy our animal need to look into the eyes of those others
gathered around a warm book; to catch the sudden intake of breath; to
caress a page as we locate that passage we've marked with highlighter
or Post-it note; to share the cup of coffee or glass of wine which gives
evidence that we're celebrating something here: books, words, communication, community, ourselves, each other.

Writing for Life

TOPICS COVERED:

Word Addiction

D. H. Lawrence and The Body

Prose as Panacea

Where the Buffalo Roamed

Giving Up on Meaning

Kitty

A Home for Words

Hypnosis

The Possibility of a Body on the Tracks

Giving Up on Sense

A Warm Loaf of Bread

The Relationship of Writer and Reader

Why I Write Fiction

SUSAN STRAIGHT

This is a true story, not embellished or even lightly fictionalized (though I wish some parts were exaggeration). I am a single mother with three daughters and a full-time job. At night, I write fiction. Many of my childhood friends are drug addicts, alcoholics, imprisoned, or dead. I am not. People give me a hard time because I don't drink anything stronger than tea, and I don't smoke at all. I am addicted, though, as strongly and passionately and unshakably as they are. If I don't read every day, imagining I'm someone else, and if I don't write every night, pretending to be someone else, I am nearly unbearable, and unable to bear my life.

This morning I woke without vision in my right eye. The pocket of flesh underneath it, the black space in a skull, had swollen and purpled as if Mike Tyson had hit me. My eye was smaller than a coin slot. I hadn't eaten anything different, wasn't allergic to anything but the chaos of my daily life. Could I blame my black eye on the previous night's enthusiastic yelling at my ten-year-old's volleyball game? Or on the minute glass shards from sweeping up the broken window caused by my eight-year-old's errant volleyball serve? Or my four-year-old's insistence on staying up until midnight, thanks to a nap on the way to the game?

Who knows? I spent two hours in the clinic peering at my students' papers, realized people were staring at what they thought was domestic abuse (except I have no husband), finally glimpsed a doctor who hovered in front of me to shrug and say, "Who knows?"

He gave me steroids for the inflammation. I gulped them down at lunch, took my children to their glamorous babysitter, who paints fingernails and eyelids, unlike me, and went to work.

Alone in the car, I thought about the story I had been writing for days. A mother is manufacturing methamphetamine in her house, cooking a mixture of Red Devil lye, Sudafed, and antifreeze on the stove. She is stirring the liquid in a cast-iron pot. I know mothers like this. I grew up with girls who became mothers like this. On my way to work, I pass women selling themselves on a particular street, and I recognize some of them from our school days.

I write fiction. That is what I live for. In the car, I thought about my story, and for twenty minutes, I was not myself.

Then I taught my class, dealt with administrative papers and student requests, explained my eye again and again. I picked up my kids.

The ten-year-old's explorer project, on Magellan, was due tomorrow. We had to host two more ten-year-olds in her group tonight.

I fed them all dinner, including the guests. I cleaned up the dishes, peered at their work on Magellan, felt the breeze from the broken window I hadn't had time to fix, moved laundry from washer to dryer, tried to answer questions about how long it took Magellan to sail around the world, and cleaned the stove.

I was dizzy from seeing with one eye. I gulped more steroids. I heard my new neighbors, a collection of skinhead surfers, warming up for the night. Loud trucks, yelling, and beer bottles. I helped my eight-year-old with second-grade spelling words. I helped my four-year-old with batteries, markers, string cheese, and her shoelaces.

Just as the Magellan project was finished, someone clogged the toilet. Just as the moms came to pick up their kids, the toilet overflowed on the plunger and me. The toilet was full of number two. I waited until the guests had faded from the porch, and then I lost it.

Was this steroid-induced rage? Or number-two-induced rage? Who knows?

We were out of paper towels. I cleaned the flood with rags, with more rags, with bleach solution, with yelling and grumbling. My daughters did not hover in the hallway. They went into the single bedroom they share, and I heard Lou Bega singing "Mambo No. 5."

I grumbled and yelled the entire time, starting two new loads of laundry, sterilizing the floor again, feeling lower than low. Nothing like body solids to put you in your place.

I gave the girls baths. I made tea. Then I told them to leave me alone.

This was it. If I were an addict like the ones I know, I would reach for the matches, the lighter, the glass, the pipe.

But I felt the headache from lack of caffeine and lack of intellectual stimulation. I had to see words. I got into bed and reached for my library books. First, N. Scott Momaday's *In the Bear's House,* a collection of poems and narratives about the wondrous animal that is his kin. Over and over, I peered at one passage about a hunter stalking the bear through canyons and ravines and forests. This was a far better house than mine, at the moment. I closed my eyes.

Television never works for me. I need silence. Not images that fade or leap away, but words I can read again, pause, think about, and touch.

And I was calm, as if the Jack Daniel's or marijuana or Darvocet of my friends had entered my bloodstream. Words like little ants, marching into my brain to whisper, "Hey, come on, stall out. We're right here."

I was gone. My daughters came to my bed with wet hair, a bowl of popcorn, a spelling test, and a list of capitals of the northeastern states. Like children of any addict, they knew when it was safe to reenter the zone.

I put my book aside. We finished homework, admired manicures, and I glanced at my own notebook on the bedside table. But it wasn't time yet. My four-year-old brought her blanket and three books. "Read to me, Mama."

"No. You read tonight. I can't. Look at my eye."

"Okay," she said, and I sighed. Usually she'd rather look at toy ads from the paper. She pointed to the cloth pages of this book we hadn't seen in weeks and said, "B-O-O-K. Book. M-E. Me. The Me Book."

I nearly cried. My last girl—the big moment. She read. I called the other girls to come and see. Then my oldest daughter asked to stay up: "Just one more chapter before bed, okay?"

When my youngest had finally fallen asleep beside me, I picked up my notebook. In it are pieces of the story—the speed lab, the mother, her children who are sleeping in the next room as she stirs the liquid on the stove.

Why write fiction? Why spend this time making up lies, paragraphs and pages of imaginative, nontruthful, embroidered tales? Why spend weeks writing a short story about people who don't talk or act or live like I do? People from whom I tried to escape years ago, people whom

I still see every day? When I sent fiction out long ago, I received polite, nearly puzzled rejection letters stating that my worldview seemed rather bleak. Really? I thought. But I can't change my world. I can only record it, by changing myself.

Nonfiction about my friends and family would be easier to sell. But I don't want to get people arrested or killed, or be either of those things myself. I am raising children. But I have to write something down, to order my dangerous and chaotic surroundings, to wrest control, to make people live again when they are gone. I can only do that with fiction. Besides, essays—though I like this, right now—don't create oblivion, disappearance, transformation.

Days earlier, my friend Holly, who writes essays and reportage for magazines, had asked me this very question in a tortured voice. "Why do I feel compelled to work on my novel? Why?"

Another friend, Kate, an editor, just took a leave from her job to work hard on her first novel. Both women are former single mothers who would understand fully, instantaneously, if I said, "Magellan project precipitated toilet overflow at 8 p.m. but here I am anyway, writing fiction."

For me, no other form of writing acts like a mind-altering substance. People have suggested "journaling" as a way they make sense of their lives. I started a journal, back in 1994. I recall clearly the first day, writing about picking up my infant daughter from my mother-in-law's house, where on the sidewalk I dodged a bullet meant for a teenage gang member/distant relative. Shortly thereafter, my then-husband came home in a dismal mood from the correctional facility where he worked; three twelve-year-olds had robbed a pizza delivery man, using a gun. I wrote all this down faithfully; it depressed the hell out of me. I wanted to leave my body behind like a lizard skin in the bushes of my front yard. That was it for my one-day journal.

Many authors write about themselves, in lightly fictionalized lives. I never do. Who wants to be me? Sometimes, on my hands and knees washing a floor, or in the car, or paying the bills, or on my hands and knees again, I don't.

Tonight, my eye is still swollen so badly I can't see well enough to sit at the computer and finish the story about the mother cooking methamphetamine. Her own homemade recipe—the vapor rising in the house, pooling on the floor, sliding under the bedroom door where her children sleep. I pull my notebook close to me. The washer is groaning, the dryer rumbling, the kids tossing around in their beds because the skinhead surfers are in full bottle-breaking, cussing, festival mode, and the police helicopter is hovering over my roof. But on the page, the silvery shimmering fills the small house in the high desert not far from here, and I am watching, afraid, transported, not really here at all.

Grace Paley

in dialogue with EMILIE BUCHWALD

Grace Paley, the fabled poet, fiction writer, and essayist, was born in the Bronx, New York, in 1922. Her collections of stories include *The Little Disturbances of Man* (Doubleday, 1959), *Enormous Changes at the Last Minute* (Farrar, Straus and Giroux, 1974), *Later the Same Day* (Farrar, Straus and Giroux, 1985), and *The Collected Stories* (Farrar, Straus and Giroux, 1994), a finalist for the National Book Award. She also published four volumes of poetry, *Leaning Forward* (Granite Press, 1985), *New and Collected Poems* (Tillbury Press, 1992), *Begin Again: Collected Poems* (Farrar, Straus and Giroux, 2000), and *Fidelity* (Farrar, Straus and Giroux, 2008), as well as a collection of poems and prose pieces titled *Long Walks and Intimate Talks* (Feminist Press, 1991).

Emilie Buchwald is the founding editor and publisher of Milkweed Editions. She had the opportunity to work with Grace Paley in 1984 as part of the Loft's Mentor Series.

EMILIE BUCHWALD: You have always pulled together the personal and political. I'm looking at your wonderful poem "Responsibility": *It's the responsibility of society to let the poet be a poet. / It's the responsibility of the poet to be a woman. / It's the responsibility of the poet to stand on street corners / giving out beautifully written leaflets. . . .*

GRACE PALEY: And also awful ones.

E. B.: *. . . also leaflets they can hardly bear to look at / because of the screaming rhetoric.* I love that. So, what at this moment in time do you see as the writer's job? Has it changed at all with the political shift?

G. P.: The political responsibility of the writer is the same responsibility that the writer has as a citizen. If she doesn't write, she should still give out rotten leaflets. The writer is an artist, and the artist's job is to respond truthfully to the pressures that are within her. Tell the truth. Often those pressures don't seem to be political, but they are. For myself, when I first began to write about women's lives, the pressure to write was intense. But I kept thinking, Nobody will read this stuff, who cares? That was in the midfifties. But my job was really to respond to that pressure within me and do it, no matter what. It's not that you try to be political, it's just that if you're truthful you can't really leave it out.

E. B.: You're one of the writers who's made it possible to enlarge the scope of what we can write about. It used to be that people thought you could only write about your personal life. Your writing brings it all in—the ethics, the politics of the world.

Another thing that I love in your fiction and in your poetry, as well, is that you have such a good sense of humor. Is it a conscious thing?

G. P.: There's no such thing as conscious humor unless you're the kind of person who wants to make everybody miserable with rotten jokes. If you've got a sense of humor, you've got it, and it's going to be there even when it's inappropriate.

E. B.: I really enjoy your *Collected Poems* and its title, *Begin Again*. It's a great title. What does it mean for you?

G. P.: It means that you really have to start all over again. You have grandchildren, you start all over again. The fact is that you can't begin again. There's no way. But you're encouraged by the fact that every day is a new day. It's always morning. There's a way of maintaining a view of the world as new. That's really what it's about. That's a poet's job particularly. One of the things I tried to do with teaching, after I was at it a while, was to keep a class of smart kids dumb. That, of course, was referring to a lot of middle-class and upper-class ideas that were quite worn out. The point was to teach things so that they'd feel new.

E. B.: As a writer, as a poet, you have kept on keeping on.

G. P.: Well, I really began as a poet. I didn't write stories until I was about thirty-five.

E. B.: What made you write stories?

G.P.: I suddenly wanted to. My kids were a little bigger and I had this business with women and what was going on. I sat down and I had some ideas and I had a voice. I don't mean that I had my voice yet, really. But I had this woman's voice that, as somebody said, was clearly right next to me. I had something to jump over and I really longed to tell stories.

E.B.: As you talk to writers, are you finding that they have different kinds of questions than they had in the past?

G.P.: Not a helluva lot different. But they're all different in the sense that they come from people in a different place. Doing readings, I've never been annoyed by questions like a lot of writers are. I mean, you should just take people where they are, or forget it, you know, go on to another business.

E.B.: What do you see for writing and publishing in the future?

G.P.: I see more trouble in bookselling than almost anything. The closing down of independent bookstores is a great tragedy.

E.B.: It's a disaster.

G.P.: That has to affect publishing.

E.B.: And also, a number of book review sections around the country are cutting the number of reviews they publish. It makes it harder for books by small presses to get to readers. It's tough. We're living in times when publishing and bookselling have continued to become conglomerated. But writers have to keep writing.

G.P.: We will. People will continue writing. Whether they write with a pencil or typewriter or computer, they'll be writing. They'll be making up words and making up people and making up histories for people who have no history.

E.B.: That's the good part, that's the exciting part.

Dorianne Laux

in dialogue with JUDE NUTTER

Dorianne Laux is the author of four collections of poetry: *Awake* (BOA Editions, 1990); *What We Carry* (BOA Editions, 1994), finalist for the National Book Critics Circle Award; *Smoke* (BOA Editions, 2000); and *Facts About the Moon* (W. W. Norton, 2005). Her poems have been published in numerous journals and anthologies. Laux's awards include a Pushcart Prize for poetry, two fellowships from the National Endowment for the Arts, and a Guggenheim Fellowship. As Pattiann Rogers rightly observes, "The world of Dorianne Laux is rich and varied with growth and decay, with grief and wit, with sex and prayer and fantasy, with those elements, tangible and ephemeral, that compose human experience."

JUDE NUTTER: You have said that, historically, all women have had is their bodies. This reminds me of Sandra Gilbert's claim that the female poet "must come to terms with the fact that as a female she is that which is mythologized." Certainly, female poets such as Sharon Olds, Adrienne Rich, Anne Sexton, Sylvia Plath, and Denise Levertov struggled to produce a "new mythology," a poetry of redefinition and reclamation. Do you view yourself as part of this tradition?

DORIANNE LAUX: I remember encouraging many of my students to stay at home, in the body, and work from there. Partly because that's just a good place to begin—what do we know better than our own containers, this flesh that feels whether we want it to or not? Whatever philosophy lurks behind this is probably darkly personal in nature. My body was misused when I was a child, and I spent a fair amount of energy and time liberating my mind from my body, transcending this world and traveling imaginatively into another. Books, literature, and song helped me to do that. It was a survival skill I learned. So for me, when I discovered poetry, it seemed to me to be a place where I could go to reclaim the body, the part of myself I had elected to leave behind in order to survive. Poetry became the portal to another level of survival, emotional and spiritual in nature. I read Sharon Olds, Carolyn Forché, Neruda; I read D.H. Lawrence—I love his poems, his philosophy.

J. N.: I'm interested in your affinity with Lawrence. Do you agree that, like Whitman, he helped usher in a new way of envisioning the body, that he allowed us to view ourselves as "spiritual animals"?

D. L.: Yes, Lawrence knew how important the body and our sexuality were to an understanding of the self, to living fully. Historically, all women have had is their bodies, and I saw that what had seemed a diminished thing to me was really a gift; that if joined with mind and spirit it was a whole thing; that it contained infinite power. I wanted to live fully, rejoin my mind to my body, to feel even pain again—but to feel. Lawrence wrote, as do Olds and Forché, from the inside out; their poems value the body, and its baseness becomes the basis of glory. What had been a container of fear, rage, and pain had been transformed, through poetry, into a powerful vessel, a ship that could take me back to this half-self waiting for me on the shoreline. I wanted to create a balanced female body, at home in the world, at home with her nature—maybe a refashioning of Lawrence's women from a female point of view.

J. N.: Was this a conscious strategy on your part when you began writing poetry?

D. L.: No, I didn't know any of this back when I began reading poetry and writing my own poems. I discovered much of it later, and some of it just now as I'm speaking to you. I had forgotten, really, how much of an influence Lawrence had on me. I began reading him again recently and recognized that vision, even images I must have unconsciously lifted from "Whales Weep Not!"

J. N.: Can you provide an example?

D. L.: Well, this section:

> Then the great bull lies up again his bride
> in the blue deep of the sea
> as mountain pressing on mountain, in the zest of life:

and out of the inward roaring of the inner red ocean of
    whale blood
the long tip reaches strong, intense, like a maelstrom
    tip and comes to
rest
in the clasp and the soft, wild clutch of the she-whale's
    fathomless body.

Years later, I wrote "The Lovers." It was one of those poems that seemed to arrive whole, but I look at those lines of Lawrence and see my theft:

And when something lifts within her
toward a light she's sure, once again,
she can't bear, she opens her eyes
and sees his face is turned away,
one arm behind him, hand splayed
palm down on the mattress, to brace himself
so he can lever his hips, touch
with the bright tip the innermost spot.
And she finds she can't bear it—
not his beautiful neck, stretched and corded,
not his hair fallen to one side like beach grass,
not the curved wing of his ear, washed thin
with daylight, deep pink of the inner body.

I loved Lawrence's sense of sexual equality—the tip of one body deep in the wildness and wilderness of another. My "deep pink" and "beach grass," that vision of the innermost spot, are really a paean to his marriage of the whales, a paean to beings at home in their bodies.

J. N.: Lawrence has often been criticized for creating women (and men) trapped in the body, defined by their biology and sex. How do you respond to that?

D. L.: I don't feel trapped by my body—I accept that I have a body and that it's inextricably linked to my mind. My mind is a body part—it's flesh and blood. Without the body, there is no brain, no thought. The body *is* its intelligence. The brain is an extension of the body's deep knowledge, and I think Lawrence knew that. I can read those works and see that Lawrence hadn't yet read Susan Sontag or Camille Paglia or even much Freud. He liked Jung. What I see more is that he was aware, beyond his time, of how important the body is.

J. N.: Personally, I think Lawrence's focus on the body creates, in most of his work, an uneasy tension between biology and politics, nature and culture—such a dialogue seems to spring inevitably out of the subject matter. Do you believe that one of our poetic responsibilities is to continue this dialogue?

D. L.: Yes. Lawrence saw that relationships between the sexes were rife with darkness and anxiety and were brutally mysterious: he was a truth teller. We can't expect him to tell our cultural or political truth, years from his poems, but if we want to write poems that reflect our current ideas about sex and gender, we must let nothing stop us. They tried to stop Lawrence. His books were banned! He was outrageous. He's *still* outrageous.

J. N.: Do you view yourself as a creator of some new mythology?

D. L.: I don't read much feminist criticism. I'm essentially a housewife, mother, friend, and teacher who reads and writes poems, though of course I am following in the footsteps of all those great poets you mention. I discovered my body; the very flesh I felt had doomed me was, in fact, my salvation. It always seemed to me that men took their bodies for granted, and that was part of why they were beautiful to me—that casual movement through the world, walking from the hips, the luscious swagger. If that vision is attached to culture, it can seem macho in the worst sense, but seen in true context, as a vision of being in the world, it's quite natural and basic to human life. I'm responding to those women poets you mention: I'm trying to continue the conversation, poem by poem, to find what more there is to say.

J. N.: The word *conversation* makes me think about narrative, about our need to write or talk out our stories. Surely, every poet distorts the literal truth to arrive at an emotional truth? For me, the story itself is secondary to the idea or understanding I am trying to get to the heart of—it's a means to an end. I'm interested in how your narratives come together, and this is a question about process as well as aesthetic. What "role" does the larger narrative play? What's the relationship between narrative and "truth"?

D. L.: You've said it well—the narrative can be so shapely and mysterious in its wanderings. I love the narrative, and, as Marie Howe says, it's in danger right now. Those of us who write poetic narratives know this when we read the magazines and journals of the day. Poetry has become such a poor, broken thing—fragmented to achieve, it seems to me, a kind of replication of the inner workings of the mind—odd associations and thought shards. But I'm less interested in that, and more interested in how those fragments can become a whole that's larger than its parts, how it can encompass more than what literally is. As for my particular narratives, yes, they are containers for an idea or feeling, and I often don't know what my idea is until I explore the feeling *through* the story.

J. N.: Yes, the narrative is instructive; it allows us, in the words of Francis Bacon, to create something out of the chaos of human existence.

D. L.: Certainly! I'm interested in how we learn from stories. So many poems are mazes of unconnected darkness: interesting, but not particularly instructive or even pleasurable. I can't imagine carrying around a poem I can't understand, a poem that only mimics the chaos in my life, my thoughts. We're steeped in chaos, why would we want more of it? If you read chaos theory you find that what seems on the surface like chaos is really a deeper order that you have to look at closely, or from a greater distance, to see. Maybe I'm not standing far enough away from some of this fragmented verse! That's always a possibility. In any case, I'm driven to leave an emotional history of my life. I think about the brain, how the body struggles to make all those connections in order to function as a brain. That's what fascinates me, the struggle of disparate elements to link up and become a whole. I'm interested in some ultimate wholeness, the Romantic synthesis Coleridge talked about. Narrative is a difficult, emotion-filled, and useful path toward this.

J.N.: You said earlier, "Poetry became the portal to another level of survival, emotional and spiritual in nature." I want to stay with that for a minute. One of my favorite poems of yours is "For the Sake of Strangers" (from *What We Carry*). This is a poem of survival, a beautiful hymn about how human connection can save us. Here, though, it's the power of the stranger, not the lover; it's the bond of a shared suffering—what it means to be human—that unites us all. I think of William Carlos Williams's lines: "It is difficult / to get the news from poems / yet men die miserably every day / for lack / of what is found there." Obviously, you believe that poetry has the power to "save" us?

D.L.: Yes. And Williams is right. That's an absolutely true statement. I think people forget that; they think it's hyperbole or a metaphysical statement seen only in terms of its abstract content. But poetry actually does save physical lives. During times of war or great upheaval, poetry is there—a scrap of paper stuffed in a pocket or lodged in the heel of a shoe. Whenever we feel lost among the crowd, unheard, unseen, discarded, we have a deep need for that intimate, singular voice speaking directly to us and for us, and sometimes that's all we need to keep from giving up and doing ourselves in. And yes, that poem is about survival, looking for and finding commonality in suffering, taking strength from the small gestures of strangers, their bodies, their faces, their being in the world. I read a *New York Times* quote of the day a few mornings ago from a woman named Susann Brady, whose fiancé, Gavin Cushny, died at the World Trade Center. She said: "Here you lost the most important person in your life, and nobody gives you any recognition. You just kind of get bypassed." That poem is about not feeling bypassed. But it's more about daily courage, going on in spite of more ordinary suffering. It's what we do every day: We get up and we confront the world again.

Writing about the Mysteries of Life

MARY LOGUE

Once I wrote a novel, a wondrous first novel that contained most of what I knew in life: waitressing, Minneapolis's West Bank area, musicians, drinking, and three women who made clothes and tangled up their lives. It wasn't a mystery. I didn't think much about what it was, except that I knew it was a novel because it was over two hundred pages long. I finished it and titled it. I was living in New York City at the time, so I sent it off to some editors and agents I had met there. They were all kind and said that the writing was good, but the plot needed work.

So I decided that, in order to learn about plot, I would write a mystery. And I did, *Red Lake of the Heart,* a novel about two sisters, one an alcoholic singer, one a dancer, both waitresses. When one sister gets killed, the other tries to find out why. I was still writing about what I knew in life, but I was doing it in a way that pushed the story forward and, I hoped, captured readers as it went. This novel was published by Dell and I acquired, among other things, the title of mystery writer. I even joined MWA—Mystery Writers of America.

I continue to write mysteries for many reasons. I've read mysteries all my life, from Josephine Tey to Raymond Chandler. I had a sister who was murdered and I helped with the police investigation of her death and will be haunted by this all my life. My favorite TV show for years was *Cagney and Lacey.* And five years after my mother's death, I can still most easily imagine her flopped out on the couch, reading an Agatha Christie. For me, writing mysteries is a noble profession.

But in the end, asking me why I write mysteries is like asking me why I bought an old farmhouse in Stockholm, Wisconsin. Why not near Ely, Cape Cod, Santa Fe? All I can say is that it works for me. That just as I learn a lot of what I need to know about living and nature by standing under the bluff on my acre of land, I have learned much of what I need to know about writing through writing mysteries.

My latest novel is what we mystery writers call a mainstream novel. But it's not so different. All novels need suspense and unanswered questions. At the beginning of a good book, writers promise their readers many things, and if they're good writers, they hold up their end of the bargain. If readers finish the book, they will know why something happened and what might come to be; they will have received a full world peopled with flawed, odd characters.

Mysteries are just more up-front about this promise, more straight-forward, sometimes more conventional. Someone is killed early on, and if you read the book you will find out who did it. But you will probably also come to know more about family, love, greed, and evil. This is the milieu of murder. People are often murdered by those who love them, by those who live close around them.

One of the hardest parts of writing mysteries is writing about evil. And yet many traditional novels take on evil in a big way: *Crime and Punishment, The Collector, Lolita.* Writing about evil is scary, saddening, and exhausting, because, in order to write about evil, you must connect with it in your life. You must feel compassionate about how far any of our emotions can take us. Haven't we all done something for money that we didn't want to do? Loved until it's made us crazy? Committed regrettable acts? We are all in it. We are guilty and we are forgiven.

There's a lot of room to move in a mystery. Many writers are using the form to write about important themes; it gives them a story to wrap their ideas around. Walter Mosley is exploring the Los Angeles Black community in the fifties in his series featuring Easy Rawlins. Elizabeth George writes complicated novels about incest and child abuse, while featuring two characters who allow her to examine the British class structure. My latest mystery, *Still Explosion,* is about a feature writer for the Twin Cities Times who is writing an in-depth story on the abortion issue. And many women writers are using women detectives and policewomen to look at women's roles in society.

It's easy to use the form of a mystery to get at the core issues of a subject because that's what mysteries do. They try to ferret out the truth. They get us to reexamine things we've taken for granted. We step into the stories and try on the different roles. And in the end, when some of the mystery is solved, we wish that occasionally this would happen in our lives: that we could get to the bottom of something and see it for what it is.

It flabbergasts me that some people disdain mysteries. But then, I'm also amazed when some writers think they've accomplished something by writing a complicated, erudite sentence that no one understands. Good writing is about telling stories, and confusion is not the same as mystery. Mystery is when everything is painfully clear: the sky is immensely blue, the land is covered with hills and valleys, and the person you most love in the world is dead at your feet. How could this have happened? Mysteries are not meant to be solved but explored— just as when someone dies, we are meant to feel it, not get over it.

There is no getting over death. It is in us and around us. Our own deaths create a kind of fuel in us, a need to understand, to see how such a death would change the world. And the world of the mystery is inexorably changed by death. Everyone is suspect; life is transformed. This is a positive thing. And often justice prevails. Death is worth something in the world of the living. We need to believe that.

I often wonder how long I'll write mysteries. They are bone-wrenching hard. One of my dreams is that I'll continue to work in the softer land of ordinary novels, where there aren't quite as many slaps in the face and knives in the back. Maybe some mystery writers can distance themselves from their material, or write about it in such a way that they can avoid taking it seriously. For me, as I explore sado-masochism and domestic abuse, as I learn about guns, bombs, forensics, I carry it all with me. Each death takes something out of me. I'm not sure how many deaths I have left to tell.

Writing the tail end of this essay down in Stockholm, I think of the deer out in the field, the new Canadian Explorer roses I will plant tomorrow, the sunflowers nodding as the train eases by on tracks by the river, and I think of a quiet, light story. Yet what if there were a body there on the tracks, down near the river? A woman no one had ever seen before? Wouldn't someone have to tell her story?

Another Poet Gone to Prose:
The Personal Essay as Quest

BARRIE JEAN BORICH

The urge to write prose came to me through a contest sponsored by Dr. Aaron Flickstein, my chiropractor.

At the time, I was trying to feel my way out of an abyss. That abyss was physical illness. I had a cyst the size of a grapefruit on my left ovary, and my immune system was so weak I had a constant cold and yeast infection in all the organs of my body. My writing, up until that time, included book reviews, film reviews, and promotional materials, but as far as art was concerned I was solely a poet.

It seems odd to me that contemporary women's poetry is so often considered a personal form. I rarely wrote about myself in poems. More often, my poems were fictions, written in the voices of characters I invented or read about in the paper. Poetry has often felt like a way into the bodies of others, a passage out of my own body.

The hundred-dollar prize that drew me to the essay form was one of Dr. Flickstein's several attempts to expand and solidify his wavering private practice by involving his patients more personally in their care and encouraging them to commit more deeply to chiropractic philosophy. I'm sure he hoped that this expanded commitment to chiropractic medicine would lead to a deeper commitment to him. This made me nervous. What if I changed my mind? Would I end up emotionally entangled in his enthusiastic worldview and the quick, sharp cracks he gave my neck and back? But I was broke, too sick to work, and had taken out a loan to pay my swelling health-care bills. I wanted that hundred dollars.

Contest participants were asked to answer a series of questions:

How would you describe chiropractic care? *The spinal cord is the switchboard of the body,* I wrote. *Alignment, the spine frees the body's circuitry.*

Describe the life of your body. *I have become aware of a double self,* I wrote. *Some hidden force has hold of me, sending up life, then death, alternately. Living fills me until my dead self punches itself to the surface. Both selves can exist at once.*

How does it feel to be in pain? *Sand slips through an hourglass funnel, and I become a dry whirlpool of stinging. The world bleaches white, until I wake with my face pressed against the cold porcelain of the toilet seat, and only a cold numbness remains in my throbbing belly.*

Dr. Flickstein awarded me the hundred dollars, but he did not save me. I lost faith in his practice and found a more compatible healer. But the writing I did for that contest stirred something that had long been dormant in me. I didn't know I could write about my own pain. Just before I wrote that first essay, I wrote in a poem, "Pain cannot be described. You can only remember that it happened to you, and that is enough." Yet here I had described pain—my pain.

I wonder if this is how Anne Sexton and all the revolutionary women poets of the sixties felt when they began to write that so-called confessional poetry. I already believed that, politically, words could make a difference in the world. Yet it had never before occurred to me that writing could make a difference in my own life. I had to leave poetry to find this out. I had to expand out of the poetic line, into the paragraph, into the rich and scattered detail of myself.

So now I write essays. These essays are my quests. I want to know: *What does it feel like to be in pain? Where did the pain start? Where did it come from? Where did I learn to hate my body? Why do I shudder when I remember a woman named Anna, whom I once loved? Why did I drink so much alcohol and smoke so much pot the year I turned nineteen? What is the pain I have always tried not to feel? Why does the landscape of my hometown, Chicago, haunt my dreams?* Every essay I have written since the first has sprung from a question I felt pressing so hard into my life that I could not breathe until I began to answer it.

When I say my essays are quests I do not mean the quest of the traditional Classical hero. This is not a physical quest, although those ancient, brawny wars may work as a metaphor for this interior quest of mine. My quest is to strike into the blood of personal truth, even when the truth makes me out to be my own villain. My quest is to drop my mask of heroism and expose the shivering child crouching behind, so I can ask her, *What do you see? What do you feel?* I need to ask so that I can sew up my wounds and live.

For this reason, my quest essay must be personal. Truth is revealed through the form of the image. The essay is about speculation, but the questions need not be asked from a lofty, chin-scratching distance. My essay is made up of stories. It is not simply memory, for memory alone does not reveal enough. It is the form in which the memory is expressed that is revealing. What memory leads to what other memory? What is the imagistic trail? I want the stories to move like snatches of film, bound together by a quick cut that leads to another image and into a meaning that none of the images can offer alone.

This practice may be therapeutic, but it is not the same as therapy. Therapy is chaotic, cluttered with stubborn, irritating silences, sodden hunks of feeling, and repetition that would bore us in art. In the essay quest, revelation occurs through the artfulness of form. Just as in film, the juxtaposition of startling images draws from us an aesthetic as well as an emotional gasp, so do the stories, the bricks, of the essay quest bring forth the language epiphany that can only come from sensory imagery expressed with formal eloquence and grace.

And so, Dr. Flickstein, I thank you for your questions, as well as for your hundred dollars. I do not recall how I spent the money, but the questions have carried me into the essay. I have not abandoned poetry, but my essay quests have changed my poetry forever. Home changes every time we leave it. I can't write a poem anymore that is not at least a little bit about me, and since I began writing essays, I am not who I was.

The Making of Sense

J. OTIS POWELL!

I have learned to stop making sense in order to allow sense to make itself known through a process of discovery. New perspectives on reality are born when one escapes the hard and sanctioned prisons that limit the field of possibilities.

For example, I was writing a poem about Sun Ra, an innovative composer, pianist, and bandleader. I wanted to write about the artist's need to escape the boundaries of the life he knew. So I wrote a phrase that was open at both ends:

> . . . is it not better to leave your body
> than to leave your mind
> or to lose

Writing that phrase was discovery. Not only did it make new sense to me, but every time a reader encounters the question, it opens infinities again. In addition to the sense implied was an inherent rhythm that rang the question like a song.

When James Baldwin, who is best known for his prose, applied his craft to poetry, the reality of how unutterable "truth" can be is evident. However, his attempt to say something meaningful and important isn't thwarted by the fact that his "truth" is unspeakable. Read this from Baldwin's "Staggerlee Wonders":

> Time warned us to ask for our money back,
> and disagreed with History
> as concerns colours white and black.
> Not only do we come from further back,
> but the light of the Sun
> marries all colours as one.

If the question in your mind is "What does he mean by that?" then the phrases are working.

We know what we know because we have made suppositions. But to tell "the truth," we must venture beyond what we think we know to what we can discover. Our recordings or recreations of inner experience are often a fusion of various levels on which an experience was had. Impressions render more truth than facts.

A strong poetic voice can be characterized by how it leaves space on a page as well as by the space it fills. Not knowing "the" answers to the questions posed in my phrase is not necessarily irresponsible writing. The answers ventured by a reader are as valid as the writer's, and leaving the questions open is valid. Space remains because nothing truer can fill it. Ambiguity is often more honest than assumptions. Consider Baldwin's "Staggerlee Wonders" again:

> History is weary
> of her unspeakable liaison with Time
> for Time and History
> have never seen eye to eye:
> Time laughs at History
> and time and time again
> Time traps History in a lie.

Baldwin doesn't spend time supporting or proving this observation; he merely shares it and goes on.

Like music, poetry often takes form according to substance, meter, and sound. Form is a vehicle for what the writer has to say and should conform to the writer's voice. Literal meaning may be secondary to the sound and music of the writer's voice. It is possible for words to assume a value beyond their meaning when what is communicated is image rather than fact.

When this happens, space and ambiguity allow variations on meaning and add weight to the text. In art, the opening of minds is desirable, even necessary. It's easy to lose sight of that in a society that makes a product of artistic expression and insists on functional forms that "make sense"—"sense" that keeps us from reexamining the tired old logic of our assumptions.

As artists we are responsible for growing consciousness. That sometimes requires experimentation. The best perspective on what is moving forward and what is standing still in our work is our own. We must continue to discover new forms in order to make new sense of the world. It's important to write what has not already been read.

The hewing of new territories may be more difficult for writers than for other artists, because everybody uses language. That can work to our advantage, however. When we leave space for the reader, we acknowledge our own ignorance, and we allow the reader to participate in the making of sense. The reader's language interfaces with ours, and something genuine has a chance to happen.

It is when we communicate thoughts and feelings without requiring the reader to believe what we believe that we are moving in a positive direction. The challenge poets face is finding ways to express truth beyond facts and beyond ourselves. The challenge poets face as persons is leaving space for the reader, the other.

The freedom not to prove every concept is a luxury of poetry writing. The planet is filled already with propaganda and rhetoric. The soul needs voice. The heart wants an advocate. Each writer's voice is different because each life sings a new song. Space offers hope that a dialogue can occur between reader and poet and that a new wholeness will be discovered.

Inside all human experience is more meaning than can be expressed in words. I feel charged with the challenge of expressing something else, something other, every time I press words to page. Unconscious and unuttered sense is longing to be made. I want to make some of it. It, after all, has been making me for a lifetime.

Theories: How Life Becomes Poetry

LINDA GREGG

Linda Gregg presented the following talk to her Mentor Series workshop.

Our poetry is about our lives because the world is there and because we need something to write about. We see a house alone by the sea in the middle of September, and we describe it or tell how it made us feel. Or we write about what we did on Christmas when we were children in California. But the hard thing is to get the life and the world into a poem instead of the poem just talking about the life. It is hard to capture the essence of the life and the events in poems beyond merely what we saw or what we did.

In a sense, my life was poetry before it became poems. I grew up in a valley surrounded by gentle hills. Cows grazed and horses wandered one by one in big pastures, and there were deer higher up among the bay trees and eucalyptus. Beyond the end of the valley was a town and beyond that a bridge and on the other side of the bridge was a big city called San Francisco. But that was far away. It was country where I was. There was beauty everywhere and order and the life with my twin sister when we rode into the hills or played in the creek or hurried home on foot through the woods as it got dark.

But there was also something invisible inside all of it, underneath it all. A world of spirits and mysteries and essences and the sacred.

It was the life inside the beauty and the order that was poetry before it entered my poems, the life that got into the poetry as truth and magic and importance even though I didn't understand and don't fully understand it now. The poetry was not saying this happened to me and then that happened to me, nor was it saying everything was pretty. When the poems succeeded, they were the essence and the spirit of the world showing themselves in things and in what happened. The place around me was beautiful, and the stars at night were so many that there seemed to be no space between them; but there were also the dark things, like the terrible pain in our family. They were mixed up—like when my father hung our pig from the tree and made the two small girls we were watch as he shot it and cut it up. There were enormous things mixed in with our grief and sorrow.

What I try to tell of in my poetry is a dim knowledge of the sacramental in all of it. In the way that the Hopi Indians come to understand that the sacred and the actual are the same thing. It is the poetry behind the beauty and behind the darkness that mostly got into my poems, I think. All of it made me a shape that can sometimes speak its shape.

It was like a marriage. I was made of that world: horses, moon, red-tailed hawks, the smell of summer, the Calling Tree, tall dry grass on the mountain hiding us from everybody, Louise and I carrying bones down to bury in our secret place, a huge blue heron caught in the woods by the creek and fighting to escape—filling the night above my head with the sound of limbs breaking. If I didn't put it into my poetry, all of it would stay invisible.

In the spring salmon would come struggling up the stream, and years later I wrote about them:

> Death looks down on the salmon.
> A male and a female in the two pools, one above
> . the other. The female turns back along the path
> of water to the male, does not touch him,
> and returns to the place where she had been.
>
> I know what death will do. Their bodies already
> are sour and ragged. Blood has risen
> to the surface under the scales. One side
> of his jaw is unhinged. Death will pick them up.
> Put them under his coat against his skin
> and belt them there. Will walk away
> up the path through the bay trees.
> Through the dry grass of California to where
> the mountain begins. Where a few deer
> almost the color of the hills will look up

until he is under the trees again and the road ends
and there is a gate. He will climb over that
with his treasure. It will be dark by then.

But for now he does nothing. He does not disturb
the silence at all. Nor the occasional sound
of leaves, of ferns touching, of grass or stream.
For now he looks down at the salmon large and whole,
motionless days and nights in the cold water.
Lying still, always facing the constant motion.

When I first read that to an audience, I was shocked by how much
I felt the atmosphere of the woods by our stream. The air was there,
and the way that place breathed. I think it's there in the poem because I lived in that world. When we live truly with things, they are
different in our poems than when we make them up; and they will
sometimes exist there even when we speak of them simply. When I
read Black Elk's last speech to the gods, about not being able to make
the tree bloom, I can hear his life in the words. His life and that
world. Just as I feel the deer exist easily in this poem when it says:

> . . . a few deer
> almost the color of the hills will look up
> until he is under the trees again . . .

And I think it's because I know about those deer forever. Really know,
and with the kind of knowing that can, with luck, get the weight and
dying and power of the salmon into poetry.

   Of course, Death in this poem is not simply a reflection of something known well. But he is a good example of how life can get into
poetry by something else, through myth: a complex truth given concrete form as King Lear, Huck Finn, or Aphrodite. Death here is also
an example of how life becomes poems by magic and unaccountably.
However, in my twenty minutes I'm not going to try to account for the
unaccountable. Instead, I want to say a few words about still another
way life becomes poetry.

After my childhood was over, I found the world was seldom poetry before I began to write about it. The world was complex and fragmented and without the inherent shape of my early landscape. When there was an essence, it was hard to get at, and the materials seemed not to have a natural form. Once a child I loved died. It was the morning of the funeral, and I wanted very much to make a poem that would preserve the importance of that death. But my mind kept slipping away, skipping around in my past, grabbing at this and that, seeming to know by instinct what it might be able to use: the picture of my grandmother, the waxed gardenias at my grandfather's funeral when I was four and tried to get into the coffin with him, the cypresses which grow in Greece where people are buried, the old women I saw out in the emptiness of an island called Santorini all in black up in fig trees, the fear and suffering men had caused me, the toughness of nature, the snake a cowboy skinned alive in front of me when I was little. The bits and pieces became a poem called "The Poet Goes About Her Business."

> Michele has become another dead little girl. An easy poem.
> Instant Praxitelean. Instant twenty-five-year-old photograph
> of my grandmother when she was a young woman with
>   shadows
> I imagined were blue around her eyes. The beauty of it.
> Such guarded sweetness. What a greed of bruised gardenias.
> Oh Christ, whose name rips silk, I have seen raw cypresses
> so dark the mind comes to them without color.
> Dark on the Greek hillside. Dark, volcanic, dry and stone.
> Where the oldest women of the world are standing dressed
>   in black
> up in the branches of fig trees in the gorge
> knocking with as much quickness as their weakness will
>   allow.
> Weakness which my heart must not confuse with tenderness.
> And on the other side of the island a woman
> walks up the path with a burden of leaves on her head,
> guiding the goats with sounds she makes up,
> and then makes up again. The other darkness is easy:

the men in the dreams who come in together to me with
  knives.
There are so many traps, and many look courageous.
The body goes into such raptures of obedience.
But the huge stones on the desert resemble
nobody's mother. I remember the snake.
After its skin had been cut away, and it was dropped
it started to move across the clearing.
Making its beautiful waving motion.
It was all meat and bone. Pretty soon it was covered with
  dust.
It seemed to know exactly where it wanted to go.
Toward any dark trees.

The old women in black up in the fig trees are a thing known well,
but they are also in themselves immense beyond the facts and without logic. Images mean and require. I could have told how I fed and
held and loved the child. But the gods showed up, the old women,
the cypresses, and the snake. When the mind, spirit, and heart in
their full size begin finding the poetry in life, it is not always comfortable. Not always nice. Myself, the world, death, and the sacred are
not always nice. Huge things happen. Unmanageable things. Poetry
and life are splendid and dangerous. Living in the city is more and
less than the sweet country of my childhood. I walked the streets of
Manhattan for six months. I thought my spirit would take care of
me. I ended up unconscious on somebody's floor for three days. Hard
things happened. My spirit was having a wonderful time walking
to the Metropolitan Museum in the December rain every day. My
spirit was singing louder and louder of its great happiness. My body
nearly died of pneumonia. A simple poetry won't make a whole out
of adult life.

     When I was in New York, I bought a toy in a children's store: a
matchbox full of small painted things—a tree, a dog, a man, and sheep.
I was living in a room belonging to somebody who was away. I put
my wooden things on a table and worked at moving them around for
a month. I thought there was a perfect order for them, and if I could

discover what it was, they would be at peace the way a work of art is complete. The poem about all that is called "The Beckett Kit."

When I look at the poem now, I see that the world as it is entered it. First there is a table. Then I finally discovered the tree should stand in the back next to the dog while the man lies with the sheep. It took two months. Then I got it right, and the poem says, "Ah, world, I love you with all my heart." It is not talking just about the world I arranged. It's talking about this world, where we are now. The Hudson River, police talking far off over a car radio, the war, jail, Oakland playing Cincinnati. The world found a home in my poetry. My poetry and I changed to let that happen. The poetry and the life are mixed together, just as the sacred and the real are. I know more about love because of that. The world is not smaller than the gods, nor is it more important than they are.

When I finished my new book, *Alma*, and gave it to Random House, I went back to Greece. I had lived four years there on different islands. This time I went to Lesbos to write my poems. After a month I knew they were shallow, so I lay on my cot and didn't move. I felt my life was at stake. I decided I was going to lie there until I was ready to write seriously. I had come to write poems about being a happy woman on a Greek island in springtime. But I discovered what I wanted was only part of it. I had to find out what the poems wanted to be. I got up and walked to the sea, sat on the ground with my back against a bank of dirt. As I sat, a pebble rolled down into my hand. But it wasn't a pebble. When I looked, it was the tiny head of a girl. A head more than two thousand years old. So I walked back to town and bought a loaf of bread. It was still warm. I took it back to my room and began writing my Her poems. Not knowing if Her was Demeter or Persephone or Aphrodite or the Earth itself. But certainly something bigger than myself, and female. As the days passed and the poems came, I also got back the stars and the warm silence of my childhood. I had not left the gods and spirits behind.

There is a communion between the gods and the human. They give to each other. And the same transaction happens between life and the poem. Just as I could see the seven-foot goddess in the months of searching and not finding her. Just as the ancient cucumbers of Praxilla are still fresh. Life and poetry become each other.

Travel Writing
and the Specter of Transience

LINDA WATANABE MCFERRIN

Linda Watanabe McFerrin is the author of the novel *Namako: Sea Cucumber* and *The Hand of Buddha,* a collection of short stories. *Namako* was named a Best Book for the Teen Age Reader by the New York Public Library. She came to the Twin Cities as part of the Loft Mentor Series, which brings four nationally known writers to Minnesota to work intensively with eight local writers selected through the Mentor Series Competition.

Of this essay she writes: "To me travel and life are analogous. My work and my philosophy are informed by my travels. . . . It seems to me that we, as a culture, are very shortsighted these days—concerned only with getting from one point to another. I've always been far more interested in the journey than the destination. In this essay I discuss literary responsibility in a world that seems increasingly in it for the short haul."

Travel Writing and the Specter of Transience

As a child, I spent years under a wide blue Montana sky, cocooned in insecurity and stiff little dresses, a minuscule mote in a landscape where square miles were the yardstick of distance.

And I saw nothing.

I didn't see the way dawn touched the short black mountains, first with bruised periwinkle fingers, then with broad rosy palms, or how twilight withdrew reluctantly at the end of long summer days; how nights unfurled, star sequined, and scented with the sharp green tang of pine forests. At the time, I didn't see much of anything. I saw the sidewalk under my feet, scored with my chalk marks; the asphalt under the wheels of my bike; and the colorful layers of my peanut butter and jelly sandwiches.

It is easy, given this simplicity, to remember a particular grade-school teacher, fond of her own voice, who read to us in the third-grade class of North Star Elementary School. Among the things she read (most of them over our heads and obviously more for her pleasure than ours) were selections from the journals of explorers Meriwether Lewis and William Clark. I remember the reading with great clarity, for this was the first time writing made me see the landscape about me.

On Friday, May 31, 1805, Meriwether Lewis, canoeing along the Marias River in the vicinity of Great Falls, Montana, wrote:

> The hills and river Cliffs which we passed today exhibit a most romantic appearance. The bluffs of the river rise to the hight of from 2 to 300 feet and in most places nearly perpendicular: they are formed of remarkable white sandstone . . . the water on the course of time descending from those hills and plains on either side of the river has trickled down the soft sand cliffs and woarn it into a thousand grotesque figures . . . nitches and alcoves of various forms and sizes are seen at different hights as we pass. The thin stratas of hard freestone intermixed with soft sandstone seems to have aided the water in forming this curious scenery. As we passed on it seemed as if those seens of visionary enchantment would never have an end . . .

The teacher's voice droned on, climbing and descending like the river the explorers followed. Gradually, what had seemed to me to be flat earth against the flat pan of the sky flickered magically and changed. The world grew round before me. I saw waterways with names like Salmon, Snake, and Musselshell unwind to crawl through serpentine beds, or plunge over precipices into granite basins. I saw a country-side teeming with wildlife—elk and buffalo and bear. I saw the trailing limbs of willows and tangles of vines. I saw Indians and smelled the buckskin of their garments.

Now, as I blinked awake and saw the panorama of my environment for the first time, I could also see what was missing. It was a beautiful world around me, but it was not the same one that Lewis and Clark described in 1805. Already much of it had passed away, buried in those meticulous accounts of elk and antelopes shot; willow, cottonwood, and box elder trees felled; and chokecherry, sarvis berry, gooseberry, and currant bushes stripped.

This did not trouble me much at the time—the universe was brand new and fresh as it came streaming into me, and I was absorbed in the first naming. That summer I watched as a bear pressed paw pads into the windows of our station wagon at Yellowstone National Park. I saw Blackfoot Indians dance in the shadows of blue glaciers in the Canadian Rockies. No matter that the Indians were dancing for a horde of loud, ill-mannered tourists, or that the bear was probably looking for another peanut butter and jelly sandwich. To me, it was of small concern that I didn't see things in their pristine, natural state. What was important was that when I met a brown boy in school who was too shy to speak, I knew a little about the history of his people, and I did not torment him as the others did—as I might have done before. Maybe a sense of sorrow and urgency began to grow in me then with those first kernels of beauty.

Years have passed, and I haven't lost my amazement or awe at the rush of the world entering me, like breathing in a great influx of air. I've lost loved ones. I've left people and places behind, and I feel more acutely than ever the sense of things passing. I'm still insecure and self-absorbed at times, still the girl in her stiff dress carefully negotiating a course in the world. But now I cover my terrain with an explorer's inquiring eye and the vigilance of a scout. The old specter of transience still haunts me, and I don't walk through the world without a certain amount of pain. I live in a space far more cramped and congested than the generous territories of my youth. The world I live in is one where rainforests and barrier reefs are disappearing; where islanders invest in karaoke equipment to please the throngs of visitors. Exploiters have replaced explorers. I cannot stem the tide, and I am caught in a desperate sense of a disappearing legacy. My sense of urgency grows.

Returning from Europe not long ago, self-satisfied and satiated with experience, I sat between a white-haired couple in their seventies. She liked the window and he liked the aisle, so I was well placed. They wouldn't hear of me moving. They were celebrating their fiftieth wedding anniversary, which we toasted with airline champagne. We traded travel stories, their favorite being a safari the previous year that took them through Masai Mara in Kenya. Conditions sounded hard in the East African bush—I was impressed by the intrepid spirit of my elderly seatmate and told her so.

"Oh yes, it's difficult," she said, "but well worth it."

I told her that I was also hoping to make a trip to Africa one of these days, to Kiambu and Samburu.

She looked at me, her blue eyes squinty, thin lips pursed.

"Well you'd better hurry, dear," she said in a voice that made it apparent she knew what she was talking about. "It won't be there for long."

"It won't be there for long." This is the exigency I carry around with me on my travels. I have confidence in man and nature. The world renews itself, but what we see from the window today passes from view tomorrow. This is what makes me travel. This is what makes me write.

We live in a world of historical context. We are poised at the edge of our literature. Our lessons are behind us, and the clean and impeccable future is before us. Communication is profuse and immediate, as is our consciousness of the interrelationship of all that exists. The records of our errors are well documented and accessible in many languages. Curiosity propels those of us who write about our journeys— we follow in the footsteps of priests and explorers, adventurers and entrepreneurs, those who leave behind their scrawls and the trails of their reflections.

In our wake we travelers often leave unhoused populations and spoiled wilderness. Through the unwincing eyes and ears of our technology, we can see the way the decisions and investments we make here and today can affect how much milk a baby in Uganda gets. We share a new concept of this planet as a finite space, denser and more difficult to navigate than ever. We have globes on our desks and ecosystems in our hands. We live in an environment fraught with hazards, and we need good guides: truthful guides who tread softly.

I think of the toothless old man Arturo, who took me down the old King's Highway toward Taxco sharing stories of *brujos* and shamans, explaining, "The Mexican culture is in an early state of menopause." I think of Connie, who showed me twilight on the top of St. George over Athens, and the fine whitewash of noon over the ruins atop the Acropolis (now mostly moved indoors). I think of Doug, who dragged me through Singapore's wet markets at dawn and ran with me through a Malaysian jungle, skirting cobras. I think of the guides I've only met in print; M.F.K. Fisher, who introduced me to the beauties of Provence; Lawrence Durrell, whose poems and prose lured me to Greece; of Meriwether Lewis and William Clark, who opened for me the window that I will never close; of hosts of other good scouts. They have given the world a treasure trove of stories. They have given the world a past, and, looking forward with intelligence and compassion, they are giving it a future.

Open Discovery in the Art of Creative Nonfiction

KIM R. STAFFORD

Last summer I was talking with a writer who moonlights with the public defender's office. (For some writers, the day job is moonlighting; the novel at night is where the warm sun shines.) We were standing by the Methow River in the north Cascades of Washington state, for the dedication of a series of poetry road signs the US Forest Service had commissioned from my father, William Stafford, and John was telling me about a custom in the practice of law called "open discovery." By this custom, the prosecutor and the defense attorney share all evidence. Every clue one discovers is given at once to the other. With open discovery, John said, once all details are shared, the DA and the defense attorney each then write a story from this evidence: Maybe it went this way, maybe that.

As John spoke, I glanced beyond his shoulder at my father's words etched on the sign by the guard rail: "Some time when the river is ice ask me / mistakes I have made." I looked beyond the shoulder of the sign, where the river itself pondered through the willows, and swung out wide into a riffle: "Ask me whether / what I have done is my life." I thought about the accused, how evidence might lean against a life— the night in question, the knife, possible motives scattered through years of trouble. I thought about my own life following the strange channel of its destiny from that place before to this place now: "Some have tried to help / or to hurt: ask me what difference their strongest love or hate has made." And John went on talking; his own research on behalf of the accused had led him beyond story to myth, to Tlingit tellings from way back that defend our kinship with the earth, with that world where woman marries bear, and the people remember their ancestry direct to salmon, eagle, cedar, and frog.

In such a place, at a certain point, human conversation dies away. We listened to the river, John and I. We listened to the water, and to the way pines took wind and passed it along, to the hiss of cars in migration from west to east, from east to west, to the soft rattle of aspen gold that swivels at its tether. I wondered how a defender, inquiring through open discovery into a life, into one night's crisis, might save that life, if that defender could get the story right. Or the prosecutor might find a stronger story. Or the old story, stronger than any, might teach the new story about deep kinship, the strangely human impulse of salmon to go home, the child's instinct of a raccoon cub at play, a girl's flight of swan, a boy's cedar poise, the old motive of the sun that feels along the ground, the moon's looming drag on all it passes. In the forest, by the road, where the Forest Service had established a sign by the river about the river, we had met. John and I turned to look at the river. We both had lost my father. Already, we knew each other well enough to hold that silence exactly between us. Having spoken a few important things, we would be equal to anything. One pure moment of sharing what we know could be the treasure we call friendship in the world. We said goodbye then; he went north, and I went south.

From that place, I go forward wondering. My father's poem ends, "What the river says, that is what I say." But what does the river say? What will I say? Next time I sit down with the open discovery of all I have met, how will the true story crawl through the pen in my hand into being? Word by word it arrives, bend by riverbend, fin by paw, defense, prosecution, killer, savior, river, road, sunlight, moonlight, letter, essay, story, song. The story will come into being by the struggle of writing what I don't quite know. A river has urgency, goes around the rock, and travels on. We translate that river in many ways. And in my writing, if it is song disguised as prose, I would call that translation of what the river says creative nonfiction. I would call it the literature of information. I would call it the musical arrangement of passionate fact. I would call it an intimate negotiation between writer and reader, in the presence of the actual, informed by some inevitable, found thread of understanding.

That thread will always be there, for the writer is the kind of teacher who invites others into the room where the evidence can be displayed, and then lets the process of discovery happen. I tell my wife I'm not ready for class; she tells me I should not be more ready than the students with answers, but be alert to meet them in the presence of their own writing. Once she says this, I'm ready. I feel my hunger for what they will teach me.

For the writer, as well as for the reader, creative nonfiction is the search for the most compelling story, or complex of stories, behind a given screen of information. In the process of the essay, memoir, fact-based sermon, informing prayer, traveler's journal, vivid profile, family saga, or other genre cousin within the tribe of creative nonfiction, the writer and reader share a certain collection of facts, chronologies, physical sensations, resonant place, a cast of characters. These truths we hold in common, and then we each—like prosecutor and defense attorney—try to find the thread of story that makes it all matter. The writer has spread out these shining things, and waited, and then, by writing, learned. The reader beholds this array of shining things, and waits, and then, by reading, invents. In the presence of these things, something will happen. The story for the writer will be some magnetic wire of meaning that binds the collection of facts into some provisionally satisfying form, some silk thread that gathers the beads. The story for the reader will include the writer's necklace, but will include other possibilities, because the facts of the story, the beads, are negotiable currency in the reader's imaginative economy. You tell me about Minnesota winter, in dear detail, with your lit thread of discovery that binds all things—icicle, nose prickle, night dog's bark—and I begin to understand my own thousand and one nights in small-town motels, traveling in the ministry of the word.

Because the raw material is fact, the writer and reader exist as partners in the open discovery of meaning. Because the work is literary, the way the facts become story is more important than some final destination of knowledge. We will want to read again. And each time we read, new deep stories may gather into our minds. In all this process, the most enticing experience for me is the discovery of the thread, the second story, the background coherence, the thing I don't know until I do. Until this happens, life is random; after this happens, life is mysterious.

Last week at a conference in Florida, I felt like a little boy newly entering the world: There behind the hotel, beyond the filled pad of the parking lot, lay miles of swamp, ribbons of bristling scrub, glittering pool and slough and casual stream, and I didn't know the names. I stood in ignorant wonder, eager as a boy. That bird flouncing a tail long as a shadow, that stunted tree writhing up from black water, that small frame house trimmed in jade green, with a madonna in the yard of white sand—I could see them in their resonance equal to that riverbank in my native Oregon, when I was small and amazed, when I told my parents, "I want to go jump into the daylight." From the hotel, I wandered. The two sailors standing by a woman on the corner, one of them kissing her long and leisurely, while the other smoked a cigarette. The turtle's triangle head pointing up from the water a block from city hall. The silk air warm and heavy on my brow. The splayed foot of the lizard on the sidewalk inside my shaggy head shadow. The fine sand of the anthill stirred to frenzy by my fingertip. At dusk, the neon vacancy sign that hurt me. At two a.m., the old man's face on the hotel TV screen without sound. At dawn, the frayed "Do not disturb" tag in my hand.

Reader, what is our story? What is mine, and what is yours? My father has died. You have been confused. My brother was a traveler. You are about to face a secret you have treasured. There you are, beside me, reading this world. Something rises up as we stare at the white plastic spoon turning and turning in slow water, under the bridge that leads to the convention center.

Voyeur in the House
of Performance Art

DIANE WILSON

"Imagination is integral to courage: The sensibility that imagines no risks does not knowingly take any, and there is no bravery in a landscape without danger."
—Georgia O'Keeffe

In the five years that I have worked for the Southern Theater, I have yet to grasp the reasons that compel artists to leave the safety of their homes to venture onto the stage. I have seen artists confront their own panic and anxiety in the last hours before an opening night, witnessed both the exultation and depression that follow performance, and wondered what motivates, what fuels the intense passion they bring to their medium. Why performance rather than film, or writing, or painting?

This question has led not to an answer as I had once hoped, but to a moment of illumination in which my understanding of theater and its relationship to writing was forever changed.

In the fall of 1993, we assembled a small group of performers from a variety of disciplines who were willing to spend six months honing their critical writing skills. Under the auspices of a grant from the Center for Arts Criticism, these performers spent hours sprawled across my living-room floor as we debated questions of art and life and writing, surrounded by pizza boxes and empty coffee cups. The results were to be published in the Southern's newsletter—of which I am the editor—and read in a final reading/performance, which was to be the *coup de grace* for the group.

At the Southern, not surprisingly, I have been a minority of one who has found the written word more compelling than a physical performance. A critical essay written by a performer, for example, reveals what the artist's process has been and illuminates the sometimes obscure historical, cultural, or family issues that were part of the original spark for creation. Thus the essay can set the stage for the performance by creating a context that will allow a deeper appreciation of the artist's work, an understanding of the ideas within the work. It can speak to the full potential of the piece as visualized in the artist's mind, reflecting more accurately than the performance the artist's reach. The performance indicates only where the artist has landed.

Providing a written context is also a way of responding to the difficulties that performance art can present to an audience, as it is essentially a form with few rules that sprawls across mediums and tends to be driven by the intensely personal vision of the artist. Without some kind of context, people are often left scratching their heads and wondering what they have just seen.

Artists writing about their own work provide a point of entry to the audience. In my ignorance, however, I overlooked an essential part of the process. I had been focusing on writing as a way of explaining a performance, rather than giving my attention to understanding the performance itself. It was only by coincidence, by the collision of artists writing critical essays and then performing for their final public celebration, that I was forced to realize that the relationship between writing and performance is infinitely more complex.

On the evening of the reading/performance, we planned to have the artists read their essays and perform a short piece in their own medium. One of the essays was written by Marcus Young, a twenty-four-year-old emerging performance artist who had written of his struggle to define art in his life and on the stage. At one point he wrote, "My definition of theatre is a whisper followed by the striking of a match followed by laughter." As I understood his words, Marcus was calling for a nontraditional form of theater that could heighten, or stimulate, an awareness of the artistry that is present in the world around us.

He also told a story about the "can man" who made sculptures from aluminum soda cans picked from the garbage; he suggested that certain venerable art institutions should be burned down and wished for "a movement that asks more of people's imaginations and less of their pocketbooks."

The artist's purpose, as I understood Marcus, is to pay close attention to all the detail of being alive. To live simply, like his neighbor who supports himself with a low-paying job and sees visions of sculptures in large pieces of dead wood. Rather than bemoaning the separation of art from life, Marcus turned the issue around and asked that we consume art with our spirits, with our daily routines, with our thinking. He said, "When we are able to strip art of its artificialities, we see that art is very simple. It is a Coke can. It is skipping. It is sunrise and sunset."

I had read the essay enough times in the editing process to have committed parts to memory, and I was quite comfortable with having made rational sense of his statements. As I sat in the theater on the evening of his performance, I was content and therefore somewhat complacent in the knowledge that I had understood the writing and was therefore fully prepared to understand the performance.

On a typical performance night someone who works for the theater usually gives a short speech to the audience. On this evening, however, the lights slowly dimmed to the point of complete blackout for Marcus's piece, "thought." There was no introduction, no scurrying stage crew carrying props to the tape marks. Only the blackout and its accompanying blanket of silence—a darkness that continued long past the point of comfort. My eyes strained to make out any kind of form on the stage, but I saw nothing. The audience was alert, and a little restless.

The silence was finally broken by the loud roar of an explosion, followed by more silence and the distant sound of a baby crying. A carefully choreographed light show by John Goodlad accompanied a sequence of unrelated sounds, all of it moving at a slow, thoughtful tempo. It was a visceral, sensory performance. There was nothing and no one on the stage; we were simply given a relationship between shifting patterns of light and sound. The theater space with its crumbling plaster walls and cracked vinyl seats had disappeared, leaving only the odd niche momentarily illuminated, or a pattern in the light grid that was suddenly made visible, or a miniature version of the theater arch

that was miraculously carved out of light and reflected on the wall. I
heard words, numbers, laughter, but without any kind of linear order
to create meaning. My sense of time and space became disordered, and
I had to abandon my attempt to organize the performance into logical
thoughts. I could listen and look, but not think.

At this point, the little understanding I had of performance was
blown wide open. I experienced a shock, a wordless jolt, of the variety
one receives after realizing that something is not what it seems—
when the vicious dog lurking on a dark sidewalk turns out to be a
frozen cabbage. Having been given what I thought were separate
pieces—an essay and a performance—I now realized that it was impossible to distinguish between the two because they were simply different
elements in an overall portrait of the artist. I had a profound sense of
suddenly knowing him in a way entirely distinct from the personality I
knew in the artists' group. It is one thing to know a person's face, laugh,
and taste in pizza; it is another thing entirely to also know his sounds,
thoughts, and vision. He, and every artist willing to risk genuine vulnerability, offer a glimpse into their souls. They stand, disembodied, in
every sound and movement that occurs on the stage.

In his essay, Marcus revealed his passion for both his art and the
world he lived in by using the old writer's rule, "show, don't tell." What
I had read was a performance, and what I saw on the stage was a form
of parallel reality, like a mirror image—the same thing is reflected, but
it is not the thing itself. The essay was written not as a context but as
its own entity. I could see the same artist's hand in each. The sense of
grace and measured tempo, the spareness, the highly organized use of
fragmentation.

By capturing the same experience in each form, Marcus may have
found a true way to convey context to the reader. The words he chose,
the juxtaposition of ideas that jumped from one topic to the next
and then slid into parentheses as if we were allowed to hear his secret
thoughts, were the literary equivalent of his performance. Sitting on
a park bench in early spring as he wrote his sound score on sheets of
graph paper, Marcus would set aside his work and write his essay.

He said he had not consciously intended it to have a direct connection to the performance. As a result of his simultaneous writing

process, however, the reader is left with similar impressions of the artist whether from the essay or the show.

Perhaps of greatest importance was the sense of revelation I felt sitting on the side of the stage, realizing that I was understanding the world in a new way. Old thinking had been momentarily disrupted and I realized that I had been refusing to listen to another language, that of the stage. In my word-bound brain, I had dismissed the power of the physical image, of movement, light, and sound as too gross to convey the subtleties of abstract thought.

I had limited my own writing by not considering the power of staging, and I had done a disservice to the performers who wrote for the newsletter by not fully understanding the relationship of writing and theater. While there remains a great need and use for context and explanation, I had overlooked the performer's unique understanding and the true strength that they bring to writing—the ability to create a performance.

I also understood, at last, that a performance like this cannot be viewed from a linear, rational perspective. The brain has to abandon its interior monologue and its tendency to invest meaning into the spectacle of performance art, where the rules of traditional theater generally do not apply. The body is the proper audience, and the appropriate response is to simply allow the performance to wash over oneself, rather than to make literal sense of it. For those of us accustomed to looking for a little meaning in our theater, it is akin to being asked to throw the paddles out of the lifeboat and simply float with the current.

And this point, of course, is where the true adventure begins. For writers accustomed to thinking in terms of arranging words and creating meaning, not using those skills means discovering a new way of experiencing the creative process. Tired writing muscles get a rest, and weaker visual muscles grow stronger. Writing forces artists to clarify concepts; performance forces writers to consider staging, to examine the visual and dramatic strength in their writing.

As a result of this personal epiphany, I began to make sense of a statement I had often heard, that the arts have the power to offer new perspectives, thereby changing the world through change in individuals. A person's deeply held convictions can shift like tectonic plates in the earth, suddenly and with little warning, altering the landscape without the conscious knowledge that one has been moving in that direction.

To step out of a comfortable niche is to take a risk. When a writer walks onto an empty stage, when a performer is faced with a blank piece of paper, they open themselves to the possibility of learning something new. In our willingness to be ignorant, there is room for discovery not only of the world around us, but of our own human potential. As Henry Miller once said, "If one must have a goal, which is questionable, why not self-realization?"

Journal Writing: From the Inside Out

ELIZABETH JARRETT ANDREW

One of the finest pieces of evidence pointing to God's existence, it seems to me, is the fact that, daily, tens of thousands of people pen their thoughts to an invisible reader. How common the journal is, and yet how extraordinary. I know the impulse: Before dawn, when the boundaries of the world are only the farthest reaches of my reading-lamp's light, I curl up in my grandmother's afghan with a cup of coffee and open my journal onto my lap. Perhaps those thousands of people who share my habit don't believe in God. Perhaps what they believe in is the ready availability of the next blank page, or the safe containment of one solid cover at the beginning and one at the end. Does the distinction matter? Do any of us comprehend to whom it is we pen our passions, or why?

"I want to write," Anne Frank told Kitty, her plaid-covered diary whose pages were hid doubly from the world. "But more than that, I want to bring out kinds of things that lie buried in my heart." Under layers of seclusion and privacy, the impulse of a young girl is to use the journal like an empty bucket, a means for hauling up from fathomless depths the watery stuff of her being. It's never enough to trust that the well is full. We drag up its contents, hand over hand, day after day, into a light which is most often concealed. And the words of our labor usually meet a fate less public than Kitty's—in other words, they are burned or hidden or forgotten. We pull up the contents of our hearts and there, in the nakedness of our own handwriting, they lie exposed, with no human reader but ourselves to acknowledge their longings and ecstasies.

For most printed matter, readership is life and breath. Two minds—the writer's and the reader's—meet on the common playing ground of the page; the dynamics between them give vitality to those otherwise inanimate words. The writer banks on the reader laughing, making associative leaps, bringing to the text the baggage and wonder of a lifetime. The reader looks for invitations to enter and engage the writer's material. Under normal circumstances, we write and read in relationship, and both parties are necessary for creation to occur.

But the journal seems to have a dead end. Unlike every other kind of writing, the possibility of a human audience destroys the journal's potential. Had Anne Frank known that her private diary would be translated into thirty languages, had she a clue to the number of adolescent hearts who would rely on her words for comfort, surely her rebellious, girlish thoughts would have been stymied. There is a hesitating, self-conscious prose which girls (not to mention adults) use when writing papers for presentations. Audience looms large then, usually sneering like a classmate or wielding a teacher's blood-red pen. Concern for what others will think infiltrates what it is we have to say; it shapes and misshapes our thoughts.

Anne, instead, conceived of her diary as an imaginary friend. Kitty is the type of soul mate most adolescents (and fewer adults—only those with enough spark of youth remaining to still inhabit the desire to be fully known) pine after. Kitty is always present, she's a patient listener, she validates Anne's opinions by mirroring them back in black-and-white, and, judging from the depth and consistency of Anne's disclosure, she is fully trustworthy. The relationship that sparks Anne's creativity is the antithesis of a human readership. It is a covenant that only imaginary eyes will read her inmost thoughts.

And yet to perceive these imaginary eyes as less than real is to do injustice to a sharp, albeit young, mind. Like any reader, Kitty lends form to Anne's entries. Anne is conscious that Kitty is new to the cast of characters and the setting of her confined life, and takes great pains to introduce her, even down to the routine details of her day—when they eat, the sad state of their potatoes, the conversation at the table. Once Kitty has been informed of the basics, Anne lengthens and deepens her discussion, as girlfriends do. Kitty is by no means a void into which Anne drains her thoughts. No vacuity could ever elicit words like "I firmly believe that nature brings solace for all sorrows" from a fifteen-year-old. Kitty has personality and exists in time, growing in awareness as Anne herself grows. That Kitty is a reader of substance is evidenced by how easily those of us who are made of flesh and bones can slip into her shoes. The path between Anne and Kitty is open and accessible. When readers walk it, we cannot doubt that Anne wrote to someone real.

Whether or not we have the wisdom to name our journal and call it a friend, none of us pens entries into nothingness. The page is still a meeting place, even if we are uncertain who or what we meet there.

A common perception is that we dialogue with ourselves in the journal—the conscious with the subconscious mind, the mind with the heart. After all, the only reader who ever opens those spiral-bound books lining my writing desk is myself. One would think that having oneself as an audience would lead to a tiresome diatribe. And at times, when I forget to be wide-eyed and optimistic, it does. Then the fact that I am in an old marriage with my journal becomes painfully evident. It's been twenty years, and I'm bored. Day after day, the same thing—a few comments about bird or wildflower sightings, a dream described in grueling detail, and some uneven, whining paragraphs. My mind wanders midsentence, and by the time it returns the sentence lacks significance, or even coherence. I stick with it out of habit, or commitment, or a drive to perpetually record things in order to spite their seeming unimportance. But then, as I scrawled in my journal not a week ago, "There are times, especially after reading a fine writer—especially a writer whose sentence structure is crisp and original—when my mind wants to construct the world into language, and does, and the prospects are too wonderful to contain." In a flurry of what is, for me, insight and fresh prose, the possibilities my journal offers suddenly multiply. The benefits of long-term stick-to-it-iveness become evident, because the wealth of complexity within one human being, even within myself, is inexhaustible. There is enough of me that is unknown that I prove to be not such a bad reader after all.

To that which is unknown and singularly unimaginable within me, I give the name Mystery. I am a romantic sort of person; I believe language and passion and need bind each of us to something far greater than our particular selves. Surely you've encountered Mystery, too, on the pages of the journal: the moment of striking clarity as pen hits page, the old entry you stumble upon in which your self of ten years ago gives biting advice relevant to your self today, the way a dream unfolds although you assumed you'd forgotten it. Mystery: Haven't we all reread a sentence or two in our own handwriting and recognized it, the ideas or beauty of the words too large to have emerged from this small brain? After a thorough ranting in the journal, haven't we at one time or another closed the covers and stood up feeling exonerated, or at the least slightly altered from before we sat down? When I write, I always have the sensation that Mystery lurks on the other side of the page and will surface as though from the depths of a still pool.

As far as I can figure, the only element necessary for the journal to be a place where we encounter Mystery is desire. Anne Frank had it. May Sarton also had it: "Perhaps we write toward what we will become from where we are," she wrote in *Journal of a Solitude,* her words straining forward as far as possible into her future. I have tremendous desire as well; I desire epiphany and connection to the heart of the universe. I write at lightning speed, hoping to break through the barrier of the page to the place I can encounter Mystery in its pure form, where it is unadulterated by language. I can't say it's ever happened, but I've come close enough to catch glimmers. There are moments when the morning sun filters through the woods to arrive dappled at my window, where it is turned to green light by the leaves of house ivy, or the mother plant, or wandering Jew; when the organic light then casts its face onto the white surface of my lap. Suddenly I am quite certain that *this* is what I'd wanted to say—this streak of sun, this hazy shadow of vine. Or perhaps this is what the demonstrative world wanted to say, and it merged with my own desire. But before long the sun in my room angles northward, leaving nothing at all on the page, and my pen races to rectify what would otherwise be lost.

It's clear that poetic sensibility resides behind my impulse to write. But I can also imagine a journal keeper who is more concrete—someone straightforward, who lives for the details of a day. This person records which flavor of ice cream she ate at noon, what outfit she wore that day, and the nasty word Kim called Wendy on the playground. I can imagine this person because I was her, and I penned these inessential details into a small book with an aluminum lock and key when I was in elementary school. Some would call it a diary rather than a journal. And there is a distinction. Record keeping is not the same as a conversation, and lists leave less room for Mystery than questions. But

even in the flat prose of my first journals resided the potential for poetry, simply because it was there that the habits of treasuring memory
and mining details for meaning were formed. Mystery lurks even in
adolescent minutiae. Or open the pages of a farmer's weather journal,
the inches of rain and temperatures recorded meticulously, and there,
without the slightest intention on the writer's part, something mag-
nificent is present: the patterns of the natural world in implied relation
to the farmer, and, underneath, the unwritten stories of drought and
abundance. Mystery lurks in the raw facts of every life.

But when, for some of us, awareness rips open our complacency
and we want more than the facts, we want understanding and connection and relationship, and we seek it out through the vehicle of
language, our desire does its work and changes the journal's nature.
A sense of obligation doesn't do it. Nor does the motivation of guilt.
Only desire, with its power to propel, makes the journal an instrument
for transformation. The monks used to say, "Go into your cell, and your
cell will teach you all you need to know." We may not be monks, we
may have no cell, but we do have four margins and a particular portion of unfilled space. We have a tremendous desire to know. Each day,
the empty page becomes our open heart; the white spread of paper
encourages us to fill as well as to be filled.

I always have an odd and undefined sense that there is a presence who
rejoices when I open my journal. "Ah!" it seems to say, "A place where
I may be heard." The pages in the first half of the journal, which are
crammed with my handwriting, have been pressed up against pages
crammed with nothing but potential in the second half. That potential,
I believe, has a voice. It has as much desire for connection as I do. The
journal then becomes a vehicle not only for expressing my yearning,
but also through which the yearning of the world expresses itself back
to me.

There are three participants in the drama. First, there is me, the
writer, with my experience which I shoulder as we all do, like Atlas
holding up the world. Then there is that open, inanimate page. Lastly,
there is what lies beyond the page—the audience, if you will, which
is no concrete audience at all but rather airy and fourth dimensional.

It is the future, the answers to questions, the source of creation, or a completely receptive reader: Mystery; my God. Driven by a longing to make myself known, I meet Mystery at a place where we are both most opened wide. The only evidence I have that this meeting has happened is that something new is born of the encounter. It is a twist of phrase; it is a striking idea; it is a vision which will carry me forward into the complicated territory of my vocation. I am left with the vague sensation of having stretched my hand as far as possible through the veil which separates this world from the next, and it has been touched there, briefly, by other fingers.

Macrina Wiederkehr, a Benedictine sister, says that prayer is mutual yearning. Our ache meets the ache of the world in a resonant chord; the result, intentional or not, is prayer. It is in the journal's nature that such connection occur on its pages.

On an impulse, I crack open an old journal and find there nothing of significance. It was an afternoon in early spring. Ice was still clinging to the shores of a small city lake, and the silly geese who never flew south for the winter were begging for bread crumbs at my knees. I was in a melancholy mood laced with a sense of freedom that came from being outdoors. I remember the day more than other ordinary days because I had called in sick, oppressed by the three busy months that remained until the end of the school year. But why did I bother to write about it? In the grand scheme of things, March 16, 1994, has little significance. No epiphany occurred, no remarkable political upheaval was printed in the newspaper, no overt dialogue took place between me and God. But something lasting happened on those pages which will survive should they ever burn—should I ever burn them—and nothing tangible be left as a witness. A moment was lifted up. The offering of the moment was received. It was a mutual and healthy exchange, with the same enduring qualities as a spontaneous phone call between friends. Little in life, I believe, is as worthwhile.

The advantage to calling the audience of our journal—the object of our prayer—God is that it's then given a name and thereby a personality and history. But Kitty, or Mother, or Mystery will do. The fact is that the journal puts us into a relationship, and because it is a communicative device, the elements which are necessary for a relationship to lengthen and deepen are present. There is desire; there is a practice of intimate expression and disclosure; there are moments, the pen idling above the page, of deep listening. Like any relationship, the journal is nourished by an investment of time. We suffer periods of emptiness as well as moments of communion. Yet there is no bottom to the well-spring, and no ceiling above which our relationship cannot grow.

Christina Baldwin calls the journal Life's Companion. But it is not the inanimate object—the bound book—which befriends us. In the material ways of creation, the journal facilitates a relationship between immaterial, creative forces. I look at the expanding shelf of spiral-bound notebooks on my writing desk, at the thousands of hours I have invested in filling pages which remain unopened and unread. All this time, I have understood myself to be writing the story of my life. If this is so, the end result hardly seems worth the effort; the closed-up prose is unpolished, rambling, and self-centered. No, the real story is written in reverse—God writing my life, creating through the journal the woman who is with every page slightly more complete, slightly more aware and receptive. Or more accurately, we both create a relationship with a life and story all its own. It is a love affair, or an old marriage, or a precious conversation between childhood friends. It is a meeting of two hearts, at which sometimes accurate minutes are taken and sometimes not. This companionship begins long before ink splatters the page, and lasts beyond the final mark of punctuation. It is as endless as the number of empty pieces of paper. It is as varied as the stories we still have left to tell.

Up-North Literary Life

WILL WEAVER

April, with its sunny days and frosty nights, is cruel to my perennials but still a reasonably good month for writing. I live five miles east of Bemidji on the Mississippi River. Spring in the Twin Cities means open water and barges and tulips outside the Saint Paul Hotel; "up north," the landscape remains chilly, bland, muted. The Mississippi outside my library window palely loiters, icebound and still. On the far shore, the palette of colors is from the Ebenezer Scrooge Crayon Collection: leafless aspen, dusty green conifer, a brushstroke of washed-blond riverbank grass. Nothing moves but a slow-flying raven and, closer in at the feeder, a few dependable black-capped chickadees. The days are lengthening, though slowly. The afternoon slant of light is higher and wider, but still without heat. Seasons *en pointe*. Nature's caesura.

This is the time of year I feel most literary. At the end of a winter's writing, I can hold the full arc of a novel in my head; I can see its assemblage, and I can make cuts unimaginable just weeks earlier. My characters' lives pulse in my fingertips. My editor in New York returns my e-mails within the hour. The whole world turns on the novel.

Then the robins arrive. Wood frogs hawk their throats in sunny ponds, and the river begins to groan and stir. As ice tectonics grumble in the night and daily heighten their pitch, I press to finish work in progress. Like someone diagnosed with incipient memory loss, with imminent derangement, I start writing earlier and earlier each morning; I wake up in the night to jot down notes. I try to leave myself a trail.

On April 16, give or take a day, it's "breakup" time on the river. Honeycombed, crushed ice slides downstream with the sound of a thousand chandeliers stirring in a summer breeze. I put my papers in order and try to muster a happy face: only a crazy person or novelist would be unhappy for the arrival of spring in Minnesota. The same day the river is clear of ice, two loons swim steadily upstream, towing summer along in their perfect wake.

Spring up north is an hour long. It's rough strife. It's hot and windy, the air thick with pine pollen and aspen fuzz, the highways littered with roadkill. Barely into May, there's blue daylight at 4:30 a.m. Birds are in full call at 5:00, the woodpeckers drumming like the Blue Man Group; a beaver, not long out of her cold, dark mud hut, thuds the water again and again with her spatulate tail.

No use going back to bed. I make coffee, look through some pages of my fiction. The sentences are flat and lifeless on the page, their effect diminished, as if written in disappearing ink, even as I read. But no time to fret over adverbs or semicolons—the dog is barking at a skunk, intervention required—and by then my wife is up, fully dressed in summer shorts and top, and has cooked eggs (it has taken her only seconds). After breakfast I'm drafted to plant peas and onions in the garden, where the chives burst through the ground when my back is turned, and the Baltimore orioles, hummingbirds, and rose-breasted grosbeaks arrive as a cohort, an avian circus blown in on a warm south wind; I hustle to cut a couple of oranges in half and nail them onto the garden fence, but a thirty-pound snapping turtle—her shell a large raku serving platter etched in the lost language of turtles—blocks the front door, she who comes every spring, programmed in her turtle brain to lay her eggs where my house sits (which is why, for karmic reasons, I cannot pave my gravel driveway). I go for a stick—she'll strike and clamp onto it—and then I can drag her away to a better spot, but when I return she has left, on the sunny side of the driveway, a scrabbled, damp-mouthed excavation softened by her own urine, a moist channel into which she has hunched out her twenty ping-pong-ball-sized eggs; I make a mental note to cover it with chicken wire against night-sniffing skunks—however, first I must mow the lawn, which is already ankle high and rising (within minutes my old mower will not handle its lushness), because I want the yard looking good for the flood of summer visitors: daughter Caitlin and her fiancé, both from Manhattan, who arrive only moments after I put away the mower. Luckily, the first peas are ripe, and a perfect complement for our lunch of fresh crappie, buttered toast, a chilly Viognier, and rhu-barb pie, Caitlin's favorite. They stay only ten minutes, then fly back to New York, which affords me a moment to write, during which I manage the first sentence of a new story: "The funeral was not all that sad," a sentence solid enough to sustain me through Bill, a pal from the old glory days at Stanford (he's getting divorced and stays only thirty seconds, twenty of which he spends online), and after him the Norwegians, a foursome of writers and filmmakers on some kind of New-World, post-emigrant research/vision quest. They want to meet me, writer and son of pioneers, and I tell them my story, how my great-grandfather, out of loneliness for the Old Country, drowned himself in the shallow lake on the home place, and whether it is that tale, or the aquavit talking, within seconds we are all weeping (I really need a nap), and when they're gone my wife and I head down to the dock to lie on the hot cedar boards for sun and a siesta with the dragonflies circling around us, and I am just drifting off when there is a violent shrilling, squalling, flapping in the air directly above. I jerk upright as a prism falls from the sky, its rainbow colors flashing, and an osprey screams at an eagle that has tried, midflight, to grab the osprey's catch—a fat sunfish that thumps onto the shore, then flips onto the dock six feet away, where it lies stunned. The raptors fly off, harping at each other, and the iridescent fish, gasping and punctured, we push back into the river; remarkably, it swims away. Enough is enough! I tell my wife, and I head to the house for a real nap—at which point Lin and Jay and Marsh and Linda, friends from upriver, arrive by pontoon, bringing champagne and a croquet set, and as their golden retrievers race about with my dog, clock-clock go our mallets, though none of us knows the colors of our stripes, and tomorrow will be one of those mornings when everyone sits around saying, "I drank too much last night," but we complete the croquet game in four minutes because I don't want to miss my son's punk band, up from Minneapolis and playing at Hard Times Saloon—yet there's still a half hour before we must leave for that, during which time the Icelanders arrive, a group of teachers, an educational exchange, and we drive them on a speed tour around the area, stopping at Red Lake Reservation, at Itasca State Park with this handsome group of people and their language that confounds all amateur linguists. "It's the language of turtles!" one of the Icelanders says, and we all laugh wildly (we've been drinking wine) while we pontoon, turtle spotting, over to Marsh's island upstream from my dock.

There we picnic and bonfire and sing Icelandic folk songs until the stars wheel out, Andromeda and Cassiopeia (what has become of the constellations of midsummer?), our cue to head to Hard Times, where, though we try to be unobtrusive in the crowd, the lead singer calls out, "Hey, Owen's parents are here!" and they launch into his original, four-second-long song, dedicated to "all mothers out there," called "Birthing Hips," the lyrics of which are lost in amplifier fuzz (we know enough to have brought earplugs), and his bearded friends who, during grade school, used to eat us out of milk and cookies, now send over drinks with names like "Car Bombs"—but quickly it's last call, the drinks need not be finished, and moments later my wife and I are out on the street.

We shiver in our summer wear. It is, we realize, Labor Day weekend. In the morning, the yard and river are quiet. The loons have gone. The last geraniums glow ruby and garnet. A tardy hummingbird, as fat as an oversized thimble, buzzes the petunias, which we have stopped watering. Inching across the driveway is a turtle the size of a fifty-cent piece; skunks got the rest, but this little one survived and is headed for the river.

My wife murmurs something about going inside to take a long, hot bath.

I go to my study.

I sit down and look around. It's a comfortable place. A manuscript lies beneath a large agate paperweight. I open a chapter at random and start reading. It's as if somebody else wrote these sentences, but they're not half-bad.

Reading the Open Book

NANCY GASCHOTT

"**D**on't you just love the joist pockets?" Kate asks me.

Together we look at the deep row of oblong openings in the brick wall above us, each space about the size of a hefty encyclopedia's spine.

"Well," I say gently to Kate, "no, I don't love the joist pockets."

Kate Bergquist is the architect for Open Book. She's brilliant, weighs about eighty pounds, and has spectacular, enormous eyes the color of aged wood. She is patient with my aesthetic shortcomings.

"I do love the building, though," I assure her. "Actually," I add, "I'm in love with it. I'm in love with this building."

"I am, too," she says.

We are standing on the first floor of Open Book at 1011 Washington Avenue South in Minneapolis, soon to be the Loft's new home. Because sections of the second and third floors have been removed, we can look up from where we are standing and see clear to three stories above us, where plastic sheeting is now tacked over the square framed window spots. The plastic sheeting flaps and moans in the wind.

Soon glass will replace the flapping plastic, and light will stream down from the roof to the third floor, where Milkweed Editions's offices will be, to the Loft offices and classrooms on the second floor, and all the way to the first floor, near the Minnesota Center for Book Arts spaces. Soon you could be sitting with a book or your journal and a big cup of latte in Open Book's café in that light.

Soon you could attend a performance in the Dayton Hudson Hall, or look for information about Graywolf Press, or SASE, or the Walker's literary programming, on the Literary Information wall. Soon you could browse in the bookstore or attend a class in one of the Loft's five new classrooms. You might sit in the Literary Commons all afternoon with a book, and then discuss that book with your book group in the Book Club Room. You could learn all about Milkweed

Editions's "The World as Home" program, or put your hands in paper pulp at the Minnesota Center for Book Arts.

Soon where Kate and I are standing a staircase will bring you to the second floor, and as you walk up the staircase you will be enclosed by the opening pages of a book, according to the inspired design of artist Karen Wirth and senior architect Garth Rockcastle. Garth says the staircase, the people climbing it, and the wall behind it will be washed in light. I like the idea of being washed in light. It sounds clean, and warm. As you walk up to the Loft you will see those joist pockets as you are being washed in light. What's not to love?

Of course, you won't *have* to walk up the stairs. You will be able to take the elevator—an enormous, sturdy thing, designed to transport an entire Loft classroom of people, or great pallets of books between floors of the bookstore. The elevator will also take you down to the lower level, where old gray stone walls will frame MCBA studio spaces, adjacent to Milkweed's warehouse and fulfillment area.

In the year that I've been working with Kate and Garth, I've learned that a building can be read, the way a book can be read. Both can be read hurriedly and superficially for plot, place, or information. Both can be read with great attention to spirit, by a reader who stops to listen to the language, relishes descriptive phrases, breathes in the nuances of design. Open Book is a nineteenth-century building being renovated with twenty-first-century values. It invites you in for a close read, to search for evidence of its history and its secrets, to notice the grace of its language.

Reading carefully, spending some time in the building, you find: two stairways going nowhere, a safe within a safe, an old confectionery, the faces of stone dogs, the faintest shadow of the *C* in an old Coca-Cola promotion. In nearly every room you will enjoy the thick, sunrise-color brick walls. You'll also encounter a few walls with puzzling remnants of curling brown paper, and you might imagine that the contractors had neglected to clean a spot of wall. But this is purposeful—a morsel of layered wallpaper remaining for your imagination, allowing you to notice the ancient subtle floral design and be inspired by the generations of people who once lived in the room where you and the wallpaper are today.

Reading closely, you might experience the building from a variety of vantage points. Stand on the mezzanine level of the bookstore formerly known as the Hungry Mind and peer out over the lobby through its windows to watch schoolchildren trying out a printing press in the Minnesota Center for Book Arts. Come to the library resource center outside the Loft offices and lose yourself in books by Milkweed writers, basking in the light of still another light well. Stand on the third-floor deck in the afternoon and watch the clouds above the Minneapolis skyline. Spend a few hours in one of the seven writers' studios and notice the changes the sun makes on the brick walls on the other side of the alley. Walk a few blocks away and be inspired by the Mississippi as it cuts its way through the middle of the country.

Open Book, as most readers of *A View from the Loft* will know, is a collaboration among the Loft, Milkweed Editions, and the Minnesota Center for Book Arts. The vision its board of directors has for Open Book is that it will be a "catalyst for artistic collaboration, bringing together the many partners who create books, from idea to finished work." It will "invite in the greater community, through engaging activities and programs designed to awaken interest, educate and provide access to the rich and joyful universe of the written word, stories and especially books."

In the spring of 1996 eighty writers and book lovers got together in a room at the *Star Tribune* building in Minneapolis to talk about the future of literature. This event, sponsored by the Loft, provided Loft board and staff with an opportunity to imagine the future, not only of literature but of the organization as well. At the end of the day, the facilitators had everyone pull out from under their tables boxes full of grade-school art project materials: pipe cleaners, multicolor construction paper, yarn, crayons, tacks, stickers. I remember that Carol Bly fashioned a fetching set of rabbit ears for herself from the materials in that box. We were invited to "build" an image of the future. Around the big room, even as some people grumbled at the hokeyness of the exercise, little sculptures were created and described by their makers. There were castles of books, circles of storytellers "heartwired" to the Loft, special libraries. Every group, in one way or another, had created a special place for books, for writing and reading, for meeting one another, for growing. Almost four years later, many of the dreams described in those construction-paper and pipe-cleaner sculptures will be a reality.

I heard once that Washington Avenue was the first street in Minneapolis to have electric lights, and that entering from outside the city at night you would suddenly find this extraordinary avenue of streetlights. I've also heard that Washington Avenue was notorious for speakeasies and prostitution. We have a photograph of the Open Book building from that era, with the streetcar rails down the center, a horse-drawn carriage on the cobblestone street, and a single teardrop-shaped street lamp overhead.

By the time this issue of *A View from the Loft* is in your hands, the huge storefront windows on Washington Avenue will have been installed, and you can watch Dick Weeks and his crew from Olson Brothers Contractors finish the year-long renovation, turning what were three warehouses into the nation's first center for book and literary arts. We expect to be moving the Loft offices into Open Book by the end of February and offering the spring semester of classes soon after.

So come and get washed by the light!

Afterword

TOPIC COVERED:

*The destruction of policies and institutions inimical
to artistic and literary freedom*

The Loft: Then and Now

JIM MOORE

It feels to me that the political and cultural situation today in the United States is similar in many ways to the 1970s, when the Loft began in a climate of cultural excitement about the possibilities of change in this country. Granted, the optimism many of us felt at that time about the "counterculture" was not borne out in the intervening years, but some of that enthusiasm did get translated into institutions that have been long lasting and that persist, in some cases, to this day. The Loft itself is an example of one such success story. As much as it has changed over the years and decades, the core purpose remains. Although this isn't the official mission statement of the Loft, I would say that its purpose continues to be to galvanize readers and writers who care about the written word in all its imaginative possibilities. Now, as then, this is an idea not always supported in the culture at large. We felt then, and I continue to feel, that an organization like the Loft can serve as inspiration, goad, and gathering place for those who believe that political change, cultural change, and artistic innovation are not only all of a piece, but also feed each other in unexpected and crucial ways.

It's important to remember that when the Loft began it was a highly informal organization, if "organization" isn't too dignified a word to use. Those of us involved with it at the beginning—most notably Marly Rusoff—tried to figure it out as we went along. We assumed that there was a strong connection between what was happening politically in the country and what was happening in the artistic world. It made perfect sense to us who were involved with the Loft at its beginning that if we saw policies or institutions that were inimical to artistic and literary freedom, we would oppose them. Yes, there was a certain self-righteousness about it all, a kind of arrogance in our approach to the political and artistic issues that were at the center of our lives. We were convinced that we understood things better than our elders did.

It's possible to look back and groan when I think about how absolutely sure I was about so many issues. At the same time, what I loved about the period was that we felt we had the right to speak out and that in speaking out we might make a difference. I'm not sure whether young artists and writers feel the same today. Of course, there isn't just one way that artists and writers will look at these questions, but my own sense of the culture today is that there is indeed hope for change and even a sense that for the first time in many years it is a real possibility. What I don't know—and what is crucially important—is whether this desire for change will get transferred into political and cultural action, whether it might result in new institutions being formed that will last beyond the enthusiasm of the moment.

I certainly don't want to idealize what it was like in the early seventies at the Loft. We were far from being a poised group of young writers with fire in our bellies and workable solutions in our heads. Early board meetings could become chaotic discussions of just how evil Waldenbooks really was. There were interminable conversations/arguments about which foundations and organizations we should take money from (and we are talking about truly paltry sums) and which must be avoided at all costs. There were a hundred different ways to go overboard in trying to take politically responsible positions during this time when political positions of all kinds were often more works in progress than well-established guidelines.

But still, I think there was something in the spirit of the times that fed our own spirit as an incipient literary organization. We were open to the possibilities of cultural and political change in ways that it seems to me the Loft still is, for all of its changes over the years. In a recent essay in the *Hudson Review* called "Apt Admonishment," Seamus Heaney writes about the importance for poets of encountering people, images, and situations that bring them up short and cause them to reevaluate their sense of who they are. This kind of "apt admonishment" is at the heart of all genuine creative work and all genuine political change. That hope for change, that sense of possibility is present in many, many classes that are taught at the Loft to this day and in many of the readings that are such an important part of the Loft's very being. These classes and readings are the Loft's way of speaking out and speaking up; as such, they offer many opportunities for "apt admonishment."

If we were overconfident to the point of being arrogant in many ways in the early seventies as the Loft was being established, we were also humble in ways that we took for granted: eccentric furniture graced our various offices, little creatures that didn't belong in literary settings scurried from one cheese dropping to the next. We sat on the floor as a matter of course if more than a few people were together in the same room at the same time. I remember readings that went on for hours and others that ended abruptly as soon as the one person in the audience walked out. There was plenty of excitement and also plenty of moments of intense anger and frustration as poets and writers tried to figure out how to act together in ways that would genuinely help the Loft and the literary community. Without quite knowing what we were doing, we were listening, almost unconsciously, to what was happening all around us. This is what writers always do, of course. It's just that the cultural moment was so alive at the time that it became possible to move that listening forward into ragged conversations and then even more ragged efforts at actions that might help writers find each other and their audiences.

At the time there were virtually no reading series, for example, except very occasional readings at the University of Minnesota. There were no poetry-writing classes being taught at the university, although there were famous poets there teaching courses about poetry. There was a community waiting to form, a community that didn't even know it was a community. When I taught what I believe was the first poetry-writing course at the Loft, we had no idea if anyone would turn up at all. I tried to spread the word, put up some signs on telephone poles, and hoped for the best. More than twenty people turned up the first night of class, crowded into every bit of space that was available in the Loft's small room above Rusoff & Co. Books on Fourth Street in Dinkytown. It was an exciting moment. I was reminded of that moment the night of the caucuses this spring when I went over to Ramsey Junior High in Saint Paul to vote. I couldn't believe what I saw: long, long lines snaking out of the school in two directions, a kind of cheerful chaos that felt moving to me in a way very similar to how

I had felt the night of that first poetry class at the Loft. We were a community waiting to come together, a community that was suddenly very much there. The mix of idealism and chaos all seemed perfectly natural and normal the night of the caucus because it was something I had experienced in the sixties and seventies.

And it seemed perfectly natural and normal, in the 1970s, that the Loft would reject money from Honeywell because they were engaged in developing antipersonnel bombs. In our own ad hoc and hit-or-miss way, we really did listen to the community around us as it—and we—struggled to find ways to turn our country around. I hope the Loft will continue to do that during this new time of political and cultural possibility. I do realize that it is a very different time from the early seventies in myriad ways, and yet, there are some similarities. My hope is that there are poets and writers already responding to—and documenting in the way that only imaginative literature can do—these changes in all their complexity, their contradictions, their failures and successes. It is too early, of course, to know whether this is happening or even how it might manifest itself in poems, novels, essays, or memoirs. But my guess is that it is, in fact, already happening and that the Loft will be a home for it when the time comes, both for the making of it and the presenting of it in front of audiences. The Loft both as a home and as a catalyst for change: maybe 2010 and 1973 are not so far apart after all.

Contributors

Elizabeth Jarrett Andrew is the author of *Swinging on the Garden Gate: A Spiritual Memoir* (Skinner House, 2000), *Writing the Sacred Journey: The Art and Practice of Spiritual Memoir* (Skinner House, 2005), and *On the Threshold: Home, Hardwood, and Holiness* (Westview, 2006). She teaches at the Loft, Hamline University, and various religious communities in the Twin Cities.

Rick Bass is the author of numerous books of fiction and nonfiction, including *The Wild Marsh: Four Seasons at Home in Montana* (Harcourt, 2009), *The Ninemile Wolves* (Sierra Club, 2004), and a collection of short stories entitled *The Lives of Rocks* (Mariner, 2007).

Sandra Benítez is the author of four novels: *A Place Where the Sea Remembers* (Simon & Schuster, 1993), *Bitter Grounds* (Picador, 1998), *The Weight of All Things* (Hyperion, 2002), and *Night of the Radishes* (Hyperion, 2005).

Barrie Jean Borich is the author of *My Lesbian Husband* (Graywolf, 1999) and *Restoring the Color of Roses* (Firebrand, 1993). She is the nonfiction editor of *Water~Stone Review* and teaches at Hamline University.

Michael Dennis Browne is the author of numerous books, including *What the Poem Wants: Prose on Poetry* (Carnegie Mellon, 2009), a picture book entitled *Give Her the River* (Atheneum, 2004), and *Things I Can't Tell You* (Carnegie Mellon, 2005). Recently retired, he taught English for thirty-nine years at the University of Minnesota.

Emilie Buchwald is the author of two award-winning novels for young readers, *Gildaen* (Harcourt Brace Jovanovich, 1973; Milkweed Editions, 1993) and *Floramel and Esteban* (Harcourt Brace Jovanovich, 1982; Milkweed Editions, 2009), and, under the pen name Daisy Bix, the picture books *Buddy Unchained* and *At the Dog Park* (The Gryphon Press, 2006). As publisher emeritus and cofounder of Milkweed Editions, she was honored by the National Book Critics Circle with the 2007 Ivan Sandrof Lifetime Achievement Award. She is currently the Publisher of The Gryphon Press.

Lewis Buzbee is the author of a number of books, including *The Yellow-Lighted Bookshop* (Graywolf, 2006), *Steinbeck's Ghost* (Feiwel & Friends, 2008), and *The Haunting of Charles Dickens* (Feiwel & Friends, 2010). He teaches at the University of San Francisco.

Marilyn Chin is the author of three collections of poems: *Rhapsody in Plain Yellow* (W.W. Norton, 2003), *Dwarf Bamboo* (Greenfield Review, 1987), and *The Phoenix Gone, The Terrace Empty* (Milkweed Editions, 1994). She is also the author of a novel, *Revenge of the Mooncake Vixen* (W.W. Norton, 2009). She has translated poems by the Chinese poet Ai Qing and by the Japanese poet Gozo Yoshimasu. She teaches at San Diego State University.

Sharon Chmielarz's poetry collections include *Different Arrangements* (New Rivers, 1982), *But I Won't Go Out in a Boat* (New Rivers, 1991), *The Other Mozart* (Ontario Review, 2001), and *The Rhubarb King* (Loonfeather, 2006).

John Coy is the author of numerous picture books, including *Night Driving* (Henry Holt, 2001) and *Two Old Potatoes and Me* (Random House, 2009). He has also written novels for young adults such as *Crackback* (Scholastic, 2005) and *Box Out* (Scholastic, 2008), and is currently completing a middle-grade series, which includes *Top of the Order* (Feiwel & Friends, 2010) and *Eyes on the Goal* (Feiwel & Friends, 2010).

Jessica Deutsch is the marketing and publicity manager at Milkweed Editions. She previously interned at Coffee House Press and the Loft Literary Center.

Kate DiCamillo is the author of many books for young readers, including *Because of Winn-Dixie* (Candlewick, 2000), *The Tiger Rising* (Candlewick, 2002), *The Tale of Despereaux* (Candlewick, 2003), *The Miraculous Journey of Edward Tulane* (Candlewick, 2006), and, most recently, *The Magician's Elephant* (Candlewick, 2009).

Mark Doty is the author of eight collections of poems. His most recent book is *Fire to Fire: New and Selected Poems* (HarperCollins, 2008), which won the National Book Award. He teaches at Rutgers University.

Heid E. Erdrich is the author of three books: *Fishing for Myth* (New Rivers, 1997), *The Mother's Tongue* (Salt, 2005), and *National Monuments* (Michigan State, 2009). She is also the coeditor of *Sister Nations: Native American Women on Community* (Minnesota Historical Society, 2002).

Laura Flynn is the author of *Swallow the Ocean* (Counterpoint, 2008) and the editor of *Eyes of the Heart: Seeking a Path for the Poor in the Age of Globalization*, by Jean-Bertrand Aristide (Common Courage, 2000).

Patricia Weaver Francisco is the author of *Telling: A Memoir of Rape and Recovery* (HarperCollins, 1999), *Cold Feet* (Simon & Schuster, 1988), *Village Without Mirrors*, with photographer Timothy Francisco (Milkweed Editions, 1989), and two plays, *Sign of a Child* and *Lunacy* (Dramatic Publishing, 1985). She teaches at Hamline University.

Brigitte Frase is a poet, essayist, and literary critic. Her work has appeared in the *Hungry Mind Review*, *Ruminator Review*, the *New York Times*, the *Los Angeles Times*, and many other publications.

Glenn Freeman has published a collection of poems, *Keeping the Tigers Behind Us* (Elixir, 2007) and a poetry chapbook, *Fading Proofs* (Q Avenue, 2006). He teaches at Cornell College.

Nancy Gaschott served as the Loft's finance director and two-time interim executive director over the course of her seventeen-year tenure at the Loft.

Diane Glancy has published a number of books, including *Pushing the Bear: A Novel of the Trail of Tears* (Harcourt, 1996), *Primer of the Obsolete* (University of Massachusetts, 2004), and a collection of essays entitled *Claiming Breath* (University of Nebraska, 1996).

Vivian Gornick is the author of many books, including, most recently, *Women in Science: Then and Now* (The Feminist Press, 2009) and *The Men in My Life* (MIT, 2008). She is currently teaching at The New School.

Linda Gregg is the author of six collections of poems, including *All of It Singing: New and Selected Poems* (Graywolf, 2008) and *In the Middle Distance* (Graywolf, 2006). She teaches at Princeton University.

Marilyn Hacker is the author of numerous collections of poems, including *Presentation Piece* (Viking, 1974) and *Winter Numbers* (W. W. Norton, 1994). In 2008, she was elected Chancellor of the Academy of American Poets.

Pete Hautman writes young adult novels, "old adult" novels, and short stories. His books include *Drawing Dead* (Simon & Schuster, 1993), *Sweet Blood* (Simon & Schuster, 2003), and *Godless* (Thorndike, 2004).

Ellen Hawley edited *A View from the Loft* for eighteen years. She has published two novels, *Open Line* (Coffee House, 2008) and *Trip Sheets* (Milkweed Editions, 1998), as well as numerous short stories and essays.

David Haynes is the author of numerous novels, including *The Full Matilda* (Broadway, 2004), *Somebody Else's Mama* (Milkweed Editions, 1995), and *Live at Five* (Milkweed Editions, 1996), as well as books for young readers and several short stories. He teaches at Southern Methodist University.

Pamela Holt was a librarian for the Hennepin County Library System in Minnesota until her recent retirement. She has served both as a member and as chair of the Loft's board of directors.

C.J. Hribal is the author of numerous books, including *The Company Car* (Random House, 2006), *American Beauty* (Simon & Schuster, 1987), and *The Clouds in Memphis* (University of Massachusetts, 2000). He teaches at Marquette University.

Lewis Hyde is a poet, essayist, translator, and cultural critic. His books include *The Gift* (Knopf, 2007) and *Trickster Makes This World* (Farrar, Straus and Giroux, 1998). A MacArthur Fellow and former director of undergraduate creative writing at Harvard University, Hyde teaches at Kenyon College.

James P. Lenfestey is the author of *The Urban Coyote: Howlings on Family, Community and the Search for Peace and Quiet* (Nodin, 2000) and numerous collections of poetry and translations, including *The Toothed and Clever World* (TreeHouse, 2006), *A Cartload of Scrolls: 100 Poems in the Manner of T'ang Dynasty Poet Han-Shan* (Holy Cow!, 2007), and *Into the Goodhue County Jail: Poems to Free Prisoners* (Red Dragonfly, 2008).

Roseann Lloyd has published eight books, including three collections of poems: *Because of the Light,* (Holy Cow!, 2003), *War Baby Express* (Holy Cow!, 1996), and *Tap Dancing for Big Mom* (New Rivers, 1986). Lloyd has been a member at the Loft since 1978, and has also taught and served as a board member for the organization.

Mary Logue's most recent books include *Point No Point* (Big Earth, 2008), *Hand Work* (Midlist, 2010), and *Dark Coulee* (Walker & Company, 2000). She has published children's books, mysteries, and poetry, and has taught for many years at the Loft and Hamline University.

Adrian C. Louis is the author of a collection of poems, *Ancient Acid Flashes Back* (University of Nevada, 2001) and the editor of *Shedding Skins: Four Sioux Poets* (Michigan State, 2008). An enrolled member of the Lovelock Paiute Tribe, he teaches at Minnesota State University in Marshall.

Linda Watanabe McFerrin is the author of *Namako: Sea Cucumber* (Coffee House, 1998) and *The Hand of Buddha* (Coffee House, 2000), and is the coeditor of the Hot Flashes: sexy little stories & poems series.

Lorraine Mejia-Green's poems have been published in *Between the Heart and the Land/Entre el Corazón y la Tierra: Latina Poets of the Midwest* (Abrazo, 2001), and in literary journals such as *Willow Springs* and *Inkwell.*

Jay Miskowiec is an editor at Aliform Publishing, a literary press that focuses on the publication of world literature in translation. He is also a translator, and his recent translation, *'El viaje triunfal'/The Triumphant*

Voyage (Aliform, 2009), was awarded the National Literary Translation Grant by Colombia's Ministry of Culture.

Jim Moore's most recent collection of poems is *Lightning at Dinner* (Graywolf, 2005). He teaches at Hamline University, at Colorado College, and through the Online Mentoring for Writers Program at the University of Minnesota. He was a founding member of the Loft and has served on its board.

David Mura is the author of *Famous Suicides of the Japanese Empire* (Coffee House, 2008), *Turning Japanese: Memoirs of a Sansei* (Grove / Atlantic, 2006), and *Where the Body Meets Memory: An Odyssey of Race, Sexuality and Identity* (Anchor, 1996). He is also a poet, and his collections include *Angels for the Burning* (BOA Editions, 2004) and *After We Lost Our Way* (Carnegie Mellon, 2009).

Nora Murphy is the author of several children's history books, coauthor of *Twelve Branches* (Coffee House, 2003), and author of *Knitting the Threads of Time* (New World Library, 2009).

Kathleen Norris is the author of *Journey: New and Selected Poems* (University of Pittsburgh, 2001), *Dakota: A Spiritual Geography* (Houghton Mifflin Harcourt, 2001), *The Cloister Walk* (Penguin, 1997), and, most recently, *Acedia & Me: A Marriage, Monks, and a Writer's Life* (Penguin, 2008).

Jude Nutter's collections of poems include *Pictures of the Afterlife* (Salmon Poetry, 2002), *The Curator of Silence* (University of Notre Dame, 2007), and *I Wish I Had A Heart Like Yours, Walt Whitman* (University of Notre Dame, 2009). She teaches at the Loft.

Shannon Olson is the author of *Welcome to My Planet: Where English Is Sometimes Spoken* (Viking, 2000) and *Children of God Go Bowling* (Viking, 2004). She teaches at St. Cloud State University and at the Iowa Summer Writing Festival.

Bao Phi is the associate director of programs at the Loft, where he curates and manages Equilibrium—the spoken-word program—and the Inroads program for marginalized writers. He is a former Minnesota

Grand Slam Champion and a National Slam finalist, and was published in *Best American Poetry 2006.*

J. Otis Powell! is a radio producer at KFAI Community Radio, a curator with the Pangea World Theater Bridges project, and a mentor, editor, and roster artist for The Givens Foundation for African American Literature. A founding producer of *Write On Radio!,* he has published two collections of poems, *Theology* (Traffic Street, 1998) and *My Tongue Has No Bone* (Porter Publishing, 2001).

Susan Power is the author of *The Grass Dancer* (Penguin, 1995) and *Roofwalker* (Milkweed Editions, 2002), a Milkweed National Fiction Prize winner. Her short stories and essays have been widely published in journals, magazines, and anthologies, including *Best American Short Stories 1993.* She is an enrolled member of the Standing Rock Sioux tribe.

George Rabasa is the author of *The Wonder Singer* (Unbridled Books, 2008), *Glass Houses* (Coffee House, 1996), *Floating Kingdom* (Coffee House, 1997), and *The Cleansing* (Permanent, 2007). He has been both a member and a mentor at the Loft.

Cheri Register is the author of *Living with Chronic Illness: Days of Patience and Passion* (Simon & Schuster, 1987) and *Are Those Kids Yours?: American Families with Children Adopted from Other Countries* (Simon & Schuster, 1990). She is a Loft Teaching Fellow and an adviser in the Loft Master Track Program.

William Reichard is the author of four collections of poems: *Sin Eater* (Mid-List, 2010), *This Brightness* (Mid-List, 2007), *How To* (Mid-List, 2004), and *An Alchemy in the Bones* (New Rivers, 1999).

Julie Schumacher is the author of *The Body Is Water* (Soho, 1995), *An Explanation for Chaos* (HarperCollins, 1998), and a number of novels for younger readers, including *Grass Angel* (Random House, 2004), *The Chain Letter* (Random House, 2006), and *The Book of One Hundred Truths* (Random House, 2008). She teaches at the University of Minnesota.

Kim Stafford is the author of numerous books of poetry and prose, including *A Thousand Friends of Rain: New and Selected Poems* (Carnegie Mellon, 1999) and *Early Morning: Remembering My Father, William Stafford* (Graywolf, 2003). He is also the literary executor of the Estate of William Stafford and the editor of *Every War Has Two Losers: William Stafford on Peace and War* (Milkweed Editions, 2003).

Susan Straight is the author of *Aquaboogie: A Novel in Stories* (Milkweed Editions, 1990), *I Been in Sorrow's Kitchen and Licked Out The Pots* (Anchor, 1993), *Highwire Moon* (Random House, 2001), a National Book Award finalist, and *A Million Nightingales* (Random House, 2006). Her new novel, *One Candle to Light a Room*, will be published in 2010 by Random House.

Faith Sullivan is the author of several novels, including *The Cape Ann* (Penguin, 1989), *The Empress of One* (Milkweed Editions, 1996), *What a Woman Must Do* (Random House, 2000), and, most recently, *Gardenias* (Milkweed Editions, 2006).

Lawrence Sutin is the author of numerous books, including *When to Go Into the Water* (Sarabande, 2009), *A Postcard Memoir* (Graywolf, 2000), *Do What Thou Wilt: A Life of Aleister Crowley* (St. Martin's, 2000), and *All Is Change: The Two Thousand Year Journey of Buddhism to the West* (Little, Brown, 2006).

Katrina Vandenberg is a poet and the author of *Atlas* (Milkweed Editions, 2004). Her second collection, *An Alphabet Not Unlike the World*, is forthcoming from Milkweed Editions. She teaches at Hamline University and at the Loft.

Will Weaver is the author of *Red Earth, White Earth* (Simon & Schuster, 1986), *A Gravestone Made of Wheat* (Simon & Schuster, 1989), and *Sweet Land: New & Selected Stories* (Borealis, 2006). He has also written books for young adults, including *Full Service* (Farrar, Straus and Giroux, 2008), *Defect* (Farrar, Straus and Giroux, 2007), and *Saturday Night Dirt* (Square Fish, 2009).

Diane Wilson is the author of *Spirit Car: Journey to a Dakota Past* (Borealis, 2006) and the founder and editor of *The Artist's Voice*, a publication of the Southern Theater in Minneapolis.

Karen Tei Yamashita is the author of *Through the Arc of the Rain Forest* (Coffee House, 1990), *Brazil-Maru* (Coffee House, 1990), *Tropic of Orange* (Coffee House, 1997), and *Circle K Cycles* (Coffee House, 2001). She teaches at the University of California in Santa Cruz.

R.D. Zimmerman is the author of numerous mysteries, children's books, and mystery games. Under the pen name of Robert Alexander, he is the author of the best-selling historical novels, *The Kitchen Boy* (Penguin, 2004), *Rasputin's Daughter* (Viking, 2006), and *The Romanov Bride* (Viking, 2008).

Acknowledgments

Lewis Buzbee, "Confessions of a First Novelist," reprinted courtesy of *American Bookseller* magazine. Copyright © 1992 by Lewis Buzbee.

Marilyn Chin, "A Mentor's Words and Words on her Words," was reprinted with permission from *The Seattle Review* XXI:1.

Lewis Hyde, "A Tall White Pine: Thinking About Prophecy," was published as an introduction in *The Essays of Henry D. Thoreau* (New York: Northpoint Press, 2002). Copyright © 1986 & 2002 by Lewis Hyde.

The following people contributed directly to the success of *A View from the Loft*.

LITERARY EDITORS
Sarah Anderson Caflisch (2002–07), Chris Datta (1981), Denise Dreher (1979), Ellen Hawley (1981–99), Jenny Hill (2000), Todd Maitland (1981), Sue Ann Martinson (1979–81), Gary Nacht (1979), Bart Schneider (2001–02), Randy Scholes (1979), Dara Syrkin (2007–10), Lucy Vilankulu (2000–01), Gerry Zeck (1979)

ART EDITORS
Randy Scholes (1979–83), Bob Williams (1987–09)

CONTRIBUTING/ASSISTANT EDITORS
Adele Bergstrom (1985), Barrie Borich (1987), Ed Burke (1984–87), Colleen Curran (1988–89), Chris Datta (1980–81), Susan Denelsbeck (1983–84), Nancy Jacobs (1989), Jennifer Jesseph (1987–89), Pat Kaluza (1979), Lorenzo Lattanzi (1979), Shawna Lucas (1985), Todd Maitland (1979–81), Jorie Johnson Miller (1986–87), Sally Nereson (1988), Rosie O'Brien (1981–83), Karen Slathar Sandsness (1980), Dara Syrkin (2004–06), Allison Wells (1987), Ed Wozniak (1985)

ASSOCIATE EDITORS
Sarah Caflisch (2007–08), Dara Syrkin (2006–07), Bob Williams (2006–09)

MANAGING EDITORS
Christopher James (2000)

MEMBER EDITORS
Rebecca Rowell (2002–03)

KALEIDOSCOPE EDITORS
Kristin Bergsagel (2008–09), Lori Wilson (2009–10)

COPY EDITORS
Mary Byers (2001–10)

PROOFREADERS
Joan Kremer (2000), Craig Morris (2001), Amy Myrbo (2000–01),
Jerod Santek (2000)

PRODUCTION
Ed Burke (1988)

GRAPHICS
Nigel Grigsby (1984)

TYPESET
John Minczeski (1979), duck type (1980–85)

AD SALES
Thien-bao Phi (2000)

PRINTERS
Haymarket Press (1984–85), Modern Press (1985–09)

Additional thanks goes to
Loft Executive Directors
1974: Marly Rusoff, Loft Founder
1975: Sue Ann Martinson, part-time Coordinator
1979: Jill Breckenridge Haldeman, Loft Coordinator
1980: Margot Kriel, Loft Coordinator
1981: Susan Broadhead, Loft Director
1994: Nancy Gaschott, Interim Loft Executive Director
1994: Linda Myers, Loft Executive Director
2007: Jocelyn Hale, Loft Executive Director

LOFT BOARD CHAIRS

Emilie Buchwald, James Dusso, Jeanne Farrar, Patricia Weaver Francisco, Margot Galt, Shirley Nelson Garner, Jim Goralski, Kate Green, Patricia Hampl, Margaret Hasse, Pamela Holt, Chris LaVictoire Mahai, Jim Moore, David Mura, Sheila Murphy, Shawn Lawrence Otto, Alexs Pate, Elizabeth Petrangelo, Mary Rockcastle, Ann Ryan, Thomas Sanner, Terry Thompson, Stephen Wilbers

The Loft would also like to thank Kelin Loe, Ellen Bogen, Laura Hedeen, Jennie Welch, and Renae Youngs of the Loft, and Jim Cihlar and Patrick Thomas of Milkweed Editions for helping this book come to life.

The Loft Literary Center

Incorporated in 1975 in a space above a Minneapolis bookstore, The Loft Literary Center has grown to become the nation's largest and most comprehensive literary center. In 2000, the Loft moved into the award-winning Open Book literary arts building in Minneapolis, Minnesota.

The Loft is a nonprofit arts organization offering services for readers and writers at every level. Programs include readings by acclaimed local and national authors, writing classes, weekend genre conferences, competitions and grants, open groups, writers' studios, and much more. The list of acclaimed authors who have appeared at the Loft over the years reads like a who's who of American letters.

Supporting Members

The Loft serves the literary community with unprecedented breadth and depth. The contributions of individuals are critical to our ability to support the artistic development of writers, foster a writing community, and build an audience for literature of all kinds. Please consider becoming a supporting member of the Loft. Learn more at www.loft.org.

Milkweed Editions

Milkweed Editions—an independent literary press—publishes with the intention of making a humane impact on society, in the belief that literature is a transformative art.

Join Us

Milkweed depends on the generosity of foundations and individuals like you, in addition to the sales of its books. In an increasingly consolidated and bottom-line-driven publishing world, your support allows us to select and publish books on the basis of their literary quality and the depth of their message. Please visit our Web site (www.milkweed.org) or contact us at (800) 520-6455 to learn more about our donor program.

Milkweed Editions, a nonprofit publisher, gratefully acknowledges sustaining support from Emilie and Henry Buchwald; the Patrick and Aimee Butler Foundation; the Dougherty Family Foundation; the Ecolab Foundation; the General Mills Foundation; John and Joanne Gordon; William and Jeanne Grandy; the Jerome Foundation; Robert and Stephanie Karon; the Lerner Foundation; Sally Macut; Sanders and Tasha Marvin; the McKnight Foundation; Mid-Continent Engineering; the Minnesota State Arts Board, through an appropriation by the Minnesota State Legislature, a grant from the Wells Fargo Foundation Minnesota, and a grant from the National Endowment for the Arts; Kelly Morrison and John Willoughby; the National Endowment for the Arts, and the American Reinvestment and Recovery Act; the Navarre Corporation; Ann and Doug Ness; Jörg and Angie Pierach; the RBC Foundation USA; Ellen Sturgis; the Target Foundation; the James R. Thorpe Foundation; the Travelers Foundation; Moira and John Turner; and Edward and Jenny Wahl.

THE MCKNIGHT FOUNDATION

MINNESOTA STATE ARTS BOARD

NATIONAL ENDOWMENT FOR THE ARTS
A great nation deserves great art.

TARGET.

Interior design by Connie Kuhnz
Typeset in Adobe Caslon Pro
by BookMobile Design and Publishing Services
Printed on acid-free 100% post consumer waste paper
by Friesens Corporation